1981

Ethics and Law in Nursing

PROFESSIONAL PERSPECTIVES

Ethics
and Law
in Nursing
PROFESSIONAL PERSPECTIVES

Kathleen M. Fenner, R.N., Ph.D.
Dean of Nursing, Lewis University

D. Van Nostrand Company
New York   Cincinnati   Toronto   London   Melbourne

D. Van Nostrand Company Regional Offices:
New York   Cincinnati

D. Van Nostrand Company International Offices:
London   Toronto   Melbourne

Copyright © 1980 by Litton Educational Publishing, Inc.

Library of Congress Catalog Card Number: 79–66065
ISBN: O–442–25643-4

Published by D. Van Nostrand Company
135 West 50th Street, New York, N.Y. 10020

10 9 8 7 6 5 4 3 2 1

To Nels Johnson,
for the lessons of love;
To Normand Johnson,
for the lessons of patience.

Preface

Nursing is faced by many legal and ethical dilemmas. Nurses are confronted daily with the difficult problem of distinguishing ethical from unethical practice and must be wary of exceeding the legal parameters of health care. Professional life in nursing now calls for increased awareness of laws, regulations, and moral issues. The purpose of this book is to help prepare students and practitioners in these areas. The text is intended for courses in trends and issues in nursing education, legal and ethical issues, and nursing fundamentals. It may be useful also in courses on medical ethics in departments outside of nursing.

In the first chapter, the rationale for studying ethics and law in nursing is established, and the conflicting state of health care is summarized. The second chapter defines ethics and analyzes the codes of ethics of various health-profession organizations. In the third chapter, the origins of personal values and the effect of these values on nursing are illustrated by the Survivability Quotient technique. Chapter 4 deals with law and legal concepts, using case studies to illustrate fundamental legal principles. Law is covered in regard to the nurse's responsibilities vis-à-vis clients, other health-care professionals, and society. The last chapter focuses on specific health care issues that have both legal and moral components. Here, too, a case study approach is used to demonstrate the analysis that precedes action.

Exercises and activities for small-group or classroom use are included at the end of chapters for reinforcement and application of problem-solving strategies. Annotated bibliographies at the end of each chapter are included for further reading.

I wish to express my gratitude to the many people who supported, guided, and encouraged me during this endeavor. Particular thanks go to Sheila Corcoran, University of Minnesota, and to Barbara Backer, Herbert Lehman College, for their reviews of the manuscript. My colleagues Drs. Douglas, Engbretson, and Rosenthal were enormously helpful and deserve both admiration and gratitude. Their consistent encouragement and advice were instrumental in the completion of this project. Marilyn Kalata and Joyce Michalowski are also gratefully acknowledged; without their tolerance and assistance, the project would never have been completed. The students and faculty of Thornton Community College have my thanks for their patience and perseverance.

Finally, I must express my greatest appreciation for the love, support, patience, wisdom, and strength of Peter Fenner, without whom I would never have survived many of life's traumas nor sampled many of its joys.

K.M.F.

Contents

5. Social Issues   127

Epilogue: Ultimate Questions, Ultimate Answers   201
Index   205

Ethics
and Law
in Nursing
PROFESSIONAL PERSPECTIVES

Gambler

He took a chance, and I lost.
He gambled, and I'm paying the dealer.
It took a risk, now I am disabled.
Everyday I live with the pain of my soul.
Everyday I cry tears of torment.
Everyday I hope and pray to be like others.
Yet I will never be.
I will be disabled forever.
A doctor took a chance.

NORMAND A. JOHNSON, 1979

1

The Mandate to Examine Health Care Ethics, Values, and the Law

"Perfection of means and confusion of ends seem to characterize our age."

ALBERT EINSTEIN

ETHICAL/LEGAL CONFLICTS IN HEALTH CARE

The value of studying ethics and legal aspects of health care is not always apparent to students of the health professions. Students intensely and competitively involved in learning the intricacies of nursing, medicine, or any of the allied health professions are frustrated by distractions that draw their academic attention from the content they see as primary—the mastery of the technology of their chosen field. This cool attitude towards ethics education is certainly not surprising in view of the current educational practices in the health professions.

Practitioners of the health professions are educated within a variety of settings, each with one common goal: to deliver quality health care. To this end, significant time and effort of faculty and students is devoted towards mastery of requisite content and application of attendant clinical skills. One area of learning—the ethical and legal aspects of health care—is frequently neglected. The absence of this material is later demonstrated in the discontent of practitioners, the dissatisfaction of consumers, and the growing involvement of legal entanglements in health care delivery. We underestimate the impact of ethics and law on the health professions. Yet a quick scan of popular literature, press reports, and government activities soon reveals the pervasive interest of society in matters such as health care ethics. Litigation and regulation in health care are the signs of great conflict and public scrutiny of the health care delivery system. Might not this turmoil result at least in part from a paucity of attention and time devoted within the professions and professional education to ethics and law in health care?

HISTORICAL PERSPECTIVE

Analysis of recent medical history (1850–1940) reveals little public outcry over such issues as medical ethics, malpractice litigation, consumer involvement in health care, or government intervention in health care planning and delivery. What has caused the public's swing from reverence of professional healers to its current jaundiced view of the health care industry? Many answers can be posited.

Increasing specialization, mechanization, and technical sophistication of health care have resulted in depersonalization of care. Relationships between providers and consumers are less personal. Although communications flow most easily between people, and less easily between people and institutions, there has been a decrease in person-to-person health care and an increase in person-to-institution health care. People are more apt to find fault and take action against disembodied entities, such as corporations, than to criticize or sue their friends. Just as fudging on income tax reports is frequently more tolerable than fudging on a friend's finances, it is also easier to take legal action against an institution than to take action against a friend or acquaintance.

The consumer has begun to anticipate high-quality, personalized care. This demand is largely generated by the media—we all expect our doctors to be like television's Marcus Welby. While the consumer's expectation of compassionate care has increased, the health care system's capacity to render such care has decreased. Fractionalization and specialization have changed the nature of outpatient care. Rather than seeing a hometown general practitioner, each family now selects services from a host of medical specialists: pediatricians for the children, a gynecologist for Mom, possibly an internist for Dad—and there are endless referrals. When true medical crises occur, all combine without a focal point of coordination. Hospital care has evolved from the ministrations of nurses and an attending physician to the application of a host of specialized technologies, each with attendant specialists. A typical hospital day for a surgical patient can include contact with: (a) the attending physician; (b) the surgeon; (c) the anesthesiologist; (d) several registered nurses; (e) practical nurses; (f) nurse's aides; (g) laboratory technicians; (h) radiology technicians; (i) social service worker; (j) dietary worker; and (k) housekeeping staff. All of these will be appropriately garbed in a uniform or suit that reveals their role to other hospital personnel, but how often can a patient discern which is the dietary aide and which is the nurse?

The result of these increasing numbers of health personnel and the increasing complexity of health care institutions is depersonalization. As consumers begin to perceive themselves as mere numbers in a huge delivery system, they grow less able to identify with, and relate to, the health professionals. The more detached clients become from the professionals who serve them, the easier it is to seek redress for perceived grievance through litigation. It is difficult to sue the local family doctor, the person who has delivered your babies, tended your colds, comforted your spouse through illness, and evaluated your health through the years. It becomes easier to express dissatisfaction through legal action when the target is not a friend, but a faceless, cold, "professional" entity.

There also seems to be a trend toward seeking compensation or remedy for perceived misfortune through legal action. Whatever the cause, many people are likely to look for someone to sue when misfortune occurs, frequently even when the responsibility for the problem cannot be placed squarely on human shoulders. Whether it is due to an increased awareness of the economic gain to be reaped from successful litigation, or an attempt to prevent future mishaps by somehow bringing a culprit to judgment, litigation for personal injury and/or personal loss is at an unprecedented high. Increasing litigiousness in society has spilled over into health care. Consequently, professional liability costs and concerns have captured the attention of most health professionals.

Furthermore, we live in a post-Watergate era: the public now scrutinizes the institutions that it once blindly trusted. Such scrutiny occasionally reveals the inevitable errors attendant on all human endeavors. There is little lay appreciation of the degree of variance and chance involved in health care. The public sees medicine as an infallible science—when, in reality, it is a combination of science, technology, faith, fortune, and magic.

One other possible cause must be suggested. Until very recently, medical intervention produced negligible results. Although the presence of physicians and nurses was frequently reassuring, it infrequently produced dramatic curative results. The fact is that good health and most cures were due primarily to the intervention of nature and Divine Providence, rather than to the medical care rendered. Maternal and infant mortality rates were reduced during the 1800's, but catastrophic diseases such as cancer, polio, tuberculosis, and pneumonia still frustrated medicine and maimed the populace.

Suddenly, around the onset of World War II, the application of medical skill took great leaps forward. Antibiotics, psychotropic medication, prophylactic health care, the technology of medical engineering, and the application of skilled nursing care greatly enhanced medicine's repertoire of life-prolonging magic. Continued public awareness of advances in theory and application of medical science was accomplished through media coverage of every development. Revelations of miraculous progress in thwarting the ravages of many long-dreaded diseases were rapidly communicated to the lay public. Dramatic evidence of the life-sustaining power of health care became apparent to society.

A curious phenomenon must be noted. Any resource, whether goods or services, if perceived as valuable, will receive attention from society. Here the key word is *perceived*. Many resources are fundamental to life; but unless awareness of their importance is attained, the resources may well be ignored, or even squandered. It would appear that the degree of society's interest is directly proportional to the degree of perceived need for the resource or service, and only tangentially associated with actual necessity. When we are comfortably protected by solidly built homes, the uses of firewood are peripheral luxuries. But once we are extracted from the artificial warmth and deposited in a cold north-woods campground, firewood becomes a necessity and its acquisition and use are prized activities, ambitiously undertaken and closely supervised.

Similarly, when professional health care had little impact on prolonging life, and health was perceived as a gift of Providence, social control of health resources was negligible. Contemporary society, however, perceives health care as a right, and medicine as a life-giving force, thus initiating both interest and intervention aimed at channeling these valuable resources in what are believed to be socially desirable avenues. As the perceived need for health care has increased, the degree and extent of attention and control that society has focused on health care has likewise increased.

Medical science, then, has become the victim both of its successes and its failures. Social control is exerted upon medicine because health care has evolved as an important social service, and because consumers are becoming increasingly aware of the human weaknesses, and occasional mistakes, of the providers of that service.

CONTEMPORARY STATUS QUO

Public intervention in health care is as much the product of success as of failure. Interest is compounded by well-publicized aspirations for even greater medical miracles. One need only thumb through the popular magazines or listen to the evening news to find coverage of new and promising therapies in health care. Everything from cures of cancer to laboratory fertilization and implantation of human zygotes is offered to the public in ways that suggest that these developments will soon become standard techniques of care. The health care industry has created both a demand for its product and an expectation of product success in the public mind. These demands create a scarcity of services. That scarcity results in public attempts to regulate health care.

Most services or products perceived as crucial to society will be vigorously regulated and supervised. The success of health care and the publicity afforded health care innovations have created the social perception of the crucial nature of health care, resulting in the degree of regulation and intervention in health care planning and implementation that much of the health professions currently decry as interference in professional judgment. Practitioners of the health professions—nurses, physicians, and allied health professionals—are at the center of the social controversy surrounding the industry. We are overwhelmed by the by-products of our success. Yet we continue about our business of delivering health service, paying little attention to the larger societal developments affecting health care—developments to which we unknowingly contribute and by which we are unwittingly affected. Many opportunities to influence the course of future health care delivery, or to increase the quality of present health care, are missed when professionals fail to take advantage of these opportunities to become agents of change.

We seem to exemplify the proverbial inability to see the forest for the trees, by being blind to these opportunities to influence social control of health care delivery within our own professions. Why are we oblivious to the forces that so pervasively influence our professional lives and the health care industry's future? How can we continue to contribute to the erosion of health care through our lack of participation in social decision-making processes? We are oblivious possibly because we are neither aware of the struggle just beyond our noses, nor are we equipped with the skills necessary to effectively contribute to the decision-making process.

The piecemeal, fact-oriented, skill-achieving nature of health professions education does little to prepare practitioners to play a role in societal decision-making in health policy. The structure of health care is that of a fee-for-service, profit-based business subject to the ebb and flow of marketplace economics. This also does little to promote health professionals' involvement in policy-making. And our ignorance of the ethical and practical ramifications of our own decisions in daily practice accelerates society's perceived need to interfere in health care delivery.

The crux of the problem is this: we have finally succeeded in making health care a positive force contributing to the quality and the quantity of life, and are now rendering a service that is perceived by society as crucial to its future; but the success of the technology of health care has increased without increased sensitivity to the ethical implications of the process. It is probable that much of the controversy that engulfs contemporary health care is due to this insensitivity to the humane dimensions of what we do. We are increasingly caught in a web of technical sophistication without the requisite touch of humanitarianism needed for the just social resolution of health care dilemmas.

Nowhere is this dilemma more easily dramatized than in the issue of abortion. Sophisticated technology makes it feasible to terminate fetal life or to support fetal life at the same point in gestation—28 to 29 weeks. The enormous debate surrounding abortion is conducted largely without the input of most health professionals. Many nurses, who may have settled the issue of abortion in their own lives, still ignore their professional role in the debate, and may indeed act in ways that are contrary to their own ethical belief. The debate over abortion is fueled by health care's technological capacity, yet health professionals have not generally been moved to take a stand on this issue. Perhaps this is because our education has failed to sensitize us to the ethical ramifications of our professional decisions.

THE MANDATE FOR ETHICAL HEALTH CARE PRACTICE

Even though health care focuses on the most precious of all resources—life itself—the consumer is often at a disadvantage when confronted with the health care system. This causes constraints and responsibilities to be placed upon the health care provider that are not present in other service arenas. It is difficult to imagine the degree of ethical conflict faced by health providers within this abstract frame of reference. A concrete example may help illustrate the problems encountered.

Dilation and curettage is an extremely common surgical procedure in gynecology, used for treatment of infertility, menstrual irregularity, and first trimester abortions. Routine preoperative care includes a variety of laboratory tests, x-rays, preoperative teaching, and completion of the usual consent form. Typically, the coordination of care is the responsibility of the nursing staff, which functions within established procedures and under medical supervision where necessary. Generally, preoperative nursing care is efficient in terms of testing, teaching, and the administration of medications. It is not usual for nursing care to focus on assessment of patient knowledge concerning the mechanics and implications of the surgical procedure. Although a preoperative pregnancy test is always completed, results are unreliable if a pregnancy is early; false negatives occur with some frequency. Given this possibility, and the fact that many women would refuse to abort a fetus, it is remarkable how little preoperative nursing care is concerned with informing patients and encouraging them to participate in the decision-making process. It is also worthwhile to note that nurses who do teach patients in areas related to ethical decision-making are frequently the targets of unpleasant responses by hospital administrators and physicians. This happens despite the fact that nowhere in the Nurse Practice Acts or Medical Practice Acts is patient education reserved solely to the physician, and despite the fact that the act of obtaining the informed consent of a patient by a nurse carries with it the nurse's legal responsibility to see that consent was truly informed and not *pro forma*.

There are many similar examples of health care practitioners failing to recognize adequately the ethical dimensions of their actions. Whenever they decide to or assist in maintaining a patient on life-support mechanisms or to terminate an unwanted pregnancy, health professionals are deeply involved in the ethical questions of modern health care delivery.

The legal, ethical, and personal consequences of our failure to become involved in the process is detrimental to the quality of patient care, the future control of health care, and the individual practitioner. This is too great a cost for society to bear: if health care professionals are to remain uninvolved in the process, who can most appropriately make such decisions? Currently, they are made by default. Would not a model of shared responsibility be more appropriate and honest?

ETHICS AND VALUES DESCRIBED

We often talk of the difference between rhetoric and reality, and of the gap between what is and what ought to be. The discipline of science and the application of this discipline in matters of health represent what is actual—what can be *done*. Nurses, physicians, and other health professionals are *doers*, people trained to apply their knowledge of the sciences to the promotion of health and the treatment of disease. Our professions devote the vast majority of education and practice to the reality of doing. Perhaps this is why the study of ethics—which appear to be unrelated to the world of practice—seems foreign to many practitioners of health care. A discussion of the concept of ethics must be framed by an understanding of the dichotomy between the world of fact and the world of aspiration, the gap between what is and what should be, for ethics are systems of distinguishing right from wrong that are based on beliefs about what should be.

Ethicists (people who study ethics as a discipline) will admit that theirs is a most complicated and murky debate, which can boggle the mind of the uninitiated with its references to epistemology and theology. The practicing nurse is rarely interested, much less equipped, to deal with this rarified atmosphere. Yet the essential components of the ethical discipline really aren't so intimidating. A quick review will suffice to equip the reader for a rudimentary discussion of ethics, both as decision-making systems and as philosophical concepts. Chapter 2 will present a more detailed definition and discussion of ethical systems.

Professional ethics represent a formalized code of behavior reflecting principles of importance to a group or profession. An ethic is a standard of behavior, evolved over time, reflecting the profession's desire to protect or insure the well-being of its clients. Nearly all professions have developed ethical codes, most of which are written and published through the profession's membership organization. A few professions have unwritten, yet tightly observed, codes of ethics. A statement of ethics reflects the profession's belief about how its members should behave, not necessarily how they do behave. Thus ethics describe what *ought to be*, rather than what *is*. Ethics are a standard of behavior to which one aspires. They provide a goal, not a description, of professional behavior. Thus the discrepancies between observed behavior and ethical codes can sometimes be attributed to the gap between what is and what should be.

Professions adopt and promulgate ethical codes as a means of establishing standards of behavior to protect the recipient of service. Such codes also serve to protect the reputation and credibility of the profession. When a code's chief purpose, however, is to protect the profession's reputation, and protection of the consumer becomes secondary, the code is no longer a code of ethics, but merely a code of etiquette. The primary function of a code of ethics is to define or outline behavior that is morally desirable by the profession in the service of consumers, not in service of itself.

Thus, the stringent and unwritten practice by physicians not to criticize each other outside of professional circles exemplifies a code of etiquette, not ethics. The traditional medical standard of confidentiality of patient information, however, reflects an ethical code, because its purpose is to protect the patient from potential misuse of personal information.

Ethical standards are enforced with varying degrees of enthusiasm and effort. Unethical conduct may jeopardize one's standing within the profession and thus threaten one's ability to earn a living. Or it may simply result in a "slap on the wrist." Unethical conduct is punished in accordance with the nature of the violation and the power of the peer group.

The American Nurses' Association publishes a code of ethics for nurses that was developed by the association membership, all of whom are registered nurses. The code reflects the values of the professional group. Yet many of the ethics embodied in the code are frequently violated in the practice of nursing. Little retribution, if any, is feared by the violators. This is due both to the fact that many nurses do not feel a commitment to these ethical standards, and to the powerlessness of nurses to control nursing practice completely.

The American Medical Association also has developed and published a code of ethics. This ethical code represents the collective wisdom of the Association's constituents, who are physicians. The code is also frequently violated with little or no consequence. However, the reason for the lack of negative feedback to violators is quite different. Physicians seem to subscribe to an unwritten yet powerful code of etiquette—"thou shalt not betray a colleague." This strong guide, plus the high degree of autonomy most physicians experience, often permits all but the most flagrant violations of the formalized code.

If no one except a few interested academics pays attention to ethical codes, and if those who do pay attention are powerless to punish infractions, then why are such codes promulgated (beside the obvious public relations benefit)? What does the future of ethics in health care hold?

Recall that ethics are statements of what should be, not what is. These ethical codes serve as guides for professionals of good conscience. They serve as a point of reflection and comparison for the conduct of service. Increasing public awareness of professional accountability has increased the demand on professionals to police their own acts and the acts of others. Today's health care client is sophisticated, knowledgeable, and assertive, and is prone to demand the level of service popularized by the media. Assaults on privacy, autonomy, and dignity are not readily tolerated in this age of consumerism. Thus, the health professional is asked and expected to be responsible for the delivery of a high standard of service. The health professions' historical role models have also led to the demand for compassionate, competent care. The self-image created by the health professions has been quite successful: the caring physician and brilliantly compassionate nurse are stereotypes that the public has come to believe in. Now we must live up to the image.

The surge of legal activity and government intervention focusing on health care delivery is also forcing self-policing as a means of self-protection. The incredible rise in liability and professional negligence claims involving physicians, nurses, hospital administrators, and allied health professionals has resulted in renewed attention to peer review and quality control as means of avoiding litigation.

Consumer pressure, peer pressure, and legal pressure: each is a force imparting change in health care practice. One outcome of these pressures has been the refocusing of attention on formalized codes of ethics. Ethical codes are a means both of serving the consumer and of protecting the profession. Yet there are more compelling reasons for examination of ethical codes than consumer pressure, peer pressure, or legal pressure.

We each do the best we can; we each like to think well of ourselves. Our behavior reflects our need for self-esteem. All persons have an internal set or standard of behaviors that reflect their personal value system—a product of living and growing within a family, culture, and society. When our personal behavior is in conformity with our personal value systems, life is easier and more satisfying: we approve of ourselves.

When we do not act in accordance with our value systems, we feel internal disharmony. A violation of one's values extracts a price in stress. These value systems spill over and affect all facets of life, including professional life. Thus, for example, physicians raised in devout Catholic households may well be affected by a value systems conflict if they choose to assist in planned abortion procedures.

Attention to the area of ethics is incomplete without correlation of ethical standards with personal value systems. This correlation can occur only after value systems have been clarified. Introspection and analysis of personal values and interpretation of value systems in view of professional ethics allows one to develop the knowledge and skill necessary for ethical health care practice without disconformity with personal standards. This involves the process of comparing personal value standards with ethical standards external to the individual, such as those held by an institution or group. This comparison can help measure the fit between a personal value standard and externally imposed ethical systems. When the two are similar, harmony may exist, permitting professional functioning to occur in consonance with ethical standards. When personal standards and externally-imposed ethics are divergent, individuals must make choices about potential external system change, or learn to live within their own value system without conflict and/or find strategies for change. The outcome of ethical disharmony is a personal toll in stress.

EXTRA CONFUSION—THE LEGAL INFLUENCE

As if the health service arena were not sufficiently confused by conflicts between professional and personal value systems, another set of compounding variables is added: the impact of legal structure, government regulations, and the threat of litigation. The law is an influence by virtue of both its real impact and its perceived threat. Each dimension—legal structure, government regulation, and litigation—needs separate examination. The composite effect is tremendous, probably equalling any force currently affecting health care.

Why examine legal influences together with ethics? Legal mandates sometimes conflict with ethical standards and values, thus compounding a dilemma. In fact, one's desire to act in a manner that is legally defensible can subvert or control the need to be ethical. More often than not, people are so concerned over legality that their concern over ethics becomes secondary. Further, sometimes the law can directly conflict with an individual's ethics. The much publicized Quinlan case, involving termination of life-support mechanisms, is an example.

Karen Quinlan's legal plight was well recorded in both the popular press and professional journals. Ms. Quinlan had been maintained on life-support equipment for an extended period of time after experiencing what had been assessed as irreversible and extensive brain damage. Her parents, after understanding the futility of anticipating a recovery to any semblance of normal existence for their daughter, requested that extraordinary means of life support be terminated. Because of the sensitive legal issues surrounding the case, Ms. Quinlan's future medical therapy was reviewed through the judicial system of the State of New Jersey. The judicial process supported the right of her parents to take such action on her behalf, and thus extended to the medical personnel involved a degree of legal protection from liability.

Family and physicians both had relinquished hope for Ms. Quinlan's recovery to a semblance of normal existence. Yet both family and physicians recognized the potential legal consequences of their decision to discontinue extraordinary life-support measures. The decision to remove exotic support equipment was first reviewed in an ethical framework by the family with the assistance of their clergy. Then, wisely, family and physicians sought judicial validation of the decision prior to its implementation. The legal battle that ensued was arduous and complex. The decision of the family, although eventually validated, withstood tremendous legal scrutiny. The potential for the force or the threat of force of law in shaping health care was well illustrated. The episode illustrates, too, the complexity of the ethical and legal dilemmas created by the technological successes of medical science.

Such conflicts between ethics and the law can only be resolved by knowledge of pertinent legal principles, skill in assessing consultation, and insight into personal ethical standards and the consequences of their violation. A capricious attitude or unknowledgeable mind can bring disaster to the individuals involved and increase the public's criticism of health care.

The prudent health professional chooses to avoid both the personal cost of conflict in violation of ethical standards and the combined personal/professional cost of legal conflicts. Avoidance requires knowledge of the law, of ethical standards, and of one's own values. Those who fail to consider the ethical and legal implications of their actions all too often pay the price, in terms of money, reputation, and happiness.

SOCIAL ISSUES AS FOCI

In reviewing ethical problems in health care, it is common to focus discussion on the dramatic social issues that present ethical dilemmas to health professionals. These include such issues as euthanasia, abortion, eugenics, allocation of scarce life-saving medical resources, behavior control, and experimentation rights. Frequently this approach bores many health professions students, who have a difficult time picturing themselves involved in such exotic situations. Students visualize themselves in more mundane capacities in health care: administering the routine procedures that occur by the millions on an everyday basis, rather than facing up to a dramatic moment of decision-making. But if we do not involve ourselves in the active debate surrounding the more dramatic issues, and if we cannot associate ourselves with the significance of the contribution of our daily practice to the resolution of these issues, then many of the crucial stands will be taken without the significant input of the vast majority of health care professionals. This would be a real loss.

Whenever nurses, physicians, or technicians affiliate with a hospital that permits abortion as an elective procedure, those professionals have committed themselves, knowingly or unknowingly, to an ethical stance. This does not mean that an individual who is opposed to abortion cannot affiliate with such an institution. But it does indicate that, before affiliating, the individual must have examined options, considered alternatives, and selected the affiliation in the belief that doing so would not produce undue stress. Allegiance to an institution, profession, or service without scrutiny of its objectives, techniques, and standards can not only be an ethically unfortunate act, but also can result in great personal loss through values conflict. The nurse working in a public hospital pediatrics unit might be rotated to surgery under conditions of short-staffing. This would certainly not be an advantageous time to learn that the hospital sanctioned an abortion procedure against the nurse's ethical standards; the behavior choices in this conflict—either to assist in the procedure or to abandon patient care—are both unacceptable. To acquiesce in assisting with the procedure could generate significant pain for the nurse; to refuse to assist in the procedure is abandonment of professional responsibilities and could generate significant professional and legal consequences for all concerned.

Similarly, the laboratory technician completing the preoperative blood work on the abortion client also contributes to the support of the process, even though unwittingly. It is important to be aware of the ethical consequences of one's professional responsibilities and be able to act in accordance with one's personal ethical standards in the avoidance of conflict and its attendant costs.

It is therefore imperative that ethics and values be examined in terms of the major social issues impinging on contemporary health care—both from the perspective of the valuable contribution that could be made by informed, active professionals, and in terms of the impact of these issues on the individual giver of care.

Even the most routine health care delivery procedures may have aspects involving ethical decisions. Few practitioners are participants in the earth-shaking developments, such as test tube babies and cloning. Yet each practitioner contributes to the resolution of issues in many small ways—from the completion of laboratory tests to assisting in, or performing, the technical procedures. The problem is to recognize in the seemingly mundane tasks of everyday practice the ethical significance that such tasks hold, and to act accordingly.

The legal ramifications of ethical decisions must be considered here too. The convergence of ethics, law, and health professions practice is frequently a less-than-gentle crash. Foresight, knowledge, and resolution strategies minimize the impact on personal lives and on social interaction. Unfortunate situations do arise, when professionals closely examine the ethical dimensions of a problem, select what they believe to be a just and humane alternative, and then are confronted with litigation derived from the unlawful nature of their act.

But the tenets of professional ethics usually can be followed within legal bounds. In fact, professional behavior that is guided by ethical mandates is more likely to be legally defensible than behavior guided by expediency. The foundational philosophy of law, as of ethics, is a concern for the protection and preservation of human rights. Thus ethical behavior is conducive to lawful behavior.

Infrequently, ethical concern will indicate a course of action of questionable legality. This can present a true Gordian knot and the professional has need both of colleagial counsel and legal advice. The rare instance when the practitioner faces such a dilemma exemplifies the need to understand the fundamental principles of law, as well as to possess self-knowledge in relation to ethics and values. Weighing difficult alternatives requires insight and knowledge.

HOPED-FOR RESULTS

The bonus at the end of the processes of value clarification, of ethical evaluation, and of legal scrutiny of major social issues, is a change in health care delivery. Change in care will be brought about by the masses of health care workers who, although not participating in the dramatic events, constitute the fabric of the system and determine its characteristics. Much of the contemporary health care system is ruled by a worship of technology over humanity, of systems over individuals. Evidence of this is found in: routine procedures done on people—who are never routine; schedules that determine client care—as opposed to client needs determining schedules; and the expenditure of wealth on exotic techniques to sustain life that is no longer human. The health care industry has, through its behavior, revealed goals that focus on technology and financial prosperity at a time when the industry's consumers demand compassion and concern. An introspective search for the values of health care might serve both to lessen criticism of the industry and to increase one's satisfaction with health care practice. Hence this text—a resource to serve as a catalyst for such searches. As we dehumanize others, we also dehumanize ourselves; as we humanize health care, we, in turn, become more humane.

Model Interview

The purpose of this activity is to give the learner an opportunity to assess the attitudes and beliefs of others concerning the occupation of nursing. The participant is instructed to administer the following interview to three nonnurses. The results or responses can be outlined and discussed in a small group setting. Compare and contrast prevailing beliefs about nursing and medicine. What patterns or trends emerge? What is the reflected image of nursing in the interviews? To what factors do you attribute this image? Would you want to effect a change in this image? How would such change be accomplished?

Interview:

1. How would you describe the occupation of nursing?

2. How do nurses learn nursing?

3. How would you describe the occupation of medicine?

4. How do physicians learn medicine?

5. Describe your image of the ideal nurse.

6. Describe your image of the ideal physician.

Exercises and Games

Spaceship Envision yourself as the captain of a spaceship bound to colonize and establish new civilizations on other planets. You will be unable to communicate or return to earth after your departure. What are the material supplies you would want to accompany you on the voyage? What are the artifacts of your cultural heritage (books, music, art, etc.) that you would want to use as the basis for establishing your new cultural system? What kinds and types of people would you have accompany you on this voyage? The answers to these questions reveal a great deal of information about you. The bringing or leaving behind of certain concepts and ideas are indicative of your personal value system.

Decisions of the captain would be telling in terms of values and attitudes. The decision to include or exclude clergy, government leaders, scientists, or philosophers, denotes the basic values and beliefs of the designer. The presence of clergy, particularly if representing only one theological persuasion, would communicate a value of that religion. Decisions to include or exclude other types and occupations of people would indicate other values and beliefs. Were one to structure a spaceship crew that was white, Anglo-Saxon, and male, the observer could readily pose several observations concerning the captain's values. Either the captain is totally oblivious of the existence of other races and nationalities, or the captain is attempting to restructure a more homogeneous society. The proposed structure also says something about the captain's awareness of the fundamental principles of biology, or that he or she chooses to make this a one-generation culture.

The spaceship exercise can allow one to discover much information about one's own values. It is sometimes helpful to write down responses to these questions and to share these with a friend in a mutual exchange. Occasionally others will perceive other values or challenge us to defend notions that we would not have examined on our own. This is similar to Uustal and Simon's concept of prizing in the process of values clarification.

Suggestions For Further Reading

Bullough, Bonnie and Vern Bullough, eds. *Expanding Horizons for Nurses*. New York: Springer Publishing Co., 1977.

> Examines recent legislative enactments and ethical problems involved in controversial clinical issues—abortion, homosexuality, and euthanasia—and the nursing professions's inherent need to stay abreast of change.

Deloughery, Grace L. *History and Trends of Professional Nursing*, 8th Ed. St. Louis: The C. V. Mosby Co., 1977.

> Major theme is the parallel evolution of the role of women and modern professional nursing. Describes a brief early history of nursing, beginnings in America, contemporary nursing, and legal aspects and implications in the field.

S. B. Simon, W. Howe, and H. Kirschenbaum. *Values Clarification*. New York: Hart, 1972.

> The first comprehensive text reviewing value formation, impact, and techniques and strategies for values clarification. Most useful in designing teaching strategies for values awareness.

Sward, Kathleen M., et al. "An Historical Perspective." Perspectives on the Code for Nurses. American Nurses' Association, 1978.
> Depicts the need of a professional code of ethics for nurses, the history of the ANA's maintenance of such a code, and its application and relevance to nurses, clients, and society.

Toffler, Alvin. *Future Shock*. New York: Random House, 1970.
> A view of society and its inability to cope with the increasingly rapid rate of change, particularly technological change. Introduces the concept of cultural lag—gap between mores, attitudes, and technological capacity. Dated, yet excellent reading.

Diane Uustal. "The Use of Values Clarification in Nursing Practice." *The Journal of Continuing Education in Nursing,* Vol. 8, No. 3 (1977), pp. 8–12.
> Examines use of value clarification in nursing practice utilizing the idea that the clearer you are about what you value, the more able you are to choose and initiate appropriate actions.

2

Ethics in
Health Care

". . . Controversy is the natural state of applied ethics."
JAMES M. SMITH

The concept of ethics has many connotations for each individual. It carries models of moral behavior, implications of what is right and wrong, and messages related to professionalism and professional rules of conduct. Many people are raised within the ethical system of an organized religion. Though possibly not identified as such, the theological system of right and wrong promulgated by a religious group is that group's ethical code. We are all also subject to social/ethical systems inculcated by our socialization experiences through life. One need only recall the strong social value placed on virginity as recently as the 1950's, and contrast that with what many believe is the contemporary American value of open sexual conduct, to note that our social system sets and revises ethical mandates that many of its participants follow as gospel.

Professional groups also have their own ethical standards. The Professional Code of Ethics of the American Medical Association delivers a message to its members about what is acceptable and what is unacceptable physician behavior. The American Nurses' Association Code of Ethics likewise represents its membership's values and standards of behavior.

What is an ethic? It is a value, a standard adhered to by either an individual or a group. It is the "what ought to be" in a world of "what is." In the most perfect of all worlds, there would be eternal justice, fairness, and honesty. That is a statement of ethical aspiration. Obviously the real world presents a different image, but the statement of ethical aspiration gives a goal—no matter how lofty or unattainable. Ethics are at the heart of our concepts of right and wrong. They exist as guides to behavior. When the phrase "situational ethic" is used, the connotation is that the standard of behavior is altered to fit the circumstances. The standard is the ethic, the judgment of what is acceptable or unacceptable in a given situation.

An ethic is certainly not a static entity. It changes and evolves as society and individuals change and evolve. The previous example of sexual ethics of the 1950s demonstrates how society changes ethical standards over time. It was once a rigidly enforced ethic of nursing never to undermine the authority of the physician, regardless of how much the nurse might disagree with the physician's judgment. We can observe a great change in the implementation of the ethic of physician authority in contemporary nursing practice. Nurses have evolved a system of ethics that places a heavy emphasis on the accountability of the nurse for the quality of patient care and the nurse's duty to act as a patient advocate in ensuring the quality of care rendered by others.

Ethical standards do not change by accident. Just as growth and experience lead to learning, growth and experience lead to change. Greater learning and experience foster the continuous reexamination of ethical systems and their modification to fit new information and expectation.

As our ability both to prolong life and to enhance the quality of life has changed, our definitions of death and ethics concerning the acceptance of death have also changed. When death was the final enemy of the healer and the moment of death was determined not by withdrawal of medical support but by nature, then the ethic of health care was to forestall death by any means possible. But the means for prolonging life have become increasingly exotic, and we now have the capacity to support life long after any semblance of humanity has evaporated. Thus our ethic concerning the acceptance of death has also altered. It is not an accident that we are witnessing enormous interest in "death education" programs and systems designed to assist health professionals in dealing with the realities of death at the same time that we witness increases in the technological capacity to forestall death by artificial means. Our view of the ethical role of the health professional vis-à-vis the dying patient is undergoing change. No longer are dying patients a symbol of our failure. They may, indeed, be symbols of our success, as we begin to value the "good death."

Ethics, then, are systems of valued behaviors and beliefs; they are declarations of what is right and wrong, of what ought to be. These systems may be subscribed to by the individual, a small group, or society in general. The system is learned through socialization, growth, and experience. Because the system is dynamic, it undergoes change concurrent with social change.

An ethical code is a framework for decision-making. It is, by nature of its use, action-oriented. We commonly speak of the "work ethic"— an ethic that values hard work as meaningful and good. The process of realizing an ethical code in a professional value system also makes one able to put that code into practice. If I have assessed my stance in regard to patient autonomy, I am then capable of implementing my position in practice—either directly in the realms that I control, or indirectly by influencing others who may have the power to effect changes.

Ethics are not static rules to be outlined and then comfortably assigned to a dusty shelf. They are professional values to be used in the day-to-day conduct of health care delivery. It is the lack of knowledge of those values that frequently places health professionals in positions that they may find uncomfortable. Knowledge of one's own personal values and implementation of values within a professional ethical code can shape the quality of health care rendered and strengthen the satisfaction received from practice.

Were not congruence of ethical codes with personal values fundamental to clinical practice, a discussion of such codes would, indeed, be an endeavor in philosophy, of little practical application. The crux of much of the controversy that surrounds contemporary health care is the paucity of ethical systems that have been applied to health care delivery—which vividly demonstrates the need for change not in *how* we practice, but *why*.

Any discussion of ethics remains conceptually mute if it does not include consideration of the crucial element of power. It is fine to engage in abstract philosophic thought, but such musings are idle gestures when one does not possess the power to put into effect the decisions rendered. Thus, the typical focus of most professional discussions of ethical crises in health care is meaningless, insofar as it usually involves such improbable dilemmas as the moral problem of cloning or the legal ramifications of extrauterine conception. The fact remains that the vast majority of practical health professionals will spend little of their real practice in the pursuit of such clinical miracles.

It is more appropriate, and a more economical use of time and effort, to focus on those dilemmas and issues in which we will have extended roles to play—roles that carry with them the power of change. All practitioners are trained in their technology to administer a facet of patient care. Thus, individual practitioners have accountability for the care given, and have the power to determine the quality and goals of their service. Whether processing laboratory tests or supervising a rotation of night nurses, health professionals have an obligation to examine their practice and to control it.

The examination of the ethical dimensions of practice is a component of value clarification. The process of examining or determining the scope of one's role, the depth of one's commitment to that role, and the degree of investment one is able to make in the pursuit of excellence in that role is the first step in self-evaluation. The recognition of the implications of actions, the values imbued in each decision in health care practice, permits the attainment of sufficient perspective as a necessary prerequisite to directed, decisive, professional practice.

Once practitioners have achieved some perspective on their professional commitment and technological competence, it becomes possible to gain insight into the degree of power they may exert over that practice.

Ethical accountability means that one is responsible for one's actions: the health care practitioner who has autonomy in her sphere of work must be willing to accept the consequences for her decisions.

It is a matter of efficiency to invest energy where the investment has the greatest potential for change. All practitioners have individual opportunities to affect health care through their clinical practice. It is not an efficient energy investment for them to focus concerns over ethical problems in their own practice, as opposed to trafficking in the rarified atmosphere of philosophers and ethicists?

So the message becomes: focus your ethical energy on daily clinical dilemmas, not on the exotic dramas we read about in newspapers. Yet, while focusing attention on realistic health care dilemmas, the practitioner must also remain cognizant of the need to plan for the future. Planning for the future is integral to any strategy for anticipating, initiating, and then coping with change. Just as we need to attend to today's problems, we must learn to plan to prevent or alleviate dilemmas created by tomorrow's changes. Revolutions in the humane attitudes needed in health care will come quietly through the actions of the masses of front-line providers, not through the pronouncements of academicians or theologians.

ETHICS AND THE USES OF POWER

The word *power* brings to mind images of revolutions, politics, clout, and muscle. One must recall that the word simply means the ability to do something, be it the power to decide the fate of nations or the power to decide the menu for lunch—both are the same noun. Each health care professional possesses power over his actions: it is the ability to control his practice within the set boundaries created by law, tradition, environment, and colleagues. Upon examination, one finds that these boundaries are not so terribly rigid; with a bit of finesse and skill, all limits, whether mental or material, can be stretched a bit.

So, as we discuss the necessity to examine the ethical implications of our clinical practice, we must also recognize the concomitant power individuals possess over the ethical dimensions of their profession. If I decide that I can no longer give a higher priority to a hospital schedule than to a patient's need for individualized care, it is within my power to effect change. The rapidity and extent of the change will be the direct result of my real power within the system and of my skill in influencing others.

If the change I seek is high on my agenda, then the skill, motivation, energy, and effort I bring to the task will be high. If the goal is peripheral to my primary objectives, I will probably spend less energy on this project. In any case, to stand aside helplessly and wring one's hands over a given situation is a waste of time and effort. If you don't like things, change them. If you can't change them, then work towards something you can change, and don't waste your energy on hand-wring-ing. All you'll get is sympathy and chapped fingers, neither of which is very desirable!

Why should we study ethics? Certainly there is ample material in the science and technology of medicine to fill a health professions stu-dent's time, without bringing in such subjects as ethics and the law. Yet it is precisely *because* there is such a wealth of scientific and technological material to be mastered that these subjects are also valuable. For it is the sophistication and complexity of health care that puts the consumer of care at the mercy of the professional.

During November of 1978, the *Chicago Sun Times* ran a series of articles titled "The Abortion Profiteers." In these investigative reports, the journalists chronicled the money-motivated, often illegal, and cer-tainly unethical conduct of some abortion clinics in the Chicago area. Many of the revelations were quite surprising to the lay public. The concept that physicians would organize care to speed individual pro-cedures because of the fee-for-service orientation of the clinics was a shock to many. The short-cuts in procedures taken to save time (because, in a fee-for-service business, time is money) were also quite enlightening. Many of the practices unveiled are the exception, rather than the rule. Yet how different are these practices from many of the routines we condone in health care, largely because we believe them to be efficient? These exposés highlighted practices that many would admit to be highly unusual: for example, omitting anesthesia and faking vital signs to cut down on preoperative time. Similar practices occur in many health care facilities and go unnoticed, because the consumer is unable to distinguish poor care from adequate or excellent care.

The language, system, structure, and hierarchy of the care delivery system remain a mystery to most people. Anyone in a white uniform is a nurse; anyone in street clothes with a knowing attitude is a physician. It is possible to humble the client by using terminology that bafflingly describes the most mundane of features. Terms such as *afebrile* and *edematous* are common to the professional and astounding to the patient.

It is little wonder that a discerning public, even though grown so-phisticated in this age of Naderism, still accepts from the family phy-sician's office the kind of demeanor, treatment, and inconsiderateness that they would complain about from a garage mechanic. The power-lessness of the patient is almost complete.

Clients can neither comprehend nor control the care for which they pay so dearly, both in money and health. Where else would one accept total loss of personal freedom, indignity, rudeness, and possibly life-threatening behavior, but as a patient in a hospital? All this with the privilege of paying hundreds of dollars per day! Our public is ignorant of the power and misuse of power in health care. Patients trust to the system for health care which, given our new-found success, has proven to be a crucial element in a long and healthy life.

Given the trust placed in health professionals, the power they have, and the potential for abuse of a quite profitable situation, it is easy to establish a rationale for the governance of health care by an ethical group of professionals.

A CLOSER LOOK

Earlier, a crude definition of ethics as a system for determining right and wrong was offered. The scrutiny of ethical dilemmas in health care mandates a more detailed understanding of the nature and process of ethics.

Small children and mildly retarded adults are capable of learning concepts of right and wrong, good from bad, acceptable from unacceptable behavior. Does this constitute the development of ethical decision-making potential? Probably not. Rather, it represents the inculcation of standards of value held by larger social groups and more powerful individuals who set about the task of teaching standards to less capable individuals for the purpose of insuring both individual and social harmony. Simply learning and utilizing a rule of behavior, such as "striking another is wrong," does not mean that one is capable of making ethical decisions.

Ethical decision-making, although based on the concepts of right and wrong, involves the determination of right from wrong within situations where clear demarcations do not exist or are not available to the decision-maker. Moreover, ethical decision-making requires the existence of a set of known value judgments whose determination is based on estimation of validity according to a known standard of ethics. In other words, ethical decision-making presupposes the existence of a system of ethics known to the individual. The decision-making process consists of analysis and interpretation of data to determine the dimensions of the dilemma and the relationship between decisional options and ethical standards. To engage in the solution of an ethical dilemma, individuals must be cognizant of their ethical systems and be able to analyze and select appropriate alternatives.

Such knowledge and skills are not easily obtained. Yet if health care is to respond to human needs, the ability to make ethical decisions is a necessary skill.

ETHICS AS A PHILOSOPHICAL ENDEAVOR

Ethics is a branch of philosophy, the discipline concerned with such seemingly esoteric concerns as the study of thought and knowledge and how thought and knowledge are obtained. The subsets of the discipline of philosophy, in addition to ethics, are *logic, aesthetics, metaphysics,* and *epistemology.* The study of the origin of ethics and the meaning of ethics is termed *metaethics,* while the study of the development of ethical systems or sets of ethical principles is termed *normative ethics.*[1]

Ethical systems—methods of obtaining an ethical decision—are frequently grouped according to the nature of the process used in the decision and the tenets upon which that decision is based. Systems that may ultimately indicate quite different individual ethical stances may thus be grouped together, in that the bases or processes by which the stance was derived are similar.

The two classes of ethical systems most frequently encountered in the literature are the *deontological* and the *teleological.*[2] *Deontological* systems are ethical systems that are founded on the discovery and confirmation of a set of morals or rules that govern the ethical dilemma to be resolved. Deontological systems include the *theological* ethical systems and other less formalized, yet equally principle-based, systems. The theological systems include the religious philosophies that influence many of us, and that continue to frame much of what is perceived as ethical decision-making. The major theologies of western culture are, of course, Christianity and Judaism. Other cultures utilize ethical systems such as those framed by the theologies of Islam, Buddhism, and Shintoism.

The remarkable feature of each of these religions is not its uniqueness, but, to the contrary, the high degree of similarity in the ethical mandates that each purports. The values that undergird each of these religions are almost universal. Each asserts a code of morals, founded upon its ethical system, that prohibits conduct deleterious to the survival of its constituents. Kieffer (p. 33) points out the possibility that religion is an evolutionary necessity providing the means for ensuring social cooperation among individuals. He further theorizes that the development and implementation of religious systems are fundamental ingredients in the maintenance of society and culture; that humans, left to instinctual levels of survival without the framework that religious codes

---

1.Kieffer, George H. *Bioethics.* Reading, Massachusetts: Addison-Wesley Publishing Company, 1979, p. 47.

2.Frankema, William. *Ethics,* 2nd Edition. Englewood Cliffs, New Jersey: Prentice-Hall, 1973, p. 14.

and promises of rewards in an afterlife provide, would be incapable of altruistic and culturally successful behavior. Thus, evolution of social systems made the establishment and maintenance of religious systems a survival necessity.

Perhaps much of our current social debate over the medical miracles, and the disasters that threaten from successes and failures in developing science indicate that the uses of religion need to be rediscovered and reexamined for transfer to the sociocultural dimension of ethical decision-making in interface with biology and the medical disciplines. Or is it also possible that evolution has propelled mankind beyond the need for formalized religious codes; perhaps it is no longer possible to promulgate religious structures that meet the complex and diverse dilemmas facing mankind today. The inability of our generation to resolve the issue of ethical poverty in the face of technological sophistication may provide the insurmountable challenge that marks the end of the evolution of the human species. Kieffer would pose ethics as an evolutionary capacity and mandate. The inability to develop this capacity and respond to this mandate could spell the close of the evolutionary chain.

The second classification of ethical systems is that of the *teleological* systems. We may classify under this heading all systems that lack hard-and-fast moral codes, but which seek the "greatest good" as the outcome of an act. The determination of the "greatest good" and the definition of what constitutes it are the demarcation lines between various teleo-logical systems.

Most deontological systems focus on a concern for principles of right or wrong; most teleological systems focus on a concern for efficiency and utility. The two classifications seem to span the spectrum from the ideal-istic to the realistic. Let us examine each in an approach to a common health care dilemma. Such examination will reveal the differences be-tween the two classifications.

The allocation of medical resources is a difficult problem. The scarcity of some life-saving equipment makes its distribution an ethical dilemma in many institutions. A situation in which there are two people in need of kidney transplantation, and only one available kidney, epitomizes the problem. What can be used as a yardstick to measure the ethical validity of the alternative decisions? If one of the candidates for transplantation is a young mother of several children, and the other is an elderly woman with few family obligations, the focus of teleological systems would require that we give priority for transplantation to the young mother on the basis that the allocation of the kidney to her would benefit both the patient and her children—thus creating the "greatest good." A theo-logical view based on the eastern religion of Shintoism would give the kidney to the older woman, because the basis of the religion is respect for age and ancestry. Western theological thought might try to invoke various notions of "justice," and might well allocate the kidney to the young mother in the cause of justice to her children. Still other religions would have us evaluate the spiritual health of each of our candidates. A humanistic view might require a concern for the welfare of each person involved, but further extend the dimensions of the problem to include the necessity of self-determination by each of the clients. Thus, a humanist would attempt to involve the principle actors in the decision-making process. Although several of the ethical systems would bring us to an identical decision, the basis of decision-making would be quite different.

The concern for right-acting would meet strictures of the deontological systems. The concern for utility would satisfy the terms of teleological systems. The premise for decision-making is different, even when the decision arrived at may be the same.

Another issue that permits the assessment of difference between deontological and teleological ethical systems is the problem of abortion. Teleological systems of ethics would permit abortion as the greatest good to the greatest number, unless the act of abortion could be construed to impinge upon or imperil the rights of the majority or threaten the existence of the group—as when a society is experiencing a decline in population, and the act of abortion would deprive the social group of future generations necessary to insure survival. Deontological systems weigh the issue of abortion from the standpoint of right and wrong. The injustice to the mother, forced to bear an unwanted child, is weighed against the injustice created for the fetus, if the fetus is perceived as a human and hence to be granted the rights commensurate with human status. The discussion of where and how humanhood is conferred, and the extent and limits of control of bodily destiny, are central issues to a deontological examination of the abortion dilemma. Although several theological systems would claim to be founded on deontologically similar principles, it would be foolish to believe that each arrives at the same conclusion when viewing this problem. In fact, many of the major western religious denominations have issued official statements concerning the ethics of abortion. Some oppose the technique under any circumstances; others give conditional sanction; and others deem it a matter of self-determination. Yet each is using a similar ethical decision-making frame.

ETHICAL CODES—ETHICS OR ETIQUETTE?

It is important to distinguish codes of ethics from codes of etiquette. Ethical codes are concerned with establishing frameworks of appropriate professional behavior in terms of the responsibility of the profession for protecting its client from unprofessional conduct. They focus on the client as the recipient of service, and in need of protection, precisely because the profession is in control of its practice and the consumer may not be capable of discerning professional from unprofessional conduct. The priority clearly expressed by a code of professional ethics is the welfare of the consumer of service. The code may also be peripherally concerned with the welfare of the profession. Indeed, the good of the consumer will, in the long range, also reflect the good of the profession.

Sections of some professional codes of ethics actually represent codes of *etiquette*, in that the focus of the code is the protection of the integrity and welfare of the professionals. The content of the code suggests a standard of behavior of professionals towards one another and a standard of behavior of the individual practitioner towards the profession in general. The priority of the code is the protection of the profession. Protection of the client may be mentioned, but only as an apparent afterthought.

An example of a code of etiquette is the segment of the Code of Ethics of the American Medical Record Association that states that the professional must behave in such a manner that honor and dignity are brought to the profession and the association. This is the *first* principle outlined in the professional code! Certainly it is worthwhile, both for clients and colleagues, that the individual should conduct himself or herself honorably. Yet the purpose of the conduct does not have as its object the welfare of the client, but, on the contrary, the honor of the association and the profession. A strange set of priorities; and one that certainly categorizes, at least, this section of the professional code as merely a code of etiquette.

The contrast between such a code and a true code of ethics can be illustrated by the analysis of the first of the principles in the American Nurses' Association *Code for Nurses*. It states: "The nurse provides services with respect for human dignity and the uniqueness of the client unrestricted by considerations of social or economic status, personal attributes, or the nature of the health problems."[3]

The focal point of this statement is the nurse's conduct towards the client. It clarifies the nurse's responsibility to give care that is dignified, regardless of client attributes or nurse prejudices. Obviously the rendering of such care brings credit to the profession of nursing, and is in the best interests of maintaining the profession's stature and reputation. Yet the priority is given to the consumer, not the profession or the association. This indicates that the statement focuses on ethical concerns for client care, as opposed to etiquette concerns for the profession. Ethical

---

3.*Perspectives on the Code for Nurses*. Kansas City: American Nurses' Association, 1976.

codes prioritize client welfare; etiquette codes prioritize professional welfare. Analysis of the codes of professional societies provides an interesting perspective on the focus and goals of each society. Nearly all of the recognized health professions have founded and maintain a professional society. Most of these have promulgated codes of ethics of varying degrees of sophistication. The degree to which the society perceives itself as a guardian of the professional *status quo* as opposed to the degree to which it recognizes its responsibilities to the consumer—is apparent in the codes.

The American Nurses Association *Code for Nurses* is accompanied by a list of interpretive statements accompanying the actual code. These statements are intended to illustrate the intent of the code. Their content further emphasizes the actual consumer-centered nature of the code and the association's concern with the welfare of the recipient of nursing care—and demonstrates that the code is a code of ethics, rather than a code of etiquette.

The American Medical Association also promulgates a code of ethics for its constituents, practitioners of medicine. The American Medical Association *Principles of Medical Ethics* demonstrate some degree of concern for the welfare of the recipient of service and for the public at large. However, much of the code sets standards of professional behavior aimed at eliminating the possibility that aspersions be cast upon the integrity of the profession. In fact, some of the provisions of the code imply that its intent is to preserve the independent nature of the practice of medicine as an entrepreneurial enterprise, bringing both economic security and independence to its practitioners. This is well and good for the profession, and there is certainly nothing wrong with the profession's seeking autonomy and economic security, but does this belong in a code of ethics? Do not such contents, rather, suggest that the American Medical Association's statement is merely a guide to etiquette?

Section 5 of the code states: "A physician may choose whom he will serve. In an emergency, however, he should render service to the best of his ability. Having undertaken the care of a patient, he may not neglect him; and unless he has been discharged he may discontinue his service only after giving adequate notice. He should not solicit patients."

This section of the code immediately puts the consumer of service on notice that, unless an emergency arises, the choice of the decision to serve is the physician's and not the client's. This is motivated by a desire to maintain the independence and free will of those who practice medicine. However, this statement in no way protects the rights of the consumer, and may actually be interpreted as setting the precedent for the denial of service to clients. If the choice of service is the physician's, the decision may be based on such grounds as the patient's ability to pay, or even the patient's race or ethnic group. I do not question the right of the association to set, nor of its members to follow, such a guide. I do question the validity of the guide as an ethical code, and find it more appropriately termed a standard of etiquette.

Let me assure the reader that the entire code of the American Medical Association does not read in such a self-serving manner. Much of the code would meet the criterion of placing priority on the welfare of the consumer. Yet portions of the code are indisputably extremely protective of the rights and options of the medical profession—a fact that leads one to speculate about the origins and intent of the code. Could it be that the association was seeking to serve two purposes with its code, that of meeting the public's quest for an ethical statement, and that of serving notice to its members about what types of professional behavior can and cannot be tolerated?

It is possible to see ethical codes as indicative of the level of moral maturity attained by the originators of the statements. Ethical codes each contain symptoms of the sophistication, or lack of sophistication, of the judgmental development of the authors. A variety of influences enter into what Boyd and Kohlberg term "development of a moral stage."[4]

MORAL DEVELOPMENT

The term moral conjures diverse images in the mind's eye. From the standards of moral behavior set by the Ten Commandments comes the idea that lewd behavior is "immoral." But the term *moral* is also used to refer, more generally, to standards of right and wrong that are engendered by the processes of learning inherent to human socialization. Boyd and Kohlberg have suggested that the development of moral decision-making follows a logical systematic form, much as Erikson has outlined for human growth and development in general.[5] The stages of moral development as posed by Boyd and Kohlberg are summarized as follows:

I. PREMORAL LEVEL

At this level the individual is responsive to cultural rules and labels of good and bad, right and wrong, but interprets these labels in terms of either the physical or the hedonistic consequences of an action—for

---

4. Kieffer, p. 36–37.

5. Erikson, Erik. *Toys and Reasons.* New York: W. W. Norton Co., 1977.

example, punishment, reward, exchange of favors—or in terms of the physical power of those who enunciate the rules and labels. This is generally the level of the young child. The level is divided into the following two stages:

Stage 1.

The Punishment and Obedience Orientation. The physical consequences of an action determine its goodness or badness regardless of the human meaning or value of those consequences. Avoidance of punishment and unquestioning deference to power are valued in their own right, not in terms of respect for the underlying moral order supported by punishment and authority.

Stage 2.

The Instrumental-Relativist Orientation. Right action consists of that which instrumentally satisfies one's own needs and occasionally the needs of others. Human relations are viewed in terms of those of the marketplace. Elements of fairness, or reciprocity, and of equal sharing are present, but they are always interpreted in a physical, pragmatic way. Reciprocity is a matter of "you scratch my back and I'll scratch yours," not of loyalty, gratitude or justice.

II. CONVENTIONAL ROLE-CONFORMITY LEVEL

At this level, maintaining the expectation of the individual's family, group, or nation is perceived as valuable in its own right, regardless of the immediate and obvious consequences. The attitude is not only one of conformity to personal expectations and social order, but of loyalty to it, of actively maintaining, supporting, and justifying the order, and of identifying with the persons or groups involved in it. At this level, there are the following two stages:

Stage 3.

The Interpersonal Concordance of "Good Boy—Nice Girl" Orientation. Good behavior is that which pleases or helps others and is approved by them. There is much conformity to stereotypical images of what is the majority or "natural" behavior. Behavior is frequently judged by intention—"he means well" becomes important for the first time. One earns approval by being "nice."

Stage 4.

The Law and Order Orientation. This orientation is towards authority, fixed rules, and the maintenance of the social order. Right behavior consists of doing one's duty, showing respect for authority, and maintaining the given social order for its own sake: "my country, right or wrong."

III. POSTCONVENTIONAL OR PRINCIPLED LEVEL

At this level, there is a clear effort to define moral values and principles which have validity and the application apart from the authority of the groups or persons holding these principles, and apart from the individual's own identification with these groups. This level has two stages.

Stage 5.

The Social-Contract Legalistic Orientation. Right action tends to be defined in terms of general individual rights and standards which have been critically examined and agreed upon by the whole society. There is a clear awareness of the relativism of personal values and opinions and a corresponding emphasis upon procedural rules for reaching consensus. Aside from what is constitutionally and democratically agreed upon, the right is a matter of personal "values" and "opinions." The result is an emphasis upon the "legal point of view" but with an emphasis upon the possibility of changing laws in terms of rational considerations of social utility rather than freezing it as in Stage 4 where "law and order" are uppermost. Outside the legal realm, free agreement and contract are the binding elements of obligation. This is the "official" morality of the American government and Constitution.

Stage 6.

The Universal Ethical Principle Orientation. Right is defined by the decision of conscience in accord with self-chosen ethical principles appealing to logical comprehensiveness, universality and consistency. These principles are abstract and ethical (for example, the Golden Rule); they are not concrete moral rules like the Ten Commandments. Essentially, these are the principles of justice, of humane reciprocity, of equality, and of respect for the dignity of human beings as individual persons.

Kieffer, in an analysis of the Boyd and Kohlberg stages of moral development, notes that the stages demonstrate a progression from the egocentric self through a variety of mid-points to a final, other-oriented stage. They also note that very sophisticated and mature individuals can be assessed as functioning at one of the lower stages, and that whole societies can be fixed at one of the lower points.

SOME PROFESSIONAL CODES OF ETHICS EXAMINED

Utilizing Boyd and Kohlberg's system of moral development, we can analyze the level of moral development indicated by the content and focus of the various ethical codes promulgated by the professional societies listed below. Each prescribes many behavioral standards for its members; some of these are quite altruistic, and others tend more towards the self-protection of the society or its members.

American Nurses' Association Code for Nurses
American Medical Association Principle of Medical Ethics
American Society of Radiologic Technologists Code of Ethics
Code of Ethics of the American Medical Record Association
American Occupational Therapy Association Principles of Occupational Therapy Ethics

AMERICAN NURSES' ASSOCIATION *CODE FOR NURSES*

Preamble

The *Code for Nurses* is based on belief about the nature of individuals, nursing, health, and society. Recipients and providers of nursing services are viewed as individuals and groups who possess basic rights and responsibilities, and whose values and circumstances command respect at all times. Nursing encompasses the promotion and restoration of health, the prevention of illness, and the alleviation of suffering. The statements of the Code and their interpretation provide guidance for conduct and relationships in carrying out nursing responsibilities consistent with the ethical obligations of the profession and quality in nursing care.

Code for Nurses

1. The nurse provides services with respect for human dignity and the uniqueness of the client unrestricted by considerations of social and

economic status, personal attributes, or the nature of the health problems.

2. The nurse safeguards the client's right to privacy by judiciously protecting information of a confidential nature.

3. The nurse acts to safeguard the client and the public when health care and safety are affected by the incompetent, unethical, or illegal practice of any person.

4. The nurse assumes responsibility and accountability for individual nursing judgements and actions.

5. The nurse maintains competence in nursing.

6. The nurse exercises informed judgement and uses individual competence and qualification as criteria in seeking consultation, accepting responsibilities, and delegating nursing activities to others.

7. The nurse participates in activities that contribute to the ongoing development of the profession's body of knowledge.

8. The nurse participates in the profession's efforts to implement and improve standards of nursing.

9. The nurse participates in the profession's efforts to establish and maintain conditions of employment conducive to high quality nursing care.

10. The nurse participates in the profession's efforts to protect the public from misinformation and misrepresentation and to maintain the integrity of nursing.

11. The nurse collaborates with members of the health professions and other citizens in promoting community and national efforts to meet the health needs of the public.

AMERICAN MEDICAL ASSOCIATION
PRINCIPLES OF MEDICAL ETHICS*

Preamble

These principles are intended to aid physicians individually and collectively in maintaining a high level of ethical conduct. They are not laws but standards by which a physician may determine the propriety of his conduct in his relationship with patients, with colleagues, with members of allied professions, and with the public.

Section 1

The principal objective of the medical profession is to render service to humanity with full respect for the dignity of man. Physicians should

---

*Courtesy of the American Medical Association. Reprinted by permission.

merit the confidence of patients entrusted to their care, rendering to each a full measure of service and devotion.

Section 2

Physicians should strive continually to improve medical knowledge and skill, and should make available to their patients and colleagues the benefits of their professional attainments.

Section 3

A physician should practice a method of healing founded on a scientific basis; and he should not voluntarily associate professionally with anyone who violates this principle.

Section 4

The medical profession should safeguard the public and itself against physicians deficient in moral character or professional competence. Physicians should observe all laws, uphold the dignity and honor of the profession and accept its self-imposed disciplines. They should expose, without hesitation, illegal or unethical conduct of fellow members of the profession.

Section 5

A physician may choose whom he will serve. In an emergency, however, he should render service to the best of his ability. Having undertaken the care of a patient, he may not neglect him; and unless he has been discharged he may discontinue his services only after giving adequate notice. He should not solicit patients.

Section 6

A physician should not dispose of his services under terms or conditions which tend to interfere with or impair the free and complete exercise of his medical judgment and skill or tend to cause a deterioration of the quality of medical care.

Section 7

In the practice of medicine a physician should limit the source of his professional income to medical services actually rendered by him, or under his supervision, to his patients. His fee should be commensurate with the services rendered and the client's ability to pay. He should neither pay nor receive a commission for referral of patients. Drugs, remedies or appliances may be dispensed or supplied by the physician provided it is in the best interest of the patient.

Section 8

A physician should seek consultation upon request; in doubtful or difficult cases; or whenever it appears that the quality of medical service may be enhanced thereby.

Section 9

A physician may not reveal the confidences entrusted to him in the course of medical attendance, or the deficiencies he may observe in the character of patients, unless he is required to do so by law or unless it becomes necessary in order to protect the welfare of the individual or of the community.

Section 10

The honored ideals of the medical profession imply that the responsibilities of the physician extend not only to the individual, but also to society where these responsibilities deserve his treatment and participation in activities which have the purpose of improving both the health and the well-being of the individual and the community.

AMERICAN SOCIETY OF RADIOLOGIC TECHNOLOGISTS
*CODE OF ETHICS**

At its annual meeting in June, 1977, the Board of Directors of the American Society of Radiologic Technologists approved the following code of ethics for radiologic technologists.

These principles are intended to aid radiologic technologists, individually and collectively, in maintaining a high level of ethical conduct. They are not laws, but principles by which radiologic technologists may evaluate their conduct as it relates to patients, colleagues, members of allied professions, and the public.

1. Radiologic technologists should conduct themselves in a manner compatible with the dignity of their profession.
2. Radiologic technologists should provide services with consideration of

*Courtesy of the American Society of Radiologic Technologists.

human dignity and the uniqueness of the patient, unrestricted by considerations of sex, race, creed, social or economic status, personal attributes, or the nature of the health problem.

3. Radiologic technologists should strive continually to improve their professional knowledge and skills by participation in educational and professional activities, and share with their colleagues the benefits of their professional attainments.

4. Radiologic technologists should judiciously protect the patient's right to privacy and shall maintain all patient information in strictest confidence.

5. Radiologic technologists shall apply methods of technology founded on a scientific basis and should not accept those methods that violate this principle.

6. Radiologic technologists shall make every effort to protect all patients from unnecessary radiation.

7. Radiologic technologists should participate in the profession's efforts to protect the public from misinformation and misrepresentation.

8. Radiologic technologists should exercise independent discretion and judgment in the performance of their professional services.

9. Radiologic technologists do not diagnose, but in recognizing their responsibility to the patient, they are obligated to provide the physician with all information they have relative to radiologic diagnosis or patient management.

Published by Journal of the American Society of Radiologic Technologists.

AMERICAN MEDICAL RECORD ASSOCIATION
*CODE OF ETHICS**

Preamble

The medical record practitioner is concerned with the development, use, and maintenance of medical and health records for medical care, preventive medicine, quality assurance, professional education, administrative practices and study purposes with due consideration of patients' right to privacy. The American Medical Record Association believes that it is in the best interests of the medical record profession and the public which it serves that the principles of personal and professional accountability be reexamined and redefined to provide members of the Association, as well as medical record practitioners who are credentialed by the Association, with definitive and binding

*Courtesy of the American Medical Record Association.

guidelines of conduct. To achieve this goal, the American Medical Record Association has adopted the following restated Code of Ethics:

I. Conduct yourself in the practice of this profession so as to bring honor and dignity to yourself, the medical record profession and the Association.

II. Place service before material gain and strive at all times to provide services consistent with the need for quality health care and treatment to all who are ill and injured.

III. Preserve and secure the medical and health records, the information contained therein, and the appropriate secondary records in your custody in accordance with professional management practices, employer's policies and existing legal provisions.

IV. Uphold the doctrine of confidentiality and the individual's right to privacy in the disclosure of personally identifiable medical and social information.

V. Recognize the source of the authority and powers delegated to you and conscientiously discharge the duties and responsibilities thus entrusted.

VI. Refuse to participate in or conceal unethical practices or procedures in your relationship with other individuals or organizations.

VII. Disclose to no one but proper authorities any evidence of conduct or practice revealed in medical reports or observed that indicates possible violation of established rules and regulations of the employer or professional practice.

VIII. Safeguard the public and the profession by reporting to the Ethics Committee any breach of this Code of Ethics by fellow members of the profession.

IX. Preserve the confidential nature of professional determinations made by official committees of health and health-service organizations.

X. Accept compensation only in accordance with services actually performed or negotiated with the health institution.

XI. Cooperate with other health professions and organizations to promote the quality of health programs and the advancement of medical care, ensuring respect and consideration for the responsibility and the dignity of medical and other health professions.

XII. Strive to increase the profession's body of systematic knowledge and individual competency through continued self-improvement and application of current advancements in the conduct of medical record practices.

XIII. Participate in developing and strengthening professional manpower and appropriately represent the profession in public.

XIV. Discharge honorably the responsibilities of any Association position to which appointed or elected.

XV. Represent truthfully and accurately professional credentials, education, and experience in any official transaction or notice, including other positions and duality of interests.

PRINCIPLES OF OCCUPATIONAL THERAPY ETHICS*

Preamble

This association and its component members are committed to furthering man's ability to function fully within his total environment. To this end the Occupational Therapist renders service to clients in all stages of health and illness, to institutions, other professionals, colleagues, students and to the general public.

In furthering this commitment the American Occupational Therapy Association has established the Principles of Occupational Therapy Ethics. It is intended that they be used by all occupational therapy personnel, including practitioners in all settings, administrators, educators, and students. These principles should be reflected in and supported by licensing laws, regulations, consultation, planning and teaching. They are intended to be action oriented, guiding and preventive rather than negative or merely disciplinary. Professional maturity will be demonstrated in applying these basic principles while exercising the large measure of freedom which they provide and which is essential to responsible and creative occupational therapy service. For the purpose of continuity the following definitions will support information in this document: Occupational therapist includes registered occupational therapists, certified occupational therapy assistants, occupational therapy students. Clients include patients and those to whom occupational therapy services are delivered.

I. Related to the Recipient of Service

The occupational therapist demonstrates a beneficent concern for the recipient of services, maintains a goal directed relationship with the recipient which furthers the objectives for which it is established. Services are evaluated against objectives and accountability is maintained

---

*Adopted by the Representative Assembly, American Occupational Association, April, 1977. Published in American Journal of Occupational Therapy Newspaper, November, 1977. Reprinted by permission of the American Occupational Therapy Association; Jerry A. Johnson, president.

therefore. Respect shall be shown for the recipients' rights and the occupational therapist will preserve the confidence of the patient relationship.

II. Related to Competence

The occupational therapist shall actively maintain and improve one's professional competence, represent it accurately and function within its perimeters.

III. Related to Records, Reports, Grades, and Recommendations

The occupational therapist shall conform to local, state and federal laws and regulations, and regulations applicable to records and reports. The occupational therapist abides by the employing institution's rules. Objective data shall govern subjective data in evaluations, grades, recommendations, records and reports.

IV. Related to Intra-professional Colleagues

The occupational therapist shall function with discretion and integrity in relations with other members of the profession and shall be concerned with the quality of their services. Upon becoming aware of objective evidence of a breach of ethics or substandard service the occupational therapist shall take action according to established procedure.

V. Related to Other Personnel

The occupational therapist shall function with discretion and integrity in relations with personnel and cooperates with them as may be appropriate. Similarly, the occupational therapist expects others to demonstrate a high level of competence. Upon becoming aware of objective evidence of a breach of ethics or substandard service the occupational therapist shall take action according to established procedure.

VI. Related to Employers and Payers

The occupational therapist shall render service with discretion and integrity and shall protect the property and property rights of the employers and payers.

VII. Related to Education

The occupational therapist implements a commitment to the education of society and the consumer of health services as well as to the education of health personnel on matters of health which are within the purview of occupational therapy.

VIII. Related to Evaluation and Research

The occupational therapist shall accept responsibility for evaluating, developing and refining service and the body of knowledge and skills which underlie the education and practice of occupational therapy, at all times protects the rights of subjects, clients, institutions and collaborators. The work of others shall be acknowledged.

IX. Related to the Profession

The occupational therapist shall be responsible for gaining information and understanding of the principles, policies and standards of the profession. The occupational therapist functions as a representative of the profession.

X. Related to Law and Regulations

The occupational therapist shall seek to acquire information about applicable local, state, federal and institutional rules and shall function accordingly thereto.

XI. Related to Misconduct

The occupational therapist shall not appear to act with impropriety nor engage in illegal conduct involving moral turpitude and will not circumvent the principles of occupational therapy ethics through actions of another.

XII. Related to Bioethical Issues and Problems of Society

The occupational therapist seeks information about the major health problems and issues to learn their implications for occupational therapy and for one's own services.

EMERGING ETHICAL THEMES

In reviewing these ethical codes written by the various professional health care associations, we can see certain basic themes emerge. These themes represent the universally-acknowledged standards for good conduct that the field of health promulgates. They can serve as the basis for the development of a universal guide to ethical decision-making in health care practice.

One universal theme that appears in one form or another in each of the listed codes is that of the client's right to privacy and confidentiality. Each professional code cites the individual's responsibility to protect client privacy as a duty. Some specify the need to observe the confidentiality of client records, while others list more general statements about the issue of privacy; but the basic obligation to observe the client's right to privacy is universal.

Many of the codes mention the obligation to respect the dignity of the individual client, regardless of race, creed, or ethnic origin. The obligation to render service to all is present in every code but one; the American Medical Association obligates the physician to render service in an emergency, but reserves the right to withhold service to clients in less extreme situations. Just what constitutes an emergency is not stated.

Each code also obligates the practitioner of the profession to continual self-development of knowledge and skills. The importance of continuing education and development is emphasized through the universal admonition to maintain professional competence.

All of the codes also obligate the practitioner to one or another form of peer review, in statements that note the professional's responsibility to protect the consumer from incompetent service. All of the codes mention the practitioner's obligation to act on the knowledge of the incompetent practice of another, although the means and extent to which the practitioner is obligated are not quite clear; nor is the concept of incompetent or unethical practice fully developed.

It is interesting to note that many of the codes also contain sections dealing with economic issues related to the profession. Although the degree to which these statements apply to ethical mandates intended to protect the client is debatable, the fact that economics are mentioned in these codes is proof of the degree to which the health care system is governed by financial considerations. Each of the statements, although ostensibly motivated to protect the clientele from unscrupulous financial gouging by practitioners, carries the distinct message that the economic welfare of the practitioner must also be protected.

A variety of other ethical and related themes emerge from analysis of the ethical codes. A comparison of the codes' treatment of major emerging themes is found in Table 2.1.

	Confidentiality	Individual Client Dignity	Professional Development	Peer Accountability	Economic Sanctions	Development of Knowledge	Protection of the Public	Collaboration with Other Professionals
American Nurses' Association	X	X	X	X	X	X	X	X
American Medical Association	X			X	X		X	
Radiologic Technicians	X	X	X				X	
American Medical Records	X			X	X	X		
Occupational Therapists	X			X		X		X

Table 2.1 Emerging Ethical Themes

TOWARD A COMMON ETHICAL BOND

We have discussed the concept of ethics as systems for determination of right and wrong within situations that present dilemmas; we have reviewed the concept of moral development and attempted to analyze the ethical codes of several health professions organizations with regard to the emerging ethical themes they contain. This discussion of ethics in health care would be incomplete if it were allowed to end without our attempting to make it relevant to the practice of the professional nurse. All of the esoteric discussion of ethical dilemmas to which we are currently treated is meaningless if it cannot be applied to the realm of practice. "The proof of a pudding is in the eating," and the strength of ethical decision-making is in its application to the real world about us.

In our review of ethical systems and emerging themes we have noted several ethical statements common to all the health professions which suggests that certain ethical tenets are universally acknowledged. These themes include the notion of client dignity, autonomy, and confidentiality. Similarly, many of the currently developing ethical systems offered by Frankema and others focus on what is becoming known as a humanist perspective. These two concepts bear relevance for the health professional in that they focus on an identical theme: the emergence of the individual as central to the decision-making process. Both in ethical deliberation and in health care practice, we are becoming more cognizant of the rights of the individual to exert control and influence over his own future. The rights of institutions, groups, and societies to modify or obliterate the rights of the individual are receiving close scrutiny. Perhaps this is the common ethical bond that will allow health care professionals to deal with the mundane, everyday ethical dilemmas more effectively and efficiently.

Edward L. Ericson, in *The Humanist Alternative*, describes ethical humanism as ". . . a philosophy and moral faith founded upon the twin principles of human responsibility and personal worth."[6] It would seem that the ethical inclination of most health professions is headed squarely in this direction. We are beginning to speak most eloquently to the issues of human dignity, individual worth, and the intrinsic good of mankind. If this is the trend of ethical thought in health care, why are we unable to allow our decision-making systems to be founded upon these principles?

It is possible that we are currently attempting to meld together two mutually exclusive concepts—those of humanism and those of the current authoritarian decision-making system that is health care. We have structured and continued to support a health care system that places the recipient of care in the least powerful of positions for decision-making, often ignoring him completely in the process of designing life-shaping regimens and professional therapeutic strategies. We assume that the client's lack of medical knowledge permanently disqualifies him from an autonomous role in the health-care structure; we relegate the consumer of care to a status only slightly above that accorded an inanimate object.

The mystique of the medical realm combined with the authoritarian structure of decision-making and power centralization make the client

---

6. Ericson, Edward L. in *The Humanist Alternative*. Paul Kurtz, editor, New York: Prometheus, 1973, p. 56.

the last and the least in the system. The hierarchy of power is such that those with most authority and knowledge are furthest from the client, and the rank of health workers seems to decrease as the amount of contact with clients increases. Pity the poor patient, who though touted as the object of the entire system, sometimes seems more like an unfortunate bystander in a system that encourages us to jockey for status and clout. No wonder that there is such a mismatch between what we say we aim to do and what we do.

Has it never struck you as ludicrous that hospitals need to promote patients' rights as a concept, when it is the patient who is the economic support of the hospital? In what other business is it necessary to remind the employees that the consumer of service has some rights too? Would you tolerate a dress shop clerk who told you what you could and could not buy or what styles were or weren't appropriate for you? Yet from the family physician to the unit clerk, the neurosurgeon to the cleaning lady, all of these health care workers are in positions of greater influence and power over a client's hospitalization than the client is frequently allowed.

Given this strange conflict between what we proclaim and what we do, a restatement of ethical standards in terms of real possibilities seems appropriate. Either we must modify our ethical objectives, or we must modify the system in order to attain these objectives. It would be ludicrous to suggest that we should revise our ethical codes to reflect our current worship of the authoritarian *status quo* over the dignity of the client; or to propose that client confidentiality and respect be sacrificed in the interests of maintaining the current scheduled health care delivery system. Yet that is, in effect, what we do each and every day that we tolerate a structure and delivery of care that does not focus on the client as the central figure in the system. Each time a nurse accords priority to transcribing a central supply bill and sends an aide to answer a client's call bell, we have given priority to central supply over client care. Small decisions like this belie our espoused concern for quality of care.

A common ethical bond focusing on the need for practitioners to view care as the primary objective of service and the consumer of care as the ultimate source of legitimate authority in the system would go a long way towards eliminating our confusion. Recognition of the fundamental goal of health care—human care—and structuring of practice to accord this goal its proper primacy would help us attain many of our loftiest ethical goals. This sounds like a simple task, and an easy criterion for judging whether each decision we make is ethical or not, but the difficulties in implementation are great. Woe awaits the nurse who dares to ask a physician to postpone his request for her services while she attends to the needs of a client. Yet who is the consumer of service? Whose needs are more significant? Nowhere in health care is the gap between rhetoric and reality more apparent than in the difference between the priority supposedly given client care and the priority actually given.

The ethical bond that is envisioned in Humanism is twofold. First, the individual is worthwhile, deserving of dignity and respect. Second, this worthwhile individual is responsible for her own actions. If we are to attend to these principles and apply them to health care practice, several modifications in attitude and application must occur.

The principle emphasizing the worth of the individual requires that we rethink and modify professional attitudes toward client care in such a manner that client dignity and respect receive first priority in institutional design and delivery of service. The strength of this principle's application can be monitored simply by assessing the degree to which current practice patterns undermine client dignity. Although in theory we act to protect client privacy and dignity, the shortcuts we use in the practice environment frequently have the opposite effect. It is not at all unusual to observe physical privacy and confidentiality of client records abused on a routine basis in the hospital climate. Whenever we discuss the interesting cases of the day while riding the elevator, casually exchange information at the change of shift, or attempt to relate a bit of fresh gossip about a client while passing a friend in the hall, our insensitivity to the worth and dignity of the individual is obvious. If we are truly to support this principle, drastic alterations in the day-to-day behavior of staff are required. Such alterations must originate at all levels of authority and responsibility in the system, from director to nurse aide. They also must be encouraged in the educational milieu, for students reflect the attitudes and behaviors of their teachers. If educators are not continually cognizant of the dignity and worth of students, how can we expect these same students to believe in the dignity and worth of the client?

The second principle, that the individual is responsible for her own actions, suggests that we must renounce our attitude of paternalistic responsibility for health care and shift the focus of control and responsibility to the client. No longer can we ask clients to follow the physician's orders without first establishing the rationale for the regimen of care. It is the client's health and welfare that are at stake; it should remain the client's decision whether or not to attend to care, and his responsibility to deal with the results of care. We must explain to the client that it is important for him to act responsibly in matters of health, for if he doesn't follow the prescribed medical or nursing regimen, it is the client, not the nurse or physician, who will be faced with the consequences. Our attitude of "taking care" needs to be modified to reflect our appreciation that we are, indeed, contractors of service, working for the client, who will ultimately determine the success or failure of the system. Making people aware of their responsibility for their own health would go far toward winning the battle for preventive health care.

CONTEMPORARY HEALTH CARE: ETHICAL DILEMMAS

The rationale for the study and acquisition of knowledge and information in ethics for health care professionals is provided only within the context of its usefulness for application in the real world that is health care. As philosophically appealing as the pursuit of ethics might sound, its efficiency and legitimacy as a scholarly effort for nurses and other health practitioners is provided solely in that the ability to transfer this information to the practice realm. As we have seen, there is great need in health care for ethical decision-making skills. At no time in the history of health care has this need been greater. The frightening prospect is that the ethical dilemmas currently facing the health care delivery system will intensify rather than abate.

The conflict of social goals, value systems, technological capacity and moral acceptability is at crisis proportions. We must deal both with the fruits of scientific success and with the problems created through our inability to cope with that success. We are faced with critical decisions regarding priorities for future research and service. We are asked to give increasingly more technologically sophisticated care with decreasing economic resources. Our ability to tamper in what was once considered the province of God and Nature has increased to proportions that rival science-fiction. Whether we consider the problems of passive euthanasia, amniocentesis, genetic screening, or control of human behavior, our clinical methodologies have become more sophisticated and are more readily applied than are our ethical guides for dealing with such developments. Our ability to make morally-based decisions has not kept pace with our ability to apply technology.

Yet many of the technological manifestations of the increasing sophistication of health care appear to be beyond the decisional realm of most nurses and health practitioners. It is difficult as a staff nurse (or hospital employee in almost any capacity) to imagine oneself having influence over the decision to prolong or terminate life, perform or act on information from a performed amniocentesis, or actually be involved in a significant fashion with any of the previously mentioned technological/ethical dilemmas. But the nurse, in particular, has an obligation to evaluate critically these and many seemingly simpler areas of ethical conflict. Her actual involvement is extensive, and her responsibility to self, client, and society is great.

Why? Nowhere is there greater potential for supporting and encouraging client decision-making than in nursing service. Nurses comprise the largest number of health practitioners, have the greatest exposure to clients in institutional and noninstitutional settings, and have earned the public's trust through their historic role in health care. Nursing remains one of the few professions not to have experienced an erosion of public confidence through disclosure of unethical or illegal activities. For whatever reason, the nurse's image remains that of a trusted friend. The continuous nursing presence in hospitals, as well as the frontline nursing care offered in public and community health clinics, schools, and industrial clinics, and independent practice settings, gives clients access to professional nursing care at a level that far exceeds that of any other health profession.

Nurses have not learned to use this fact to the full advantage of the health care consumer. Because of the structure of the health care system, under which most nurses are paid by and accountable to institutions, nurses frequently do not perceive their first obligation as being to the welfare of the client. If paid by a hospital, one is more likely to behave in ways that please the powers that be in that institution than to try to satisfy the consumer of services rendered. A refocusing of attention on the actual consumer of care, the client who foots the bill for the process (with or without insurance assistance), would do much to reorient nursing to the original objectives upon which the profession was historically based and upon which its future viability rests.

The professional efforts of nurses in the health care system are a most significant force. Nurses' potential impact on the quality and quantity of health care is phenomenal. Their task is to learn to use their extensive power and resources for the design and delivery of health care that is more than simply efficient and effective: they must learn to use their power to design and deliver health care within an ethical framework. Nurses can be influential in the process of shaping the health care future of our society.

Revolutions are said to be won in small battles, not large wars. Any significant change in the humaneness of health care will result not from the pronouncements of medical authorities and acknowledged leaders (although their leadership would certainly promote change); it will be extracted from the small, everyday efforts of the vast numbers of health professionals in practice. The individual's recognition of his responsibility for his own practice could form the foundation of a health care system in which the recipient of care is no longer an inconvenience in the process, but is instead the proper object of service.

The reorientation of health care to recognize and meet its true priorities of service, client care, health promotion, and enhancement of the quality as well as the quantity of life, will occur through the efforts of the many, not the pronouncements of a few. If each practitioner were able to change her attitude and orientation in her practice, the massive revolution would be almost complete. Small decisions and small changes are the foundations of large decisions and large changes.

Where does one begin? The starting point of the process of modifying practice is to reflect an ethical perspective with a view to the intrinsic worth of the individual and the recognition that the ultimate responsibility for the state of health or illness, like the responsibility for any other facet of one's life, rests on the shoulders of the individual.

Where else but in health care can we observe the operation of a large bureaucratic system that treats its consumers as helpless, passive dolts incapable of taking responsibility for decisions and actions central to the maintenance of health? Where else would the fellow footing the bill tolerate such indignities, injuries, and insults? Lack of respect for the worth of the individual and lack of appreciation of the individual's ultimate responsibility for health outcomes go hand in hand. When we devalue the client by treating her as if she were a helpless child, we create the necessary environment for robbing her of decision-making control and set the stage for her tolerance of the myriad indignities that accompany contemporary health care. Recognition of client worth and appreciation of client responsibility are the first steps in the process of change.

The practitioner will undoubtedly ask, "Even if I make these changes in my philosophical approach to practice, the larger system will remain the same, so how does this help?" The answer has two aspects: If each practitioner were able to exert a bit of change, the cumulative effect could be a great deal of change. We can ultimately be accountable only for our own practice, but we can hope to change the practice of others indirectly, by acting as role models. The potential impact of the change in orientation of each individual practitioner is large. This potential impact is made larger still by the effect of this attitudinal change on the consumer.

We tend to see ourselves and to perform according to the expectations of others around us, particularly according to our perceptions of the expectations of those we view as being in positions of authority and power. The client behaves and performs according to the expectations that he perceives the decision-makers within the health care authority structure have of him. Thus, if the client believes that he is expected to behave like a dolt, incapable of effective decision-making for health care, he will behave accordingly. After all, the professionals have all the advanced knowledge and skill in this mysterious field; surely if they say the client's a dolt, he's a dolt. But what would happen if suddenly the opposite message were received?

The impact of an alteration in practitioner attitude on the behavior of the consumer of care could be phenomenal. Should we begin to treat clients as if they were capable of control over their own future, even control over small, seemingly insignificant decisions, sweeping changes in the attitude and demands of the consumer of care might occur. The expression, "give them an inch, and they'll take a mile," could be delightfully applicable in this situation.

Envision a situation in which the consumer of care suddenly is aware that it is she who is footing the bill and will ultimately bear the consequences of care. Can you image the active role this consumer might want to take in the decisions affecting her care?

This is currently happening in many environments and many ways. From the inclusion of consumer representation on health planning agency boards, to the growing realization that clients have rights of access to information recorded on their health records, we are beginning to witness public recognition that the ultimate authority for health care decisions should rest with the object of those decisions. Can you imagine how this movement would be accelerated if nurses and other health professionals were to start acknowledging the client as the ultimate target of their service and, thus, as the final determinant of care design?

Some institutions have begun to modify the delivery of nursing care in such a fashion as to permit the client increased determination over the conditions and timing of service. The methods include incorporating client objectives and input in nursing care planning; allowing client preference for scheduling of routine care procedures; and providing for client direction of some aspects of service, such as when to have personal care performed or when to complete routine treatments. These are, admittedly, token efforts, yet they represent a beginning. These seemingly small changes are the first steps in the long process of reorienting both the system and the client to the realities of responsibility in health care. One can only guess at what larger changes may eventually be the result of such small beginnings.

The ethical perspective of the individual practitioner determines the care that practitioner will give. A perspective that incorporates the recognition of the intrinsic worth and dignity of the individual, and that focuses responsibility on the individual, will set the stage for the delivery of care that promotes individual dignity and responsibility. This, then, may lead to the modification of the self-image of the client, ultimately increasing the client's ability to seek and obtain more humane standards of service. How does this process relate to resolution of contemporary health care ethical dilemmas?

The appropriate decision-maker in the resolution of a dilemma is the individual who will bear responsibility for the consequences of the resolution. If it is my life that will be terminated, my future welfare that will be affected, or my lifestyle that will be altered, then I am the ultimate authority for decision-making control. It is simply unjust and inhumane to deprive the individual of authority over her future and then to ask her to bear the consequences for decisions made. A typical health professions response to this statement is, "How can the patient make decisions when he is not prepared with adequate knowledge of the facts upon which such decisions rest?"

The role of the health professional should be to share information and alternatives with clients to ensure that decisions are based upon whatever knowledge is available. Usually there is a lot less complexity to a situation than we, in our professional conceit, would like to believe. The client's expectation of health care should include his preparation for making an informed choice. It is our obligation to render advice, information, and support. It is not our obligation to deprive the client of the ultimate authority for the decision unless we are also prepared to shoulder the consequences of that decision.

The case of Mary Northern provides an excellent example of the manner in which we attempt to make decisions for clients and then expect them to live with the consequences. Ms. Northern was a 72-year-old victim of frostbite and subsequent burns. At the time of her hospitalization, the attending physicians decided that amputation would be necessary to save her life. Ms. Northern refused to give consent for the amputation procedure. The State of Tennessee, in which she was a resident, brought suit to declare her incompetent to make the amputation consent decision. Her lawyer argued that she had the right to take responsibility for the decision, and was competent to do so. The court battle was resolved when the state was granted the right to give consent for Ms. Northern, but the resolution was never implemented, as her condition deteriorated beyond that in which surgery could be safely performed. The difficulty in the Northern case is that the health professionals involved were more than willing to assume the decision-making authority for Ms. Northern, but did not have to bear the consequences of their decision. Had the amputation occurred, it is doubtful that the 72-year-old woman could have experienced sufficient rehabilitation to resume her previous independent lifestyle. It is likely that she would have required long-term institutional care, accumulated considerable debt, and been reduced to living a life much different from what she was used to and probably repugnant to her. Health professionals would have imposed their personal priorities on Ms. Northern and then have left her to contend with the results. Her determination both to live and die as she chose, no matter how different from the strategies we would have personally selected, merits respect and admiration.

I believe that a health care system that recognized client worth and responsibility, even in the most insignificant of matters, would foster more assertive client behavior. The recognition that final authority for all decisions must rest with the client would contribute to the humane resolution of many of the contemporary ethical dilemmas confronting health care.

Exercises and Games

Self-Description: An exercise that is helpful in the process of attaining awareness of one's own values is that of self-description. Simply describe yourself in a brief, newspaper format style. Use as few words as possible, just what is absolutely necessary to give the reader a quick but thorough image of you.

Analysis: Did you begin your self-description with role titles, such as wife, mother, husband, father? Or did you choose to begin by stating occupational information, such as nurse or student? Possibly you began your self-description with physical information, such as height, weight, or skin color. Did you choose to describe yourself by relationship to others, such as, "the daughter of prominent lawyer . . .?"

Your choice of descriptive terminology is quite telling. It allows you to evaluate what you think are the most important characteristics about yourself. If you see your role as a wife and mother as a significant, you probably perceive your family role as having the most weight. If you choose to describe yourself in terms of professional status, it is most probable that you value your vocational self-image and relate a strong part of your identity to your profession.

Suggestions for Further Reading

Amundsen, Darrel W. "The Physician's Obligation to Prolong Life: A Medical Duty Without Classical Roots—What the Hippocratic Corpus Does Not Say." The Hastings Center Report, Vol. 8, No. 4 (August 1978), pp. 23–29. Examines the physician's duty to prolong life in relation to treating the terminally ill, assisting in suicide, and the relevance of the Hippocratic Oath.

Bandman, Elsie L. and Bertram Bandman. *Bioethics and Human Rights.* Boston: Little, Brown and Company, 1978.
Fundamental theme is that the right to the enjoyment of good health is a necessity of life as vital as food, shelter, and safety. Health care is viewed as a consumer product. Functions of health providers and rights of consumers are discussed.

Beauchamp, Tom L. and Seymour Perlia. *Ethical Issues in Death and Dying.* New Jersey: Prentice-Hall, Inc., 1978.
  Attempts to define brain death, irreversible coma, standards for determining human death, and the technical and ethical implications. Explores the ethics of suicide, its morality and rationality, euthanasia, and the significance of life and death.

Bedau, Hugo Adam and Michael Zeik. "Case Studies in Bioethics—A Condemned Man's Last Wish: Organ Donation and a 'Meaningful' Death." The Hastings Center Report, Vol. 9, No. 1 (February 1979), pp. 16–17.
  Examines issue of choosing one's own method of dying and new legal implications if "meaningful" death prospects are executed.

Bereiter, Carl. "Morality and Moral Education." *The Hastings Center Report,* Vol. 8, No. 2 (April 1978), pp. 20–25.
  Examines moral education, particularly in the public school system, and the pedagogy of values. Discusses Kohlberg's cognitive-developmental approach, implements value clarification, and examines legitimate function of public education.

Black, Peter McL. "The Rationale for Psychosurgery." *The Humanist,* Vol. 38, No. 4 (July/August 1977), pp. 6, 8–9.
  Discusses *pro* and *con* views on performing psychosurgery; defines psychosurgery. Conclusion stated reveals techniques will not be banned provided psychosurgery remains a potentially important facet of contemporary medical care.

Brody, Howard. *Ethical Decisions in Medicine.* Boston: Little, Brown and Company, 1976.
  A self-instructional text focusing on the physician's interface with medical ethics. Contains a comprehensive review of medical ethical dilemmas.

Bullough, Bonnie and Vern Bullough, eds. *Expanding Horizons for Nurses.* New York: Springer Publishing Co., 1977.
  Examines recent legislative enactments and ethical problems involved in controversial clinical issues—abortion, homosexuality, and euthanasia—and the nursing profession's inherent need to stay abreast of change.

Carr, Arthur C., ed. "Man and Medicine." *Journal of Values and Ethics in Health Care,* Vol. 3, No. 4 (1978), pp. 229–309.
  Attempts to explore possibility of humane nursing and quality care in our present efficiency-oriented scheme of organized health care.

Chinn, Peggy L., ed. "Ethics and Values." *Advances in Nursing Science,* Vol. 1, No. 3 (April 1979), pp. 1–99.
  Depicts ethics as a science integral to and necessary for nursing practice by promoting a philosophical commitment to the profession in dealing with issues such as the right to die and mental health and the aged.

Coene, Roger E. and Carol Levine. "Choosing Between Dialysis and Transplant." *The Hastings Center Report*, Vol. 8, No. 2 (April 1978), pp. 8–10.
Examines decision-making process and available options in cases of dialysis and transplant, including ethical costs and benefits of organ donation involving family members and resultant changed lifestyles and behavior due to deficit.

Davis, Anne J. and Mila A. Aroskan. *Ethical Dilemmas and Nursing Practice.* New York: Appleton-Century-Crofts, 1978.
An introductory text for nursing's interface with ethics. Review of ethical systems and capsulization of common ethical dilemmas, including abortion, behavior control, and death and dying.

Gorovetz, Samuel, et al., editors. *Moral Problems In Medicine.* Englewood Cliffs: Prentice-Hall, 1976.
Medical reference reviewing moral philosophy, physician-encountered dilemmas, legal concepts, and contemporary social problems. Collection of articles by leading scholars in each discipline. Advanced comprehension required.

Hardin, Garrett. *Exploring New Ethics for Survival—The Voyage of Spaceship Beagle.* Baltimore: Penguin Books, Inc., 1972.
Suggests that technology cannot solve the "population problem." Discusses concepts such as population responsibility and whether parenthood is a right or a privilege.

Heifetz, Milton D., and Charles Mangel. *The Right to Die.* New York: Putnam, 1975.
Candid neurosurgeon discusses brain death, the right to die and refuse treatment, and the effects of such decisions on the social fabric.

High, Dallas M. "Is 'Natural Death' an Illusion? An Ideal In Search of a Meaning." *The Hastings Center Report*, Vol. 8, No. 4 (August 1978), pp. 37–42.
Attempts to discuss notions of natural death, define the natural death concept, and analyze moral and individual implications. Briefly discusses the California Natural Death Act.

Humber, James M. and Robert F. Almeder, eds. *Biomedical Ethics and the Law.* New York: Plenum Press, 1977.
Introductory anthology viewing biomedical ethics as a discipline utilized in such decision-making areas as abortion, mental illness, human experimentation, human genetics, and dying; each is examined with regard to legal influence.

Kelly, Lucie Young. *Dimensions of Professional Nursing*, 3rd Ed. New York: MacMillan Publishing Company, Inc., 1975.
Overview of non-clinical aspects of nursing, including nursing history, growth of practice in U.S., current status, religious and legal aspects, and an overview of organizations, publications, and career opportunities.

Kieffer, George H. *Bioethics: A Textbook of Issues*. Reading: Addison-Wesley Publishing Company, 1979.

Presents a broad spectrum of opinions frequently encountered in ethical and scientific literature. Primarily intended for a non-specialist with little or no training in philosophy or ethics. Explores medical and non-medical issues—from human experimentation to our obligation to future generations.

Krawczyk, Rosemary and Elizabeth Kudzma, "Ethics: A Matter of Moral Development." *Nursing Outlook* (April 1978), pp. 254–7.

Proposes that seminars, rather than formal courses of theoretical ethics, contribute more to moral development of students. Cites moral development stages according to Kohlberg; provides a dilemma discussion and student responses.

Kurtz, Paul, ed. *The Humanist Alternative: Some Definitions of Humanism*. New York: Prometheus Books, 1973.

Concise paperback outlining humanistic approaches to problem-solving, mankind, and how humans can enjoy a significant life.

Kurtz, Paul, ed. *Humanist Manifestos I and II*. New York: Prometheus Books, 1973.

Suggests religious influences on economic and scientific changes. Manifesto II broadens concepts presented in Manifesto I, with in-depth discussions of ethics, the individual and democratic society, and the world community.

Leopold, Aldo. *A Sand County Almanac*. New York: Oxford University Press, Inc., 1966.

The land ethic: the community concept resting on the premise that an individual is a member of a community of interdependent parts, implying respect for fellow-members, hence for the community as well. Attempts to define concepts of right and wrong in the current philosophy of values.

Levine, Carol. "Ethics and Health Cost Containment." *The Hastings Center Report*, Vol. 9, No. 1 (February 1979), pp. 10–13.

Examines service and resource allocation, ethical issues, models for health care proposed by Charles Fried and H. Jack Geiger, review of the need for psychotherapy, and the role of the expert.

Nelson, James B. *Human Medicine—Ethical Perspectives on New Medical Issues*. Minneapolis: Augsburg Publishing House, 1973.

Explores a variety of ethical issues in medicine. Issues discussed are flavored by religious-humanistic overtones and the intertwining of ethical decisions is stressed.

Orem, Dorothea E. *Nursing: Concepts of Practice*. New York: McGraw-Hill Book Co., 1971.

Provides a basis for organized nursing knowledge. Proposes

structural frameworks of nursing relevant to concepts and principles involving ethics, values, the law, and nursing as a human service.

Paterson, Josephine G. and Loretta T. Zderad. *Humanistic Nursing.* New York: John Wiley and Sons, Inc., 1976.
   Suggests that nurses have the opportunity to co-experience and co-search with patients the meaning of life, suffering, and death, and in the process, may become, or help others to become, more human.

Pelligrino, Edmund D. "Medical Morality and Medical Economics." *The Hastings Center Report,* Vol. 8, No. 4 (August 1978), pp. 8–11.
   Concludes that "cost containment" flavors the work of health planners, economists, legislators, and physicians. Explores traditional canons of medical morality, and cost consciousness and public policy.

Potter, Van Rensselaer. *Bioethics—Bridge to the Future.* New Jersey: Prentice-Hall, Inc., 1971.
   Promotes the formation of a new discipline, bioethics, to marry two cultures of science and humanities. Explores societal involvement flavored by biological roles as well as the role of the individual in relation to his environment.

Prescott, James W. "Abortion and the 'Right-to-Life': Facts, Fallacies, and Fraud." *The Humanist,* Vol. 38, No. 4 (July/August 1978), pp. 18–24.
   Discusses the ethical implications of abortion, citing cross-cultural studies that indicate significant statistical support of anti-abortion views.

Rowan, Carl T. "Health Care Inhumanity." *Chicago Sun-Times,* 22 March 1979, p. 64, cols. 1–2.
   Examines health care given to those patients without medical insurance and promotes the idea of a health care system revision in order to accommodate all patients.

Shannon, Thomas A., ed. *Bioethics.* New York: Paulist Press, 1976.
   Religious and humanistic overtones flavor a wide variety of ethical issues, including abortion, severely handicapped, death and dying, research and human experimentation, genetic engineering, and social involvement for health care accessibility.

Stein, Leonard I. "The Doctor-Nurse Game." *Archives of General Psychiatry,* Vol. 16 (June 1967), pp. 699–703.
   Analyzes relationship between the doctor and nurse, depicting "rules" of the game and preserving forces such as rewards and punishments, strength of the set, need for leadership, and sexual roles. Examines roles and preparation of nursing and medical students.

Steinfels, Margaret O'Brien and Carol Levin, eds. "In the Service of the State: The Psychiatrist as Double Agent." *The Hastings Center Report,* Vol. 8, No. 2 (April 1978), pp. 1–24.
   Investigates conflicting roles of psychiatrists in mental institutions; examines moral dilemmas in military practice, role of psychiatrists in

prisons, review of psychiatric institutions, conflict, and professional etiquette.

Sward, Kathleen M., et al. "An Historical Perspective." *Perspectives on the Code for Nurses.* American Nurse's Association, 1978.

Depicts the need of a professional code of ethics for nurses, the history of the ANA's maintenance of such a code, and its application and relevance to nurses, clients, and society.

Szasz, Thomas S. "Aborting Unwanted Behavior: The Controversy on Psychosurgery." *The Humanist,* Vol. 38, No. 4 (July/August 1977), pp. 7, 10–11.

Dr. Szasz tastefully and candidly critiques psychosurgery by endorsing the policy that physicians who advocate such a procedure constitute a threat to our personal freedom and dignity. Compares issue to abortion.

Vaux, Kenneth. *Biomedical Ethics.* New York: Harper and Row Publishers, Inc., 1974.

Proposes sources of ethical insight involved in decision-making and planning. Suggests that most genetically-based ethical decisions are not the result of broad speculating questions, but rather of day-to-day choices. Religious connotations flavor genetics discussion.

Veatch, Robert M. *Case Studies in Medical Ethics.* Cambridge: Harvard University Press, 1977.

Discusses morality in medicine, principles of medical ethics, and such special problem areas as abortion, genetic engineering, behavior control and experimentation, right to treatment, refusal, and concepts of death and dying.

Veatch, Robert M. *Death, Dying, and the Biological Revolution—Our Lost Quest for Responsibility.* New Haven: Yale University Press, 1976.

Examines the ethical dilemma of technology and the concept of death and dying. Defines and analyzes patient rights regarding treatment refusal and choosing not to prolong life, as well as right and obligation to have the truth.

Visscher, Maurice B., ed. *Humanistic Perspectives in Medical Ethics.* Buffalo: Prometheus Books, 1973.

Examines a new ethical framework resulting from advanced medical technology by reviewing common ethical issues such as the right to die, human experimentation, use of psychotropic drugs, the sanctity-of-life principle, and others.

Wertz, Richard W., ed. *Readings on Ethical and Social Issues in Biomedicine.* New Jersey: Prentice-Hall, Inc., 1973.

Concise anthology exploring a wide variety of ethical issues, giving the arguments of both sides in most cases. Critically examines justification of issues for current practice.

3

Values in Health Care

"Most people would rather defend to the death your right to say
it than listen to it."

ROBERT BRAULT

Health care is a service rendered by professionals, who apply their specialized knowledge and skills in a uniformly competent manner to all who come under their care, regardless of ethnic background, religion, age, race, creed, or other individual differences. Few practitioners would disagree with this statement. Yet it is untrue. Irresistably we each are influenced by a host of factors beyond our control. We are the sum of our experiences and our culture. Thus, if I am raised within a society that values brunettes and demeans blondes, and I am a brunette, the care I render to a blonde may well be influenced by my attitude toward blondes. Whether I am aware of that attitude or not, it is inextricably involved in my behavior.

We are each a product of our experience, background, culture, family, and education, and each of these in turn reflects a range of attitudes and values. What are *values?*

The term *value* denotes worth or significance. A mink coat and a diamond ring are said to be of great value; that is, their possession is coveted and sought after by many. Much energy is devoted to acquiring material goods, as they are highly valued by many people. *Social* and *cultural* values are also sought after and coveted, but in a different way. Most of us would state that we value freedom, and to that end our government has gone to war and sacrificed the lives of many of our fellow citizens. Freedom is a value we all share. Other values may be held by only a few people, or by a single individual: these may be termed *personal* values.

Individuals receive countless messages from birth to death. Many of these messages are related to values or concepts of worth. The mother who reinforces aggression in her son and extinguishes assertion in her daughter is teaching each child a value about his or her behavior: that boys are to be aggressive and that girls are to be passive. These messages are reinforced by the entire social structure in most instances, until they are an ingrained feature of the individual's personality—part and parcel of the person.

Values can be either personal or social. Most individuals value security. Additionally, most societies also value security. Yet in any society one can find people who are unable to conform to this social value. These people, although they may demand safety and security for themselves, are unable to respect this right in others. Society values security at a sufficiently strong level to take corrective measures when conformity to this value is violated. Thus we develop systems of confinement for those who do not conform to this particular social norm.

We are the "value products" both of home and culture. Each of us is exposed to a variety of different personal and collective experiences that influence, shape, and mold our plastic sense of values throughout life. Much of what shapes our concepts of acceptable or unacceptable behavior stems from the efforts of parents and significant others during childhood. These messages are modified by teachers, friends, and wider social group influences to which we are exposed as we emerge into adulthood. Even in adulthood, it is impossible to predict accurately the life patterns of values.

Value judgments, like ethical judgments, are judgments of worth. We value that which we hold worthy. The almost universally high valuation of family, although varying among different cultures, demonstrates that all of humanity has value systems—concepts and ideals that are judged to be worthy of support, promulgation, and continuation.

Personal values are concepts that the individual holds worthy in his own life. Whether it be the universal trait of valuing one's own survival, or the highly individual value placed upon a particular religious belief or political philosophy, each person develops a system of concepts of worth. Few people, however, have experienced opportunities to *clarify* their values to the extent that they can easily verbalize their value system.

Values are obtained in the process of growth and development. We reflect many of the values with which we were brought up. Homes and families that place a heavy emphasis on the importance of family life produce adults to whom family life is also most likely to be important. Parents and school systems that strengthen and emphasize children's acceptance of responsibility will produce independent children. As the once popular song held, "you have to be taught to hate," similarly, children must be taught to value.

The word *value* has a positive connotation. One visualizes things good and desirable, such as freedom and truth. Yet values also imply negatives, for if we value truth then it follows that we do not value dishonesty. Values are a series of choices, few of which are intentionally or consciously made. We choose truth, probably through childhood experiences that reinforce the comfort we experience in truth and the discomfort of dishonesty. The choice of truth as a value was not a conscious or intentional decision.

VALUES CLARIFICATION

Values are the concepts, ideals, behaviors, and significant themes that give meaning to our personal lives. They are the composite result of life's experiences; family, friends, culture, education and benchmark occurrences (personal crisis and aftermath). *Values clarification* is the process of assessing, exploring, and determining what these personal values are and what priority they hold in our personal decision-making.

Values clarification is a growth-producing process that permits one to assess controversial issues from a personal perspective by clarifying her position and exploring the basis for that position. In this process, one explores her beliefs to determine what she has informally valued; and, conversely, to discover those beliefs which may not be highly valued, but to which she has been giving lip service. Clarification provides a means of self-understanding that permits one to behave in ways appropriate to her personal value priorities.

The clarification of personal value systems allows one to set priorities of action that concur with her internal value agenda, and to avoid values conflict. When one is cognizant of what does or does not hold worth on a personal basis, it is far easier to decide just which battles are worth waging.

The process of values clarification involves many component processes. These include *choosing, prizing* and *acting.*[1]

During the clarification process, one *chooses* those actions which allow him to select the values most congruent with personal priorities. In order to choose, one must be *free* to choose—hence, aware of alternatives.

Prizing allows one to rank values according to personal feelings and inner awareness. The prizing activity is accompanied by the sharing of values with others, so that a value is cherished when disclosed and revealed to others. The process of self-disclosure allows one to affirm and further clarify one's values. It is probable that only positions that have been carefully examined and found to be integral with individual value sets will be freely shared with others. Certainly one will not hold personal value systems up to the acknowledgement and scrutiny of others if those systems are not well defined and personally affirmed prior to sharing.

The *acting* stage in the values clarification process involves the incorporation of values as guides to action. The clarification of values is a meaningless ritual if it does not produce greater congruence between values and actions.

---

1. Uustal, Diane. "The Use of Values Clarification in Nursing Practice." *The Journal of Continuing Education in Nursing,* Vol. 8, No. 3, 1977.

Strategies for values clarification have been outlined by Uustal, Simon,[2] Dalis and Strasser,[3] and others. These strategies focus on exercises and techniques for personal clarification of value systems. Such strategies are best used in small groups, since the process of values clarification involves the assertion of one's values during the prizing stage.

Various techniques permit one to attempt to inventory value systems, and thus to seek insight into personal concepts of worth. Although many people think that personal values clarification must involve disclosure, it is possible that private efforts at clarification are also useful. Such attempts are certainly better than none at all, and may even prove to be highly effective.

IMPACT OF PERSONAL VALUES

Value systems are much more than simple statements of what we, as individuals, treasure and hold in esteem as principles of life. They provide the framework, whether or not acknowledged, for many of our daily decisions and actions. The value one places on health, along with one's individual health knowledge, is influential in determining which health practices one engages in, or which principles of health care one abuses. The value we place on the life and worth of others is influential in determining how we will both perceive and respond to others. Thus, it is logical to conclude that personal value systems have a tremendous impact on professional practice in health care.

If a personal value system places a high priority on health-promoting behavior, it is more difficult for the individual to understand and empathize with the individual who chooses to ignore or even abuse his health. Delivering care to the client who reflects a value system that we do not support is a difficult challenge. Awareness of our own value systems allows us more readily to identify situations in which we are involved in value system conflict, and allows us to attempt to shield both ourselves and the client from unnecessary stress associated with the conflict.

Areas in which each person is likely to hold strong values include religious beliefs, sexual orientation, familial attachment, prejudices regarding other ethnic groups (blacks, Hispanics, whites, Jews, and so on), and beliefs regarding appropriate roles for others (women belong

---

2. Simon S. B., W. Howe and H. Kerschenbaum. *Values Clarification.* New York: Hart, 1972.

3. Dalis, Gus T. and Ben B. Strasser. *Teaching Strategies for Values Awareness and Decision Making in Health Education.* Charles B. Slack, Thorofare, New Jersey, 1977.

in the kitchen, children should be seen and not heard). The problem of values clarification is compounded when we hold, or attempt to hold, two conflicting values.

It is possible for the individual to have thoroughly clarified a personal value system, only to find that the conditions of her life do not allow her to adhere to this system without great stress. It is possible to be caught between one's own values and those subscribed to by the larger group or by the authority structure. Such conflict can cause great stress.

If one is employed in a hospital where surgical sterilizations are performed and she discovers that such procedures conflict with her fundamental values, then the resultant conflict needs to be reduced or minimized. Options in such a situation may be: to attempt to change the larger authority structure (probably a futile effort); to leave the situation; or to attempt to resolve the discrepancy between one's personal value system and that of the larger structure.

Frequently the grounds for conflict resolution exist and simply need to be explored. For example, the professional caught in the conflict outlined above could invoke other values, including those which project a nonjudgmental attitude toward clients, and resolve the conflict by assimilating values that can accommodate both perspectives.

The resolution of conflict when one holds two contradictory values at the same time is less complicated than it appears. Recall that the process of values clarification involves a kind of informal ranking. We prioritize our value beliefs in order of the strength and importance each holds. Although I may value individual freedom quite highly, my belief in personal and public safety might rank even higher on whatever internal value system I have clarified. Thus, when faced with the issue of depriving others (for example, suspected violent criminals) of their freedom, I am able to resolve the conflict quite readily by recognizing the strength and priority of one value over the other.

Value systems affect and influence our health professions practice in numerous ways. It is most important to clarify our values and find ways to minimize both our own values conflict and the potential negative impact of values conflict on the care of our clients. To allow ourselves to structure care within a framework that is not founded upon self-evaluation, self-esteem, and self-understanding would be to short change ourselves and our public.

SURVIVABILITY QUOTIENT

We have defined the concept of values and speculated about the impact of value systems on health care. But what is the extent of this impact? Just how much can a simple thing like personal attitude affect the care we give? For example, if a health practitioner is privately anti-semitic, does it follow that a Jew in his care will receive less competent or careful service than others? A new strategy can be used to answer that question. The strategy needed to appreciate the impact of value systems on health care may be called a *survivability quotient*.

Let us pretend that we are able to observe two clients as they enter the same metropolitan hospital for identical procedures. Both are young women who are pregnant. Both seek therapeutic abortions. One is the daughter of the chief of medical staff. She is in the second trimester of pregnancy and has learned after amniocentesis that she is carrying a malformed fetus. After much soul searching and consultation with family and clergy, she has made the difficult decision to terminate the pregnancy. She is college-educated, outgoing and sociable, even if a bit depressed at the turn of events before her.

Our second client is also in the second trimester of pregnancy. She is listed as an unemployed hostess, although it is commonly known by the staff that she supports herself by prostitution. Her financial obligations for the hospitalization are being borne by state welfare, which is why she waited until now for the abortion—an earlier termination would have necessitated her paying the bill herself. Outpatient care is not covered by her welfare status. (First trimester abortions can be safely performed on an outpatient basis; second trimester terminations are most judiciously done in a hospital environment with a minimum of twenty-four hours of observation after the procedure is complete, thus requiring hospitalization.) The second client is not very sociable, preferring to keep to herself. Furthermore, she is of Latin American origin and not able to speak English as fluently or quickly as the hospital staff.

Let us imagine that both our clients have undergone their second trimester termination procedures and are now resting in the recovery room. If both these women were to experience sudden complications, such as hemorrhage, do you think the staff response would be identical? We would like to think so; but probably not. The speed and care received by our first client is assured, even if she weren't the boss's daughter. Our sympathy would be with her as she struggled through a very human problem. She is affluent, able to communicate in our language, and similar to those giving care in many ways. The second client has many factors working against her. Not only is the staff likely to disapprove of her actions, but they are also less likely to be able to communicate with her in an emergency situation because of the language problem. The crucial edge in timing and care can be lost or found on the basis of ease of communication. The survival of the first client in an emergency situation is enhanced by her congruity with the value systems and life-styles of the health workers caring for her. The survival of the second client is endangered by many factors, including social status, language, ethnic origin, and lifestyle. Different degrees of care can be predicted even though the admitting diagnosis is identical.

Of course the circumstances portrayed are extremely unusual, and not about to happen, right? How can one be sure? A brief look at a typical day in any hospital will demonstrate the degree to which professional care is influenced by values and attitudes. The extent to which these pre-formed opinions actually affect quality of care can only be guessed at. But that they have some effect is unarguable. Objective, single-standard care does not exist, because humans are not automatons. We each bring our life experiences, culture, family background, and a host of other influences with us as we enter the health care arena. There is nothing magical about assuming the mantle of professionalism that automatically removes the influence of lifelong learning.

One can extrapolate the concept of a survivability quotient to formulate an actual sliding scale of predictability of survival. Attributes that heighten one's potential for survival will be given positive numerical values, while attributes that detract from the potential of care are given negative values. In this manner, a client's potential for survival or success in a particular hospitalization experience can be plotted, and a numerical predictor of survival obtained, simply on the basis of non-medical, non-health-related factors.

	Positive	Negative	Neutral	
Age				
Race				
Sex				
Sexual Preference				
Education				
Financial Status				
Language				
Appearance				
	————	————	————	Subtotals
			————	Total

Table 3.1. Survivability Quotient

The value of various attributes within the survivability quotient may change with different environments and circumstances. Usually one would expect the care of a Black client to be adversely affected by race, but should the environment in which care is given be that of an urban hospital in a predominantly black neighborhood and staffed by black professionals, the circumstances are quite different (probably not different enough, however, for a white client to be jeopardized by racial prejudice. Rarely is being white a disadvantage in our predominantly white culture).

The survivability quotient is a gimmick intended to illustrate the influence of values on health professionals. Perhaps the point is brought home most sharply if one imagines a situation in which someone collapses on the street. A crowd gathers around the victim, and it soon becomes obvious that the person is in severe distress. You are standing there, and recognize the need for extreme lifesaving measures to be instituted immediately. Artificial respiration is required. How do you imagine yourself reacting? Visualize the victim's face. What images do you conjure up, and how do you respond to the act of giving mouth-to-mouth resuscitation with each? Picture, in your mind's eye, the victim as an attractive young woman of twenty, obviously well kept and of good stature. Most people would not be repulsed at the thought of instituting resuscitation on this victim. But what if the victim were an older-looking black man with a heavy beard? The response of most people is hesitation. In fact, instances of failure to resuscitate a victim in distress are frequently related—not through inability, but through hesitation. The hesitation can be shown to be a reaction to an individual's physical characteristics. We simply don't like to get close to people who are somehow different, or who do not meet our images of what is appealing or acceptable. Other taboos also enter into play. It is more difficult for a man to initiate resuscitation to another man than on a woman, because of the implication of male-to-male physical contact. Even the dire circumstances of a life-threatening emergency are not sufficient motivation to overcome some hidden values and learned behaviors. If the immediacy of an emergency cannot overcome these attitudes, what of the day-to-day routine of hospital care?

An awareness of the effect of personal values on one's behavior, and the detrimental impact that these values can have on health care, is not sufficient to counteract long-held notions. But it is important that conscientious health professionals at least be aware of the fact that these influences on behavior exist. This is a first step towards change.

Ethical Dilemmas

Place yourself as the actor in each of the following case situations. As the individual responsible for decision-making, what alternatives do you choose? After selecting a route of action, defend your stance on the basis of the ethical decision made. What do you do? What are the motivating factors for your decision? What is the ethical rationale for the decision? To whose benefit does the decision work? Who will deal with the consequences of the decision? How do you feel about the alternative you choose?

Case A. Plug Pulling You are the night nurse on a large medical nursing unit in a community based hospital. Several of the patients under your care are quite ill. One, in particular, is a heartwrenching case. A seventy-year old woman who had previously lived independently has been treated for chronic congestive heart failure complicated by late onset diabetes and obesity. She is rarely alert, frequently confused and occasionally completely disoriented. Her prospects for ever returning to a semblance of her former existence are quite dim, this according to both her attending physician and the consulting specialists. During the night she suffers an episode of acute respiratory distress. You are faced with the decision to either institute immediate resuscitation measures, reviving her for a predictably grim future; or to allow her to expire, knowing that no one will question your judgment, since it is obvious that you were blamelessly occupied with the care of another critical patient. You must make your decision within a matter of seconds.

Case B. Cheating Classmates It is midterm examination time in your nursing program. You are in the midst of the quite competitive sophomore year. Just previous to your entering the test site for the examinations you observe several of your classmates secreting notes into their purses. During the examination you watch these same individuals as they quietly consult their notes. You are aware that many of the students in your class are in fragile states in terms of grading and face the jeopardy of academic dismissal if they are not successful on the examinations.

Case C. Innocent Error You are the team nurse on a postpartum obstetrical unit. Today you have a quite busy schedule, having received several new mothers onto your unit within the last twenty-four hours. One of the mothers, a young woman of twenty-two, is scheduled to receive prophylactic Rhogam during your shift. You draw the medication and administer it as ordered, only to discover that you've injected her roommate by error. You know that neither patient suspects anything is wrong and that you could probably simply administer an injection to the correct patient and try to forget the entire incident without reporting it.

Case D. The Mediocre Samaritan You are late for a very important appointment in another town. On your harried drive you take a shorter route along a country lane, only to come upon an injured driver leaning against an automobile in the ditch. Obviously his injuries are not too severe because he is able to stand upright next to the car. Yet he appears in distress. Your delay in stopping to help may be personally disastrous for the successful completion of your appointed business.

Suggestions for Further Reading

Judith E. Barret. "Values Clarification as a Teaching Strategy in Nursing." *Journal of Nursing Education,* Vol. 17, No. 2 (February 1978), pp. 12–18.
    Examines purpose and establishment of values clarification, primarily for nursing students without instilling any particular set of values. Utilizes workshop proposals and exercise strategies to acknowledge student's values.

Carl Bereiter. "Morality and Moral Education." *The Hastings Center Report,* Vol. 8, No. 2 (April 1978), pp. 20–25.
    Examines moral education, particularly in the public school system, and the pedagogy of values. Depicts Kohlberg's cognitive-developmental approach, implements value clarification, and examines legitimate function of public education.

Peter McL. Black. "The Rationale for Psychosurgery." *The Humanist,* Vol. 38, No. 4 (July/August 1977), pp. 6, 8–9.
    Discusses *pro* and *con* views on performing psychosurgery, defines psychosurgery, conclusion states reveals techniques will not be banned provided psychosurgery remains a potentially important facet of contemporary medical care.

Bonnie Bullough and Vern Bullough, eds. *Expanding Horizons for Nurses.* New York: Springer Publishing Co., 1977.
    Examines recent legislative enactments and ethical problems involved in controversial clinical issues—abortion, homosexuality, and euthanasia—and the nursing profession's need to stay abreast of change.

Arthur C. Carr, ed. "Man and Medicine." *Journal of Values and Ethics in Health Care,* Vol. 3, No. 4 (1978), pp. 229–309.
    Attempts to explore possibility of humane nursing and quality care in our present efficiency-oriented scheme of organized health care.

Phyllis Chesler. *Women and Madness.* New York: Doubleday and Company, Inc., 1972.
    Examines mental health treatment of women based on biological definition rather than consideration of being human or adult. Attempts to view women and mental health through the eyes of a clinician.

Lawrence Corey, Steven E. Saltman, and Michael F. Epstein. *Medicine in a Changing Society*. St. Louis: The C. V. Mosby Company, 1972.
  Reflection of medical students' and teachers' combined contribution in defining and exploring areas of change in the American health system, including the hospital and society, community health planning, and medicare/medicaid review.

Seymour L. Halleck. *The Politics of Therapy*. New York: Harper and Row, 1971.
  Promotes the idea of psychiatry and community mental health influencing social fabric, thus giving psychiatry political meaning.

Judith Hole and Ellen Levine. *Rebirth of Feminism*. New York: Quadrangle/New York Times Book Co., 1974.
  Defines women's rights and liberation and explores history of such. Illustrates the rapid growth of the women's movement and defines feminist concerns, tactics, and goals.

"Instructor's Resource Book" *Redesigning Man—Science and Human Values*. New York: Harper and Row, Inc., pp. 5–8, 30–60.
  Selective array of developmental concepts with accompanying scripts and filmstrips—microbial concepts, eugenics, transplants, implants, exploring man's mind, fetology, and the search for immortality.

Lucie Young Kelly. *Dimensions of Professional Nursing*, 3rd Ed. New York: MacMillan Publishing Co., Inc., 1975.
  Overview of non-clinical aspects of nursing, including nursing history, growth of practice in U.S., and current status', religious and legal aspects, and an overview of organizations, publications, and career opportunities.

George H. Kieffer. *Bioethics: A Textbook of Issues*. Reading, Mass.: Addison-Wesley Publishing Company, 1979.
  Presents a broad spectrum of opinions frequently encountered in ethical and scientific literature. Primarily intended for a non-specialist with little or no training in philosophy or ethics. Explores medical and non-medical issues—from human experimentation to our obligation to future generations.

Paul Kurtz, ed. *The Humanist Alternative: Some Definitions of Humanism*. New York: Prometheus Books, 1973.
  Concise paperback outlining definitive humanistic approaches to problem-solving, mankind, and how humans can enjoy a significant life.

Paul Kurtz, ed. *Humanist Manifestos I and II*. New York: Prometheus Books, 1973.
  Suggests religious influences on economic and scientific changes. Manifesto II broadens concepts of Manifesto I with in-depth discussions of ethics, the individual and democratic society, and the world community.

Robin Lakoff. *Language and Woman's Place.* New York: Harper and Row, 1975.
    Comprehensive analysis of how women view themselves, and
linguistic influences on society's assumption of women's place in society.

Dorothea E. Orem. *Nursing: Concepts of Practice.* New York: McGraw Hill Book
    Co., 1971.
    Provides a basis for organized nursing knowledge. Proposes
structural frameworks of nursing relevant to concepts and principles
involving ethics, values, legalities, and nursing as a human service.

Josephine G. Paterson and Loretta T. Zderad. *Humanistic Nursing.* New York:
    John Wiley and Sons, Inc., 1976.
    Suggests that nurses have the opportunity to co-experience and co-
search with patients the meaning of life, suffering, and death, and in the
process may become, or help others become, more human.

S. B. Simon, W. Howe, and H. Kirschenbaum. *Values Clarification.* New York:
    Hart, 1972.
    The first comprehensive text reviewing value formation, impact, and
techniques and strategies for values clarification. Most useful in
designing teaching strategies for values awareness.

Thomas S. Szasz. "Aborting Unwanted Behavior: The Controversy on Psycho-
    surgery." *The Humanist,* Vol. 38, No. 4 (July/August 1977), pp. 7, 10–11.
    Tastefully and candidly critiques psychosurgery by endorsing the policy
that physicians who advocate such a procedure constitute a threat to our
personal freedom and dignity. Compares issue to abortion.

Thomas Szasz. *The Second Sin.* New York: Anchor Press/Doubleday, 1974.
    Brief collection of fresh and often humorous thoughts focusing on
matters such as sex and the family, drugs, schizophrenia, and
psychiatry. Cites the Old Testament on the knowledge of good and evil, and
calls the knowledge of clear speech the "Second Sin."

Diane Uustal. "The Use of Values Clarification in Nursing Practice." *The Journal
    of Continuing Education in Nursing,* Vol. 8, No. 3 (1977), pp. 8–12.
    Examines use of value clarification in nursing practice utilizing the
idea that the clearer you are about what you value, the more able you
are to choose and initiate appropriate actions.

Charlotte Wolff. *Love Between Women.* New York: Harper and Row, 1971.
    Attempts to define the lesbian background, typical characteristics,
impact on family life, and applicable psychological theories of
homosexuality.

Gordon Wolstenholme. "The Health of All Peoples: A Question of Human
    Values." *Society for Health and Human Values* (22 October 1978), pp. 5–15.
    Proposes integration of human values and science and improvement
of health care status worldwide by such techniques as a world health
service cooperating with WHO, frequent retraining and use of
appropriate equipment.

4

Legal Concerns of the Health Professions

"It ain't no sin if you crack a few laws now and then, just so long as you don't break any."

MAE WEST

Health professionals are frequently awed by the law and the influence of legal constraints on the delivery of health care. Much professional literature, conference time, and conversation deals with the ways in which law mandates health care. A good deal of effort is expended by physicians, hospitals, and nurses in order to protect health professionals from the possibilities of legal complications. Yet there is little to be awed of in a reasoned consideration of legal concepts and the legal/medical interface.

An opportunity to eavesdrop on any professional gathering will rapidly give one the impression that health professionals do not control health care—lawyers do. This is simply not so. As one begins to understand the concepts and mechanisms of law, he soon gains a healthy respect for legal constraints but also realizes that our preoccupation with the threat of litigation is misconceived and self-generated.

It is important that the nurse understand his legal responsibilities and rights in the performance of his discipline. Yet it is equally important that the individual practitioner recognize that the legal system sets *guidelines*, not rigid rules for practice. Legal constraints should facilitate effective professional functioning within reasonable boundaries. It is useful to know basics of law and the legal system, the mechanisms that implement the system, and the rights and responsibilities of the competent professional under the law. Such working knowledge should help the practitioner keep out legal entanglements. It can also allow one to practice in confidence, free from unrealistic fears.

The first step in attaining fluency in the basics of the interface between law and the health care industry is to gain a comprehension of the origins, types, and applications of law.

LAW AND SOCIETY

Laws are the rules of conduct that protect the social fabric. Prior to the formation of social groups, laws were not necessary. Where humans do not interact socially, legal systems rarely exist. The structure of governments and legal systems grew from the need to manage complex human interactions. As society becomes more complex, the accompanying legal system becomes more complex. Simple, homogeneous groups have little need for complex sets of regulations to govern their affairs. As a group becomes more complex, its need for adherence to a consensus of accepted rules of conduct becomes more acute.

A small group requires simple rules. The more homogeneous the group, the simpler the rules; the closer its members are, the more easily they will adhere to the rules they establish. As groups become large and heterogeneous in membership, the need for more complex rules and more sophisticated mechanisms for rule enforcement increases.

A Cub Scout den led by one of the boys' mothers is usually a small group and homogeneous in makeup. The need for rules of organization and conduct is fairly minimal, as the den is engaged in few activities that involve interaction outside of the membership. The participants do not have sophisticated needs, nor have they developed sophisticated ways of interacting with others. Simple respect for the level of noise, commitment to nonviolence, and a little discipline in pursuing goals or activities are all that is usually required of the governance system. But as the members of the group become older, interact with other groups, seek recognition from the larger parent organization, or engage in activities outside of the small group, the need for more sophisticated rules and more active rule enforcement increases. Thus, a den or even a pack of Cub Scouts does not need the sophisticated rules and regulations that the national organization, Scouts of America, employs. As the number of individuals involved, the heterogeneity of the group, and the complexity of tasks and skills increase, the need for an organized system of rules and regulations—and a mechanism for the enforcement of this system—also increases.

Society as a whole is much like our little Cub Scout den. When human interactions were on a very small scale, say in a European village in the year 500, the need for rules of conduct and their enforcement was minimal. A village was classically homogeneous, its members having the same ethnic background, religious aspirations, and everyday concerns with maintaining life and family. Rules of conduct were developed through group understanding of what threatened the fabric of life in the village, and through tradition, which also evolved mostly along lines guided by the need to ensure survival. Thus property was passed by father to eldest son because sons farmed, while daughters married, moved, and contributed to someone else's farm. The crime of killing or stealing another's livestock was dealt with severely, because such acts threatened the acknowledged primary goal of human existence, survival. Social life was unsophisticated, people were homogeneous, and the need for a complex legal structure did not exist.

As class differences evolved, and some people earned a living by managing the work of others, manufacturing goods or selling services, complex social systems developed. Large groups of heterogeneous people living in close proximity made necessary a formalized system of governance to maintain the welfare of the larger social group. As these groups interacted with other neighboring groups, the need for mutually acknowledged rules of conduct became more acute. Soon systems of governance evolved that were based on power, religion, and monarchy.

Thus, as social systems evolve, participants become more sophisticated and heterogeneous, interactions increase, and the need for forms of governance founded upon mutually acknowledged rules of conduct becomes more apparent. Complexity breeds regulation. Evolution frequently generates complexity. The health care industry is no exception.

Until the 1940s, the impact of health care on prolonging life or drastically improving the quality of life was negligible. Health was a function of chance and good fortune. Doctors and nurses, the only health professionals who existed in any great numbers, concentrated their efforts on a few techniques of disease remediation. Medical care was delivered largely by general practitioners, as there was little content in which to specialize. Nursing care focused on the comfort measures. Most of the advanced technological capabilities and knowledge we take for granted have been developed since the Second World War. Thus, since a largely homogeneous group of caregivers rendered a relatively simple service that did not produce more than negligible results, the need for a sophisticated system of governance of health care did not exist. The interface between health care and legal forces was minimal and sporadic.

Since 1940 the health care industry has achieved a technology and knowledge never before dreamed possible. Medical specialties have generated subspecialties that have devised subsystems of referral and consultation. Nursing too has broadened its role and deepened its knowledge base. Nursing focuses on clients, wherever they may be found—both in and out of formal health care facilities. It renders care with the objective of preventing illness, promoting optimal health, and encouraging client autonomy and accountability for health. Nurses function in all sorts of relationships with other health practitioners. The scientific and theoretical base of nursing is undergoing an explosion in both breadth and depth.

There are also some two hundred fifty allied health professions currently functioning within the health care system. These include everything from physical therapists to electroencephalograph technicians. Each separate vocation brings its skills and functions to the increasingly complex health care system.

In addition, consumers are increasingly sophisticated. Contemporary health service recipients are better educated and better informed than any of their predecessors. Public education has promoted literacy. Many school curricula incorporate rudimentary health education as required courses at either the elementary or secondary school level. The public's level of knowledge regarding health, although still woefully inadequate, is much greater than ever before. All the communications media are full of information pertaining to health, illness, or accessing care. Magazines, from *Time* to *Family Circle,* routinely carry articles aimed at increasing the reader's health knowledge. Thus the client population has had both its expectations of care and its knowledge of services raised. The typical client is beginning to see herself as a consumer, active in the process of health care.

Then, of course, one must take into consideration the increasing litigiousness of society. Litigiousness is the willingness to seek remedy through legal mechanisms. Not long ago, a family experiencing the birth of a cerebral palsied child accepted the fact as an act of God or fate. The same occurrence today is much more likely to find the family evaluating legal alternatives for assessing medical responsibility for the misfortune. The tendency to seek legal redress for misfortune, whether or not justified, is greatly increasing. Professional liability suits have multiplied at an astronomical rate in health care.

As society becomes more complex, its needs for systems of regulation become more complex. So, as health care has become more complex, its needs for more sophisticated systems of regulations also increase.

The burgeoning degree of interface between law and health care is the direct product of health care's successful growth in capability and capacity. The legal complications currently arising in health care are a byproduct of the system—a useful byproduct not previously recognized as being useful.

The legal complexities, although somewhat frightening to the unknowing, have caused a tremendous surge of accountability and evaluation in the practice of the health disciplines. No longer can an institution assume little or no responsibility for the actions of its employees and staff. No longer can an individual practitioner work unscrutinized by his peers. The legal principle of accountability for the quality of care has decreased the susceptibility of the health care system to the whims and wishes of a few professionals and opened the system to a degree of health examination by its constituents and its consumers.

The process is not without discomfort, but it is relatively painless and certainly useful.

ORIGINS OF LAW

Contemporary law evolves from two sources, *legislation* and *judicial decision*. Law created by elected legislative bodies (federal, state, and local) is termed *statutory*. Law created by judicial decision is termed *case* or *common law*.

Statutory law is written by individuals within the legislative bodies in response to perceptions of need for social regulation. When governments became aware of the abuse of medical privileges and quackery practiced in the name of medical care at the beginning of this century, laws to regulate the practice of medicine and to establish minimum standards for medical practice were enacted. These are titled the Medical Practice Acts and are fairly uniform in content from state to state. Similarly, a governmental concern for protection of the citizenry from unsafe nursing practice later motivated the Nurse Practice Acts—statutory laws governing the practice of nursing within each state.

The purpose and function of statutory law is to maintain or promote the rights of the state to uphold the social order and/or to protect the rights of the individual. Law that deals with the protection of the rights of the individual is *civil law*. Violations of civil law are frequently termed *torts*. Such violations include acts that harm the individual or the individual's property, but do not present a grave threat to the rights of society as a whole.

Civil law covers such mundane topics as corporate contract law, and more exciting-sounding areas such as slander and libel. Each is concerned with the protection of individual rights, which in turn ensures the maintenance of the social fabric. The violation of these laws does not directly infringe on the state's rights to maintain the social fabric.

Criminal law is concerned solely with actions that directly threaten the orderly existence of society. It deals with acts that may be aimed at individuals, but which are also an offense against the state. That is, to tolerate such actions would directly endanger the state's right to maintain an orderly social existence. The crime of assault and battery is an excellent example. If you are quietly walking down the street and someone rushes up, says, "I'm going to clobber you!" and proceeds to hit you with her fists, you have been a victim of the crime of assault and battery. Certainly no one feels the results of the blow more directly than you do—so your rights to an unmolested peaceful existence have been violated. Yet the state's rights have also been violated, because the state has a vested interest in ensuring the safety of its citizens in the conduct of normal affairs. Thus, the attacker has committed a crime. She has violated both civil and criminal law. The state may choose to prosecute the criminal offense, and you may choose to seek redress through litigation for the civil violation.

Most of the interactions by health professionals with the legal system deal with civil laws. Little of health care's legal concerns focus on criminal law, because health care usually has to do with the relationship between individuals: the consumer of care and the provider of care, or employee and employer. Occasionally a situation arises where the interaction involves both civil and criminal law, or simply criminal law. These are usually extreme circumstances, such as gross negligence or willful assault and battery. The typical health professional, adequately prepared and conducting himself in a reasonable manner, can be assured that there is very little potential for criminal violations in his practice.

The simplest way to distinguish criminal from civil law is to assess the impact of the violation. If the act detracts only from an individual's rights, it is probably civil. But if the action detracts from both an individual's and the state's rights, or only from the state's rights, it is probably criminal. Defrauding the state of funds by a public official is a criminal act that may not deprive any one person of his rights to a large degree, but certainly impairs the state's rights to function. Fraud by a public official is prosecutable as a criminal act. Defrauding an individual citizen may also deprive the citizen of her rights over property. Such fraud may lead both to criminal and civil actions. By contrast, fraud in a contract between corporations may lead to civil actions only.

Criminal and civil law can have their origins in either judicial decision (common law) or in legislative action (statutory law). Statutory criminal or civil law is enacted by a legislative body and enforced by testing through the judicial system. A law written to protect the rights of minors to equal educational opportunity is tested when an individual or institution feels that law has been violated and brings suit for remedy of the violation.

Frequently the results of a suit brought in the testing of statutory law generates case or common law. The Bakke decision is an excellent example. Allan Bakke applied for, and was denied admission to, the medical school at the University of California at Davis. He brought suit, contending that his admission had been denied because of a minority quota system that mandated the admission of less qualified minorities over more qualified white males. Bakke's suit was finally heard by the Supreme Court, which ruled that the medical school would have to admit him and revise its affirmative action admissions procedures to encourage the retention and recruitment of minorities without the use of quota systems that denied due process to white males. The Bakke case was seen as significant because of its case law potential.

A ruling by a court becomes precedent for all lower courts within its jurisdiction. The Supreme Court's ruling sets precedent for all courts in the United States. Thus, while the Bakke decision was important for Allan Bakke, it was equally significant for anyone involved in affirmative action, college admissions, and other social action programs. The Court's narrow ruling relieved much of the anticipated stress on the admissions systems that had been feared. Yet the precedent for further litigation was also founded. It established case or common law dealing with the formation and implementation of affirmative action programs.

A celebrated example of case law that strongly influenced health care is the Darling case (*Darling vs. Charleston Community Memorial Hospital*). The case dealt with alleged inadequate medical and nursing care rendered to an 18-year-old with a fractured leg. The care resulted in the eventual amputation of the leg due to circulatory impairment from an improperly applied and unsupervised cast. The resultant suit succeeded in gaining damages from the hospital. The significance of the suit was in finding the hospital responsible for the negligence of a physician practicing on its staff. Until this time, hospitals had not been found responsible for the services of physicians not in their direct employ. The Darling case has become common law and is frequently cited in the preparation of legal textbooks and as a precedent in other medical negligence suits. It stands as influential case law.

Thus judicial ruling provides important interpretations of the existing common and statutory law. The testing of statutory law through suit, such as the Bakke decision, provides the framework for the interpretation of law in practice. For example, the testing of laws governing (or, more accurately, forbidding) midwifery in the State of Illinois provided the health professionals concerned with guidelines for working under this law. The legislative process is interpreted through the judicial system. And, occasionally, the precedent established by the judicial system motivates the passage of statutory law by the legislature. The attempts of state and local legislatures to enact statutory law regulating abortion in response to the Supreme Court decision that legalized abortion (*Roe vs. Wade*) is an example of legislative response to judicial decisions. Both legislation and judicial decision shape, interpret, and develop law.

PRINCIPLES OF LAW

Our system of law is quite confusing to the casual observer. But the law rests on a few simple principles that are frequently cloaked in complex terminology. Just as health care has a particular language that sometimes serves only to confuse the lay person, law also has a complex jargon. Both medicine and law can point to certain fundamental principles that undergird the labyrinthine structure of the disciplines.

The fundamental principle upon which all law is based is *a concern for justice and fairness.* It seeks to protect the rights of one party from infringement by the actions of another party. It serves to set guidelines for conduct and mechanisms for the enforcement of those guidelines. Thus, whether the focus of attention is a murder trial or a corporate dispute over patent rights, the goal is to pursue the promulgation of rules of conduct that protect the rights of the parties involved, and assure a just outcome for the process. Certainly the system does not always appear to work in ways that are just, nor can all people agree with the outcomes of the process all of the time. But it does provide a more orderly way of managing our increasingly complex social system than does any alternative. Complex and imperfect, our legal system is evolving in the attempt to change with a changing society.

The second principle of law is that it is plastic: it is characterized by *change.* Society is ever-changing, undergoing evolution in its human systems and technologies. As change occurs in the social structure, change in the legal system is also necessary. A consideration of the legal ramifications of euthanasia was merely philosophic until current technology made the prolongation of life an ethical and legal dilemma. Now that the problem is upon us, the legal system, through both the judiciary and the legislature, is seeking to set guidelines that will result in fair and equal parameters for health care professionals.

The legal system is frequently in a position of reacting, as opposed to acting. This is because social change and technological advancement occur rapidly, and frequently without hint of the problems to follow. Amniocentesis, the process of evaluation of amniotic fluid for determination of some fetal defects, was developed and implemented before many of the legal and ethical problems the procedure would create were revealed. It was only after the procedure became available that some of the legal difficulties were apparent.

Amniocentesis that reveals the presence of a malformed fetus may generate legal questions, such as: What are the physician's responsibilities to reveal information to the client? What are the father's rights and responsibilities in relation to the information revealed?

Many of these questions have yet to be clearly sorted out. Many more questions will be raised as the technique becomes more reliable and comprehensive.

A third principle of law is that an action is judged on the basis of a universal standard of what a similarly trained, *reasonable and prudent* person would have done under similar circumstances. That is, every physician is not expected to have the same capabilities. Nor is every nurse expected to function at the same level. It is recognized that each person's experiential and educational level may be different. Yet all are expected to function as the reasonable person with similar preparation and experience would function.

An example of the doctrine of reasonable and prudent conduct would be the judgment applied to a suit following a pedestrian's injury incurred by tripping over a wire placed by a homeowner across the front steps of a home. The reasonable and prudent homeowner typically does not string a wire across steps without good cause. If the steps had recently been poured with cement, then it may be decided that the action was reasonable and prudent. If the wire was strung because the homeowner didn't like salespeople coming to the door, then the action may be found to be negligent, and the injured person may recover some form of compensation. The standard applied would be the actions the reasonable and prudent person would have taken under similar circumstances.

A fourth principle of law is that each individual has *rights and responsibilities*. The failure to meet one's responsibilities can jeopardize one's rights. Persons imprisoned for failure to conduct themselves in a responsible manner experience a loss of their rights to freedom of movement. Rights are fundamental powers or privileges that each person possesses unless revoked by law. Responsibilities are the obligations that are attendant on one's rights. For example, the registered nurse has a right to practice her profession within the constraints dictated by law; violation of the responsibility to observe those constraints can result in the revocation of the nurse's right to practice. Most Nurse Practice Acts prohibit nurses from prescribing medications for their clients or performing surgical procedures. A nurse found to have acted irresponsibly, by performing a surgical procedure or prescribing a medication is in danger of having the right to practice nursing revoked.

Justice	a fundamental concept of fairness extended to each individual
Change	law undergoes continuous change in keeping with social and technological evolution
Reasonable & Prudent	rule of conduct by which individual actions are evaluated
Rights & Responsibilities	each individual possesses both inherent rights (powers) and attendant responsibilities

Table 4.1 Principles of Law

These four principles of law provide a base upon which many of the processes of the legal system function (Table 4.1). There is a complex language that accompanies every nuance of the law. But this language is much like medical terminology: understanding of the basics allows one to comprehend many of the important parts of the system. Also, like medical terminology, legal jargon is used to eliminate the participation of the uninitiated in the system. Just as physicians can talk over the heads of patients and thus sometimes justify their role when the care needed is quite simple, lawyers can talk over the heads of clients and thus justify fees when the tasks to be accomplished are relatively simple. That is not to say that the practice either of medicine or of law is founded upon obfuscation, but that a bit of fluency in the language of the discipline can promote understanding and application of its fundamental principles without sophisticated preparation.

What follows is a brief introduction to legal concepts and their characteristic application in health care. It should not be mistaken for a first-aid manual or how-to-do-it guide, but as simple information designed to give the practitioner the guidelines for legally safe and responsible practice, a sensitivity to the impact of law on health care, and the ability not to have professional practice paralyzed by the fear of litigation.

LEGAL ROLE OF THE NURSE

The health professional usually views the legal system with fear and awe, rather than with an eye to understanding his role in the system. An understanding of the role, or more accurately, the roles, that the practitioner plays in the legal aspects of health care is conducive to legally responsible and personally satisfying practice. The principles and mechanisms by which law and health care come into contact are related to the roles that the provider and consumer fill.

There are three roles that the health professional moves in and out of in the process of completing her professional and personal responsibilities. These include the role of provider of service; the role of employee or contractor for service; and the role of private citizen. These roles are played simultaneously. Each role, in keeping with the underlying principles of law, has two dimensions: the rights that are attendant on each role, and the responsibilities that are mandated by these rights. Just as we previously examined the principles of law and found that there are four distinct yet intertwining principles (justice, change, reasonable and prudent conduct, and responsibilities attendant to rights) which are inherent, we now observe that there are three distinct and interdependent legal roles of the health professional, each with rights and responsibilities obliged by the inherent rights.

The role that most concerns practitioners, although possibly not recognized as such, is the role of provider of service. It is fear over litigation resulting from provision of consumer care that preoccupies the profession. Care is rendered directly, when a nurse administers a medication, or indirectly, when the charge nurse assigns a procedure to a subordinate. This role inspires much of the unnecessary posturing that results from the fear of legal suits. Elaborate charting guidelines, unnecessary and costly medical care, fortunes in professional liability insurance premiums, and volumes of policy and procedure manuals—all are designed with the goal of preventing litigation arising from the conduct of the practitioner in this role.

The role of employee or contractor of service is much less known and less frequently scrutinized, but also very important. This is the role that mandates the practitioner's rights and responsibilities in relation to his employers, partners, consultants, and other professional colleagues. Some attention has been paid to the employee's rights to bargain collectively versus her responsibilities to provide service. This is only one of the many dimensions of this complex, and frequently baffling, role. The rights and responsibilities of employees and contractors of service are not widely known by professionals. But it is here that one's economic security, professional future, and peer relationships are based. We need to examine the rights and responsibilities we each have, as staff attached to a health care institution; as supervisors of the services of others; as consultants to the services of others; as independent practitioners contracting (formally or informally) to render service to others; and as members of a peer group of professionals.

The third and probably most important, yet least understood, role that the health professional plays is that of citizen. The vast significance of this role is that all other roles, rights, responsibilities, and privileges are awarded because of the inherent rights and responsibilities of citizenship. Our unique form of democratic government grants these rights as inherent: civil rights, property rights, and right to due process. Each of these rights forms the foundation for the extension of the other legal relationships of the health professional. For example, it is the right to due process that protects psychiatric clients from indiscriminate incarceration without just cause. It is also the right to due process, and other civil rights, that govern much of the legal relationship between employee and employer. Nondiscrimination assurances, security, and fairness in hiring/firing practices are all covered under these fundamental rights of citizenship. These rights, which evolved from British law, are guaranteed and protected by the United States Constitution and by the many laws and statutes that have been generated for the interpretation and implementation of the Constitution. It is also these rights that may be revoked when the attendant responsibilities are not fulfilled. In the summer of 1978 it was disclosed that a few members of the ethnic communities of Chicago's south side had allegedly served in official capacities in Nazi extermination camps. As these individuals are brought before the legal system, their rights to citizenship and its attendant privileges will be scrutinized and possibly revoked. Until proven to have falsified immigration documents and achieved citizenship in a fraudulent manner, these individuals will be protected by the right of due process—among others, the right to a fair and impartial hearing. Should citizenship be revoked, the rights and responsibilities they enjoy will be diminished and other appropriate steps in the pursuit of justice will follow.

By examining the three roles that they play, and the rights and responsibilities of these roles, any health professional will be better able to practice within the parameters imposed by the legal/medical interface.

THE ROLE OF PROVIDER OF SERVICE

Nurses have as their career objective the provision of competent nursing care aimed either at disease prevention and cure or health promotion. The consumer's welfare is the acknowledged concern of the health care system. Thus it is logical that much of what we do and say focuses on the promotion of client health. It is incongruous that the lion's share of litigation in health care is originated by consumers who are disgruntled with services they have received. What are the fundamental rights and responsibilities of the provider of service that must be observed to assure both competent and legally responsible practice?

The major standard by which the competency of services provided is evaluated is also one of the main concepts of law introduced earlier in this chapter: that of reasonableness and prudence. The care provided must meet the standard of care; that is, what would have been done by the reasonable and prudent professional with similar preparation and education and under similar circumstances. This introduces several subconcepts: liability, standard of care, duty of care, and contractual obligation and fulfillment.

In a given health care situation, a client retains and may expect recognition of his rights: civil and property rights, due process, and contractual rights. The provider of care retains and may also expect recognition of her rights: civil and property rights, due process, and contractual rights.

Here follows a thumbnail sketch of each of these subconcepts:

Liability. Simply, one is responsible for obligations and actions under one's own area of commitment. Example: a charge nurse is liable for her actions and the actions of those supervised in the process of fulfilling the commitments commensurate with the position of charge nurse; failures to meet these responsibilities would result in the nurse's liability for the resultant injury.

Standard of Care. Standards by which one's acts or failures to act are judged; what the reasonable and prudent person would have done under similar circumstances and with similar preparation. This is the standard of care applied to judge the liability or correctness of an act or failure to act.

Duty of Care. The professional's responsibility to render care that is established by the presence of a formal or informal contract. Without a duty to render care, the professional may not be held liable for care rendered under some circumstances.

Contract. The existence of a legal relationship that may be expressed (formal, written, or unwritten) or implied (informal or unwritten). A contract consists of an offer, its acceptance, and an exchange of goods and services. Both parties must agree to the terms, there must be a consideration or promise of consideration in return for the service or goods offered, both parties must be legally competent to enter the contract, and the contracted service or exchange must be legal.

It is, perhaps, easiest to understand the dimensions of the legal rights and responsibilities of the provider of health care by examining vignettes illustrating the legal principles and mechanisms involved.

Case Study: A patient enters the emergency room of the hospital for treatment of a lacerated arm resulting from an industrial accident. The admitting clerk records appropriate identifying and insurance information and then refers the patient to the ER (emergency room) nurse for evaluation of the need for immediate medical attention. The nurse observes the injury, questions the patient and summons the staff ER physician, who, in turn, also scans the wound and orders an X-ray and preparation for suturing the laceration. The physician requests a stat dosage of xylocaine (anesthesia) for local use prior to suturing. The nurse draws the medication into the syringe and hands the syringe to the physician, who injects the forearm area using standard procedure. Suddenly the patient begins to experience shortness of breath, reports a constricted feeling in his throat, and then collapses. Resuscitation measures are started and successful; the patient recovers after a harrowing experience, which includes a brief hospital stay and discharge follow-up. The cause of the episode is recorded as acute allergic reaction to xylocaine. After discharge, the patient brings suit against the hospital, nurse, and physician, claiming that the reasonable and prudent provider of care would not have administered anesthetic to a patient whose medical history was unknown without first evaluating the patient's history and attempting to rule out the presence of allergies.

The hospital disclaims responsibility for the professional performance of its licensed staff; the nurse disclaims responsibility, as prescription of medications is the legal right and responsibility solely of the physician; and the physician disclaims liability because the emergency status of the situation justified the waiving of normal medical procedures in favor of maintaining the patient's life and preventing permanent disability.

Several legal principles are interwoven in this most complicated situation. Let's look at the vignette from the point of view of each of the participants:

	RIGHTS	RESPONSIBILITIES
PATIENT	1. to competent care. 2. to respect for his existing civil, property, and due process rights (including the right not to have health status impaired without cause).	1. to fulfill obligations of the contract. 2. not to infringe on rights of others.
HOSPITAL	1. to expect institution's rights will be respected. 2. to receive consideration for fulfilling contract obligations. 3. to competent and loyal service from employees.	1. to supply and supervise competent staff. 2. to provide safe and functional equipment and facilities.
PHYSICIAN	1. to expect own rights to be respected. 2. to safe and functional equipment and facilities. 3. to compensation for service. 4. to competent assistance.	1. to act as a reasonable and prudent physician. 2. to render care commensurate with the standard of care.
NURSE	1. to expect own rights to be respected. 2. to safe and functional equipment and facilities. 3. to compensation for services. 4. to competent assistance.	1. to act as a reasonable and prudent nurse. 2. to render care commensurate with the standard of care. 3. to fulfill contract with employer.

Table 4.2 Rights and Responsibilities

Given this complex dilemma, whose rights should prevail, and who is responsible for any liability incurred?

The elements of a contract existed between the patient and the hospital. Both parties (the patient and the hospital) were legally competent to enter into a contract. Legal competence is judged by majority (legal age of consent) and mental competency. There was an offer of service (health care) and a promise of consideration (reimbursement through insurance coverage). Both parties agreed to the terms of the contract, the patient by giving consent for care, the hospital by offering care. The activity (health care) was legal. Therefore, it appears that the patient did, indeed, have a valid contract with the hospital.

The physician, by virtue of receiving staff privileges at the hospital, is an agent of the hospital, and, therefore, the hospital cannot disclaim responsibility for the physician's actions (recall the Darling case). The nurse is a salaried employee of the hospital and, therefore, also cannot be disclaimed, according to the doctrine of *respondeat superior* ("Let the master answer"). This legal doctrine, ancient in tradition, focuses on the responsibility of the master (employer) for the conduct of the servant (employee). *Respondeat superior* does not prevail if the employee's actions were extraordinarily inappropriate and beyond the bounds of expectation (foreseeability) by the employer. That is, had the physician hit the patient in the face, the hospital could disclaim responsibility, unless the patient could prove that the hospital had reason to expect the physician to behave in such a manner.

The nurse is also covered under the doctrine of *respondeat superior*. As an agent of the hospital by virtue of employment, the nurse's conduct is the hospital's responsibility, unless she is grossly negligent without the hospital's having cause to anticipate such conduct.

The doctrine of *respondeat superior* does not, however, excuse either the physician or nurse from responsibility for their own actions. Each person is responsible and accountable for his actions or failures to act.

We have established the presence of a contractual relationship between the hospital and patient, the responsibility of the hospital for the actions of its agents, and the responsibility of the physician and nurse for their own actions. The next determination must be one of injury. Injury may be physical impairment, such as having one's arm amputated or one's car destroyed. Or injury may be the psychological stress and inconvenience incurred through someone else's irresponsible actions, such as the psychological stress of grief after a loved one has been injured. This is frequently termed "pain and suffering." For liability to be found, the patient must prove that he suffered some form of injury. Our patient believes his hospitalization was unnecessary, that the situation, although not permanently disabling, was life-threatening and, therefore, constitutes "pain and suffering," and that both the hospitalization and the pain and suffering were the direct result of the incompetence or negligence of the hospital's staff members.

This last aspect introduces the important concept of cause. Cause is proving that a negligent (irresponsible) act occurred, that there was an injury, and that the negligent act caused, or significantly contributed to, the injury. It would be futile to prove that the staff was negligent in performing service, and that there was an injury, unless one could also show that the injury suffered was caused by the negligent service. Also, the patient must not have contributed to his own injury or the defendant may not be found liable. This is termed *contributory negligence;* the plaintiff (the individual bringing suit) must not have substantially contributed to or aggravated the situation. If our patient had known he was allergic to the medication, had been asked if he had any known allergies, and had deliberately withheld information that resulted in his receiving medication that generated an allergic reaction, the entire episode might be dismissed because the patient had contributed to the negligence.

There are times when the issue of showing cause is not the responsibility of the plaintiff. These situations arise when the injury is such that the plaintiff did not have any knowledge of, or control over, the cause of the injury, and cannot reasonably be expected to have exercised input into the situation. The classic example that is always given of this doctrine, termed the doctrine of *res ipsa loquitur* ("the thing speaks for itself"), is the postoperative patient who has a surgical tool remaining within a body cavity. It's a safe bet that she wasn't born with a clamp in her abdomen, nor had she acquired one during a normal life's activities, yet here's a bit of metal that certainly doesn't belong there postoperatively. The burden of proof therefore falls upon the individuals responsible for the surgery. They must satisfactorily explain the presence of the clamp as not demonstrating professional negligence. Perhaps they can claim a new theory of spontaneous generation!

So here we have our patient claiming injury, our hospital having responsibility, and our health professionals also having responsibility. How would you decide this one?

We are back to the original principles introduced as underlying the structure of our legal system: justice, reasonable and prudent conduct, change, and inherent rights with their attendant responsibilities. Justice would dictate that, if an injury is confirmed, the person responsible for the injury should remit damages (monetary reimbursement for assessed liability). The principle of change would ask that the situation be evaluated on the basis of current technology and the standard of care prevailing at the time of injury. The idea of reasonable and prudent conduct would ask if the conduct of each of the participants in the situation (patient, physician, nurse, and hospital) was commensurate with what a reasonable and prudent person of similar education and experience would have done under similar circumstances. That is, would a competent physician, practicing in an emergency room situation, have conducted herself in the same fashion our physician has? Would the competent nurse have paralleled our nurse's behavior? And would a reasonable and prudent person of our patient's education and experience, and in these circumstances, acted in the manner in which our patient acted?

In our legal system, judgment is arrived at through the use of *adversarial process*. When going to court, being sued, retaining legal counsel, submitting evidence, or whatever, we present our case, the other side presents its case, and we rely on the adjudication of differences through an impartial third party.

As the patient's representative, we might ask why a medical history was not obtained prior to the administration of any medications to rule out possible allergies. Wouldn't the reasonable and prudent physician and nurse have wanted a medical history prior to taking any action?

The defendant's representative will ask why the patient did not reveal the presence of the allergy to the physician or nurse prior to treatment. Does this not constitute contributory negligence, a breach of the patient's responsibilities in the contractual relationship with the hospital, physician, and nurse?

The ultimate outcome of the adversarial process is determined by the judiciary—the court system. If one participant is dissatisfied with the initial outcome, there is the recourse of requesting an appeal to a higher court, a process which may be followed until the case is accepted and reviewed by the highest court that has jurisdiction.

This sketch depicts a complicated and involved situation for the purpose of illustrating the many principles of law which shape and govern health care. Yet there is rarely a case which reaches the point of litigation that is not complex. Any subject as emotionally charged as one's own health is always complex. Disappointment over outcome; dissatisfaction with service; unanticipated injury; inconvenience: all serve to compound the potential for litigation.

The outcome of litigation in such an involved and complex case would be difficult to predict with accuracy. Yet my judgment is that negligence could not be proven. I view the actions of the principals involved as reasonable and prudent, given the emergency nature of the situation, the technological level of the service rendered, and the information at hand. However, the slightest alteration in the circumstances of the incident could alter a finding of negligence. Had the patient given any indication of previous allergic episodes connected with the administration of any medication, a finding of negligence might be forthcoming.

The vignette illustrates many of the rights and responsibilities inherent in the professional's role as a provider of service. These include the responsibility to provide safe and competent care commensurate with one's preparation and circumstances, to fully inform the recipient of care of the consequences of various alternatives and outcomes of care (the client must give *informed* consent, not simply consent), to provide adequate supervision and evaluation of subordinates whose services are in one's domain of responsibility, and to respect the rights and responsibilities of other participants in the health care process. Rights inherent in the professional's role as provider of service include: the fulfillment of the terms of a contract, whether expressed or implied (consideration in return for service rendered), the right to expect reasonable and prudent conduct by others participating in care delivery and by the recipient of care (including the patient's obligation to provide accurate and honest information as requested), and the right to have the provider's rights and responsibilities respected by other participants in the care-giving process.

Both the rights and responsibilities attendant on the professional's role as a provider of service appear to involve simple principles of logic and fair play. Most of what is written as law reflects these same fundamental concepts of logic and fairness. It is the interpretation of what is logical and fair that carries with it the confusion and debate. What one person sees as only fair and just in any situation, can also be interpreted by another as a grossly unjust act or consequence. It is in the judgment that the controversy arises.

THE ROLE OF EMPLOYEE OR CONTRACTOR OF SERVICE

The nurse has another role to respond to as an employee or contractor of service. Whether a written contract for employment is negotiated, with terms and conditions outlined in advance, or the employee is simply hired and begins service, the professional again carries certain rights and responsibilities in relation to the employer or recipient of contracted service.

Again the essence of contract law requires four elements: (1) the act to be contracted for must be legal (hence, one cannot legally contract for a physician to commit active euthanasia under most state laws, because this would be seen as a contract for homicide); (2) the parties to the contract must be of legal majority (of age) and competent to enter a legally binding agreement (free of mental impairment); (3) there must be an offer and acceptance of the service to be contracted; that is, there must be mutual agreement about the service to be contracted; and (4) there must be consideration or the promise of consideration.

Thus the elements of a contract entered into when a nurse is employed by a clinic are as follows: (1) the nurse's employment is a legal act, and the duties to be performed and the services rendered are legal; (2) both the nurse and the employer, the corporate entity of the clinic, must be of legal majority and competent to enter the contract; (3) there must be an offer of a position, and the acceptance of the offer by the nurse, all of which is clearly understood by both parties; and, (4) there must be compensation, or a promise of compensation, for the service to be rendered: the nurse must be offered a salary or the promise of a salary.

If any of the elements of a contract are missing, a contractual relationship between the nurse and the clinic does not exist. For example, were the clinic in the business of providing illegal treatments and the nurse aware that her services were being sought to assist in the delivery of illegal treatments, a contractual agreement would not exist. Or if the nurse were simply to interview for the position without actually accepting the appointment to the staff, and later the clinic were to claim that she had violated (breached) the contract by not reporting for duty, the nurse would be free of responsibility by demonstrating that there had never been an acceptance of the clinic's offer of employment.

The specifics of contract law seem both reasonable and relatively simple. Yet many complications can arise under the conditions of a contract. For example, a physician hires an office assistant under a verbal contract. Later, at the receipt of the first paycheck, the assistant claims that the physician offered more salary than was received. The contest of truth becomes a matter of one individual's recollection as compared with another's, unless the terms of employment were either witnessed or written.

The complexity of contractual relationships increases when one realizes that a contract can either be expressed or implied. That is, the terms of a contract may be acknowledged and agreed to formally in a written or oral statement of contract; or the contract may be informal or implied, as when a patient presents himself to a physician's office for treatment and the physician agrees to see the patient. Such an informal implied contract is binding, even though neither party may be particularly aware of the specifics of the contractual relationship into which they have entered.

The violation of the terms of a contract can result in litigation and the award of damages or similar means of recovery. For example, the physician who accepts a patient for care has entered into an implied contract for the delivery of competent medical care to that patient. Justly, the physician may expect adequate compensation for service rendered. A patient who fails to provide compensation for service (that is, fails to pay the bill) has violated the terms of the contract, and thus may be shown to have terminated the contractual relationship. Certain circumstances would prevent the physician from withholding service, even if compensation were not forthcoming, such as in emergency situations or when the failure to render care could result in death or permanent injury. Yet the obligations of the patient, within the contractual relationship, must also be recognized and undertaken in good faith.

Similarly, an employee may violate or have his employment contract violated by an employer, thus terminating the contract. The employer who fails to compensate the employee according to the terms of the contract has terminated the contract and may have released the employee from further obligation to the employer. Again, there are circumstances where this rule may not apply. If a nurse on duty were to fail to receive her paycheck because of some secretarial or bookkeeping error, the nurse would not be permitted to simply withdraw nursing service at that point, particularly if to withdraw care would endanger the health or safety of patients under the nurse's care.

Collective bargaining efforts currently occurring in many health professions, particularly nursing, prompt questions about the legality of striking by practitioners. Does the nurse maintain responsibility for any harm that might befall clients as a result of the strike? The legal concern here is with the concept of abandonment. Clients have the right to expect that care will be reasonably administered in a consistent fashion. The nurse who withholds care without affording the client prior warning may be held responsible for any injury that results. Should the nurse give adequate notice of withdrawal of service, allowing the client, or in the case of collective bargaining, the hospital, to make alternative arrangements, the nurse would probably not be held liable for injury. Should the employer not respond to notification of a withdrawal of services by employees, and client care be diminished to the extent that harm occurs, the employer would, most likely, be held responsible for the injury.

Again, let us analyze the nuances of employer/employee and contractual relationships by the use of a sample case vignette.

Case Study. A patient is admitted to the hospital for a routine hernia repair. Pre-admission tests and admitting information are adequately managed. The patient is prepared for a simple surgical procedure by his physician, who reviews with the patient the specifics of the procedure, possible complications, expected results, and recovery potential. The patient's consent is obtained.

During the surgical procedure, the usual routines of operative technique are observed, including the close attention to retrieving from the patient's incision any surgical instruments that may have entered. A few days after the procedure, the patient complains of abdominal pain and distention. Radiologic evaluation discloses the presence of a sponge in the patient's abdomen, an unexpected surgical result. The patient brings suit against the surgeon, operating room supervisor, scrub nurse, and hospital for the unanticipated injury and the required surgical extraction of the wayward sponge. The physician disclaims responsibility for the error, claiming that the sponge-count was kept and verified by the operating room nurses, who are hospital employees, and was not the supervisory responsibility of the surgeon. The hospital disclaims responsibility, claiming that the surgeon was operating as an independent contractor and not under the supervision of the hospital and, furthermore, that the operating room staff, while assisting the surgeon, were the surgeon's agents and therefore not the responsibility of the hospital. The nurses disclaimed responsibility, saying that they were acting within the confines of established hospital procedure as hospital employees, and also that they were under the supervision of the surgeon, who was responsible for the operative procedure.

The proof of injury, under these circumstances, is usually shifted from the plaintiff (injured party) to the defendant. The legal doctrine involved is termed *res ipsa loquitur* ("the thing speaks for itself"). It applies whenever the circumstances under which an injury occurred are entirely under the control of the defendant in the case, and when the plaintiff cannot have known or contributed to the circumstances, nor can he adequately attest to their occurrence. In this case it is obvious that the client didn't arrive in the hospital with a sponge placed in his abdomen, nor could he have contributed to the placement of the sponge, since he was unconscious during the procedure. Therefore, the circumstances of the alleged injury were entirely under the control of the defendant and the burden of proof is shifted from the plaintiff to the defendant(s).

It should be noted that all of the parties to this case have acknowledged that a negligent act did indeed occur. It is difficult to disclaim negligence in the face of such irrefutable evidence as a sponge removed from a previously spongeless abdomen. Thus, defense against an award of damages can only be found by demonstrating that the patient, in some way, contributed to the negligent act—a distinct impossibility—or by showing that responsibility for the negligent act lies elsewhere.

Responsibility for this example of medical misplay will be determined by evaluation of contractual relationships between the patient, hospital, physician, and nurses. Thus the hospital, having hired the nurses and admitted the surgeon to staff privileges, has established a contractual relationship with both. The hospital, having admitted the patient, thus offering service, and accepted the patient's promise of consideration for service, and probably insurance reimbursement, has established a contractual relationship with the patient in which certain minimum standards of service are implied. The physician, by accepting the patient as a client and accepting the patient's offer of compensation, and by offering to perform the surgical procedure, has established a contractual relationship with the client, the elements of which must be fulfilled. The nurses, as employees of the hospital, have a duty to render competent nursing care under the terms of the employer/employee contractual relationship. If the surgeon is extended control of the operating room staff as a necessary element of the surgical procedure, then it is also possible that the nurses will be seen as agents of the surgeon. The responsibility of the surgeon for the conduct of the nurses might be found under the concept of the "borrowed servant"—the surgeon is supervising the nurses as agents whose service is loaned by the hospital to the surgeon. What a tangle!

Again, the act of negligence would be hard to deny. The responsibility for negligence is controversial. Were it my decision, I would allot responsibility for the actions among all parties named. The surgeon is responsible, in that he had a duty to the patient to see that the procedure be accomplished within the standards of care normally associated with such a routine operation, and because he failed to ensure that the persons assisting in the surgery were accomplishing their tasks within the framework of the standard of care. The nurses share responsibility, for failing to act in accordance with the actions one would anticipate from a reasonable and prudent surgical nurse; and the hospital must answer for its failure to supervise the quality of care of physicians and nurses operating within its bounds and domain. Additional factors, of course, could alter such a judgment. Had the nurses notified the surgeon that the sponge-count was off, and had the surgeon insisted on completing the procedure without regard for the advice of the nurses, then I would be tempted to place responsibility squarely on the shoulders of the attending physician, and relieve the nurses of responsibility for the negligent act. The responsibility of the hospital for the quality of care its medical staff renders would remain unchanged. Again, this is nothing more than my opinion. Each and every case and circumstance adds factors that may alter the outcome of the litigation involved.

In summary, then, the essence of the health professional's rights and responsibilities as a provider of care are: (1) to provide competent care commensurate with the standard of care that could be anticipated by another person of similar training and experience; (2) to provide adequate supervision and evaluation of those under one's authority for the quality of care given by them; (3) to observe employer's rights and responsibilities to clients and other employees; (4) to fulfill the obligations of the contracted service adequately; and (5) to adequately apprise the employer of circumstances and conditions that impair the quality of care rendered, and to report observations of negligent care by others when and where appropriate.

Rights include: (1) the right to consideration in return for service; (2) the right to provision of adequate working environment and conditions; (3) the right to adequate and qualified assistance where necessary; and (4) the right to respect of all other rights and responsibilities.

THE ROLE OF CITIZEN

Much is said of our rights and responsibilities as citizens. Here we will simply review the fundamental rights of the individual under our legal system. It is the rights of citizenship that protect patients from the negligent acts of health care professionals, and it is also the rights of citizenship that protect the health professionals from having their own rights violated. These fundamental rights include: (1) the right to protection from harm; (2) the right to a good name; (3) personal property rights; and (4) rights to due process.

SIGNIFICANT LEGAL THEMES

The concept of law as a discipline governing human interactions to ensure maintenance of the social fabric involves several basic themes. The health practitioner who is aware of these few themes is equipped with the fundamental knowledge for legally sound practice.

Rights and Responsibilities as a Provider of Care

The nurse has an obligation to direct his or her practice and, when in a supervisory capacity, the practice of others so that: (a) damage to the recipient of service is prevented, knowing that damage can be physical, psychological, or material; (b) a standard of care is maintained, where such a standard of care is the quality/quantity of care comparable to what other recipients of service receive in similar circumstances from practitioners with comparable preparation and experience; (c) contractual obligations are fulfilled, where contractual obligations are the agreed services the recipient can reasonably expect the provider to furnish. A private duty nurse employed by a family has contracted to perform nursing services and can be reasonably expected to fulfill these services according to the prevalent standard of care; and (d) the recipient's fundamental rights are not compromised. The recipient's rights that are frequently placed in jeopardy in health care are rights to privacy, confidentiality, informed consent, and protection from bodily harm. Clients, particularly when their rights are placed in jeopardy by hospitalization and the dependent state induced by physical or mental impairment, have the privilege of expecting that their fundamental rights will be protected by those assigned to care for them. This expectation is part of contracted service. When agreeing to enter the institution for care, the client does not forfeit fundamental rights and responsibilities.

Thus the notion of a Patient's Bill of Rights is ridiculous.[1] These rights are *inherent;* they are neither to be granted nor withheld by the institution. The necessity of publication and dissemination of such a "Bill of Rights" simply underscores the pervasive extent to which health care professionals have violated clients' rights in the course of service.

Also, the nurse must practice in such a way that the rights and responsibilities of other members or subordinates in the health care team are respected. Aides, orderlies, practical nurses, technicians, physicians, volunteers, and client family members all are involved in the repertoire of health care. Each of these people possesses all the various inherent rights with attendant responsibilities. It is obligatory that their rights also be observed and protected in the course of health care delivery. A client's family also has the right to expect confidential information to remain confidential. A physician has the right not to have her reputation maligned unjustifiably or without cause. An orderly has the right to physical safety and does not have to perform functions that are at unreasonable risk.

Rights and Responsibilities as an Employee or Contractor of Service

The nurse must fulfill and can expect others to fulfill certain obligations and functions inherent in the employee/employer and contractual relationships:

---

1. Gaylin, Willard. "The Patient's Bill of Rights." Editorial, *Saturday Review of Science,* Vol. 8, No. 3, 1973.

(a) The service promised is performed within the limitations and terms specified. An institution hiring a nurse because of his previous knowledge and experience in coronary care may expect the nurse to have greater competence and skill (and thus evidence a higher standard of care) than the inexperienced or general duty nurse. Conversely, the coronary care nurse agreeing to employment can reasonably expect the terms of employment to be fulfilled as promised, namely that employment be within coronary care. Should the nurse suddenly be assigned work, for example, in pediatrics without just cause, and for an extended or unreasonable period of time, the terms of employment may have been violated and the contractual relationship nullified. The responsibility of institution to employee or employee to institution in no way precludes or supersedes the responsibility of both to the recipient of care. A short-staffing crisis without warning could justify the institution's reassignment of staff. Refusal to administer care under these circumstances could be perceived as abandonment by the nurse. Conversely, the nurse has an obligation not to allow himself to be assigned responsibilities for which he is not competent.

(b) The employee is bound to protect and promote the good name of the employer. The privilege of employment accords the obligation not to engage in unjustifiable criticism or information-sharing about the employer. Employer information is considered to be as confidential as client information, and thus must be protected. Thus, a nurse employed by a large hospital may not spread unfounded criticism of the hospital's performance simply because of his dissatisfaction with employment conditions.

(c) The employer is obligated to fulfill the terms of employment and provide a safe, functional employment setting. Employees may expect functional equipment, safe surroundings, and adequate provisions for protection of their welfare in emergency situations. Thus, the staff nurse can expect equipment on the unit to be in safe operating condition. Should she be injured due to unsafe equipment attributable to employer negligence, damages may be awarded against the employer. Similarly, the nurse may expect the hospital to have secured fire equipment and designed evacuation procedures. Should she be injured due to the hospital's failure to reasonably prepare for the protection of employees and patients in a fire situation, the nurse may recover damages from the hospital.

(d) Both the employer and employee, or any parties to a contract, must observe the fundamental characteristics of a contractual relationship: (1) the service contracted or performed must be legal; (2) the parties to the contract must be of majority (age) and competent; (3) there must be both an offer and acceptance; and (4) there must be consideration or the promise of consideration (payment or return).

The Licensure Overlay

Professional and technical nurses, and many other health care practitioners, are required to obtain a license to practice their skills. Licensure is a function of state government. It is designed to fulfill the state's responsibility to protect the general public from unsafe practice. Licensure can be permissive (optional) or mandatory (required). Nurse licensure is mandatory in all states of the United States of America; that is, you must hold a valid license to practice nursing, except under limited, defined circumstances, such as when delivering nursing care to a member of your own family. The philosophy or rationale for licensure for public protection is that the skill licensed is sufficiently sophisticated and the potential harm of incompetent practice sufficiently great to warrant the state's acting in the public behalf.

Nurse licensure is regulated by state legislation, termed Nurse Practice Acts. Although different from state to state (and each nurse is strongly urged to review the Practice Act in her state), the Practice Acts do share some common features. Each act is generally administered through a State Board of Nursing. The Act empowers the state to control nursing through the Board. The Board promulgates rules and regulations to ensure the efficient and effective administration of the Practice Acts. Boards of Nursing are generally responsible for: (a) setting policies and procedures for granting, suspending, and revoking licensure; (b) establishing means for review and approval of educational programs preparing nurse graduates; and (c) establishing and maintaining voluntary or mandatory continuing education requirements.

The Nurse Practice Acts contain specifications regarding: (a) requirements of candidates for nurse licensure. (May include age, citizenship or citizenship intention, education, and evidence of moral character, physical health, etc. Some of these requirements are quite nebulous and, therefore, difficult to interpret or enforce); (b) requirements of candidates for endorsement (Endorsement is the process of receiving licensure in one state on the basis of licensure in another state); (c) specification of grounds for licensure revocation; (d) specification for empowering and comprising the State Board of Nursing; and (e) a definition of nursing's scope and function. (This may include specification of definitions for practitioners and various levels of nursing).

There is currently growing criticism of the effects of state-enforced mandatory licensure for many of the professions. Although designed to protect the public, many people perceive licensure as a means of obtaining economic and vocational security for the professions licensed. The role of licensure in ensuring homogeneity and quality in care, as opposed to its role in protecting practitioners from "outside" competition, needs to be evaluated. Undoubtedly, as new health roles and knowledge develop, old assumptions and structures will change. The permanency of mandatory licensure cannot be predicted.

Summary

Law is a social discipline, concerned with the maintenance of the social fabric and generated by the heterogeneity and complexity of society's population. Law originates in statutory and judiciary actions. Law that focuses on the protection of the rights of the state to maintain the social fabric is criminal law; it governs actions which, if tolerated, would disrupt society. Law that extends to the protection of individual rights and property rights is termed civil law. Most of the interactions in which health professionals encounter the legal influence on health care are within civil disputes. Rarely is a health professional involved in criminal law.

Three overriding legal principles can be detected in an analysis of the law. These are: (1) a concern for justice, as defined by the just consequence of an action; (2) use of the concept of a reasonable and prudent person as a standard for the evaluation of the appropriateness of acts or decisions; and (3) a focus on the dual principle of rights and responsibilities, according to which each right has its accompanying responsibility and the failure to fulfill responsibilities may lead to the curtailment of rights.

Nurses who are able to frame their practice within a system of ethical decision-making, who are cognizant of both their rights and responsibilities, and who attend to the standards of safe practice as promulgated by the profession, are not likely to find themselves involved in legal imbroglios.

AN OUNCE OF PREVENTION . . .

No message should be easier to give to nurses than that of the desirability of prevention over cure. Nursing has long recognized its responsibility to promote health, rather than simply attempting to cure disease. Why then are we so loath to take our own advice when it comes to our dealings with the law? Possibly the old adage, "Physician, heal thyself," is appropriate here. Nursing would do well to recognize that curative strategies are never as efficient as preventive strategies.

Safe, ethical nursing practice makes legal entanglements unlikely, and usually results in excellent nursing care. Safe nursing practice is the delivery of nursing care in accordance with established procedures utilizing the best of prevailing standards of care. Safe practice is the simple result of adequate nursing preparation and conscientious nursing practice. Simply caring enough to want to do a good job and attempting to keep up with advances in one's field are the foundation for safe nursing care.

Ethical nursing practice entails the clarification of and conformance to an internally established standard of ethical decision-making and implementation. Ethical decision-making is a frame of reference for the solution of problems. It allows the implementation of guidelines or rules that consider factors other than sheer expediency, particularly considerations that incorporate a view to the broader consequences of decisions in terms of moral and social impact on both the prime agents in the situation and extending to agents with peripheral involvement.

The nurse who engages in practice that conforms to the minimum acceptable criteria for safe practice and who frames her nursing care within a structure of ethical considerations will probably stay out of trouble with the law. Recalling the basic principles of the law will reveal the rationale for this effect of safe and ethical practice.

The law is structured to ensure justice and maintenance of the social fabric as its first priorities. Systems of law are enforced when these priorities are threatened. Usually, health care professionals who encounter legal difficulties find themselves dealing with civil law—the law that governs noncriminal interactions. Civil law focuses on protecting individual rights and responsibilities. Recourse to perceived violation of individual rights is through civil litigation. Among the legal entanglements involving health care, and particularly nursing, most deal with civil litigations. In civil litigation, the judgment as to whether conduct was responsible or irresponsible is based on fairly simple principles that relate the acceptability of an action to the standard set in the community of peers for that action, the degree to which obligations incurred are fulfilled, and the prudence of the actors in the incident. The law establishes, and the judicial process enforces, minimal standards for acceptable fulfillment of these principles. That is, the law is not concerned with excellence, but merely with acceptable conduct of civil interactions.

The nurse who focuses care within a framework built on knowledge and skill of safe practice and who attempts to complete the obligations of professional service within a perspective of ethical standards is aiming practice at levels of care that surpass the legal minima. Any nurse who aspires to provide high-quality nursing care will probably evidence practice that is amply satisfactory from a legal standpoint.

Communication Skills

Some experts in the field of communication espouse the view that much of what is awry in human affairs is the result of poor communication, rather than incorrect action. Nowhere is the powerful effect of inefficient interpersonal communication more apparent than in health care.

Imagine the situation in which the client is an elderly black woman with minimal education. Her comprehension of information and procedures rendered during hospitalization will be directly proportional to the ability of the staff to relate to her in terms that are dignified and appropriate to her level of understanding. Should she be experiencing a urinary tract infecton and the attending physician attempts to explain that she has "bugs" in her urine, a state of hysteria could be easily induced. Although staff have one meaning for the term "bugs," the client has another. Such incidents are totally preventable if adequate communication strategies are employed. Should the client sustain any real or perceived injury from the incident, the liability of the staff would have to be determined. Although this incident seems farfetched, it is one which in fact occurred, and it produced substantial harm to the client's self-perception and wasted huge amounts of nursing staff time in efforts to redress the grievance perceived by the client's family. The end result of the interaction was the expenditure of more staff time and effort on the compensation for the incident than was necessary for the therapeutic care of the original health care episode, a waste of energy, and an affront to the dignity of all concerned.

The power of effective communication is frequently underestimated by health professionals. But, as our less-than-perceptive physician demonstrated so clearly, words carry meanings and strengths that go well beyond simple definition. We need to learn to respect the clout of verbal and non-verbal communication. We can begin to employ this power for the benefit of client care and in the prevention of legal entanglements in health service.

Many of the classic court cases that have produced medical malpractice law appear to have been founded upon, or to have involved, substantial miscommunication. The knowledge of what information to share, with whom to share it, and how, has marked the difference between life and death and, later, between the awarding of damages and a finding of no fault in many instances. The case of *Tarasoff v. Board of Regents* is an excellent example of a communication problem. Angela Holder summarizes the case as follows:

A student under treatment by a university health center psychologist
said that he intended to kill his former girlfriend. The psychologist
believed him, and arranged with two staff physicians to have the young
man hospitalized. The Chief of the Service ordered him released. He
killed her. Her parents sued the university for failing to hospitalize the
young man, or alternatively, to warn her or them of the threat. The
court upheld their cause of action.[2]

The inability of the responsible professionals in the university's
counseling and health service to act on information that they possessed
may have contributed to the girl's death and was the basis for the finding
against them by the court. The appropriate action in communicating the
suspected violent intent of the young man might have prevented a tragic
scenario from occurring.

Equally unfortunate, yet not so obvious, instances of miscommunication occur daily in most health care institutions. The range of lost
meaning and misuse of information extends from the innocent sharing
of confidential information to the intentional misleading of clients in
attempts to reassure a terminally ill person when reassurance of recovery
is a blatant lie. Each instance of miscommunication, in addition to de-
tracting from the quality of care, enhances the potential for legal ramifications of professional actions.

Miscommunication can be defined as relaying or failing to relay
information, and, by doing so, impairing or defeating the accomplishment of the desired goal. It can also be seen as the relaying of inaccurate
or incomplete information. Holder reports a case, *Moyer v. Phillips*, which
involves a physician who, in the course of completing a required physical
on a truckdriver, reported that the truckdriver was an alcoholic. This
information cost the truckdriver his job, even though he had a seven-
year driving record without incident. The physician was found to have
committed libel against the plaintiff. The physician's error in communicating information that damaged his client, and which may not have
been borne out by facts related to the client's performance, resulted in
the physician's liability for these actions.

Beyond one's ethical obligations to ensure the accuracy and appropriateness of communications, it is a legal necessity for health professionals to recognize and appreciate the impact of the powerful information
to which they are privileged. Failure to comprehend the degree of import
of information gained during the performance of most professional duties
can have disastrous legal consequences. The expression, "discretion is
the greater part of valor," is nowhere more appropriate than in health
care.

2.Holder, Angela. *Medical Malpractice and the Law*. (New York: Wiley) 1978, p. 275.

Client/Provider Rapport. There are other aspects to the dimensions of communication in health care, some of which have direct bearing on the relationship between health care and the law. None of these dimensions is more mystifying and subtle than that which accounts for the extensive impact of client/provider rapport on legal ramifications of service. An observable but inexplicable phenomenon is that of the health care consumer who may have experienced a serious incident of mispractice or malpractice at the hands of a professional, but who chooses not to bring action, or simply is unaware of the need to bring legal action, largely because of the relationship the client and provider of service have maintained. Yet one can see other instances where a professional has performed a remarkably competent service for the consumer of care and the client chooses to bring suit, even capriciously. The degree of communicative relationship established by the provider of service with the consumer of service may well be responsible for this phenomenon.

We are much more likely to be forgiving of a friend's shortcomings and less likely to be sympathetic toward an institution. The provider of service who has established and maintained a personal relationship with her client is often seen as a friend or teammate by the client in his battle to gain or maintain health. The provider—nurse, physician, aide, or orderly—who seems mostly concerned with time and efficiency, thereby demonstrating little outward concern for the client's personal response to illness, is likely to be perceived by the client as less than a friend and colleague in the quest to obtain health and well being. The provider of service who is able to communicate concern and compassion to the client, able to demonstrate genuine interest in his welfare, is much more likely to be perceived as a supportive friend in the health care process. The key concept is in the word *perceived*. Frequently, one is able to observe providers of service who may have little or no contribution to make to the client's actual care, yet are able to attain and maintain a high level of regard in the provider-client relationship through rapport established. The provider is perceived as a therapeutic agent and is thus treated as one. There are other observable instances where a particular professional is instrumental in efforts to obtain or maintain client health, but the efforts and talents of these professionals are, for some reason, not apparent to the client, and are thus undervalued or not valued at all.

The concept of perception of support or non-support has a high degree of relationship to a client's willingness to engage in legal action for perceived wrongs. Clients will accept the fact that providers of care are, indeed, human, and, as humans practicing an art with many variables and conditions of change, may not always be able to obtain the results they seek. Yet other consumers of service, partly because they think that health care is a science whose results can be predicted with certainty, anticipate that care will always bring the promised or hoped-for result.

The consumer of service who has been led to a high expectation of the results of care, who does not perceive the providers of care as allies in the health struggle, and who may be unrealistically optimistic in his expectations, may be likely to perceive care as inadequate when the anticipated results are not obtained. Such a client is more likely to seek remedy for perceived disservice.

Again, the strength of the rapport between provider and consumer is frequently the crucial factor in the client's decision to seek or not to seek legal remedy. We simply don't often sue friends unless a considerable wrong is involved. We are more likely to bring suit against faceless institutions without compassion that have the economic resources to award the damages.

It is often said by physicians (out of earshot of nurses) that nurses save physicians from malpractice suits more often than either group would like to admit. The meaning of this statement is that the nurse's continuous contact with clients which permits them to establish a rapport and relationship that is frequently closer than that which exists between the client and the physician. Although the physician may be seen as the agent with authority over the client's welfare, particularly during a prolonged hospitalization, the nurse is seen as an ally in the process—simply because of the amount and type of contact that occurs between the nurse and client. Thus, when events unfold in the course of care, the nurse is more able to explain them, and sometimes to compensate for the perceived aloofness of the physician. Moreover, the nurse is often the family's main or exclusive contact with the health professionals caring for their loved one. The nurse's ability to maintain an effective channel of communication with the family can assist her in supporting and maintaining the primary client during health care, which lessens the chance of client dissatisfaction with service. The client's satisfaction with health care is related to levels of support obtained; if the client's family and the nurse have rapport, the overall level of care is enhanced.

The nurse's ability to communicate with clients and their families, and, conversely, to relate information about the client back to the physician, often determines the success or failure of a health care episode. The role of the nurse in prevention of legal entanglements for other health professionals and for herself is frequently underestimated. The power of the nurse to effect satisfactory care and ensure effective communications needs to be recognized and promoted more efficiently and rewarded more adequately. We do clients and professionals a disservice to do otherwise.

Effective, efficient, accurate, and appropriate communication, both verbal and non-verbal, remains a most powerful influence in determining client satisfaction with care. Nurses, as well as other health professionals, would do well to emphasize this concept in practice.

There are several means by which information is communicated, or miscommunicated, in health care. Each of these means has differing legal consequences. Although prior to practice, professionals are schooled in the rudiments of each, a review of the fundamental principles of these concepts and their legal ramifications is in order.

Charts and records are documents associated with a client's health care, and should always be treated as legal records—which they are. A client's chart is considered a subpoenable document, expected to stand as an accurate reflection of the course of events and the progress, or lack of progress, obtained from the client's hospitalization. It is a reflection of the care given, and is expected to depict such care accurately. Regardless of the course of events that actually occurred, the material contained in the chart is considered reflective of the care given. It is evidence of the competence or incompetence of the health professionals rendering service. It is imperative that all institutional records related to client care be afforded a high degree of accuracy and diligent care.

Nurses are often unmindful of the significance and implications of chart contents. Many instances in which the accuracy or completeness of hospital records is disputed demonstrate the legal power of written records. In *Gonzales v. Nork,* the strength of the plaintiff's case was based on the documentation in the client's record that demonstrated the physician's negligence in inappropriately performing a laminectomy procedure and spinal fusion on a client, despite lumbar myelogram findings within normal limits and without consultation. The physician's progress notes, in this case, contained assurances of the client's improving condition. Yet, the corresponding nurse's notes for the same period and client, contained evidence of the client's deteriorating condition and painful response to the procedure. The negligence of the defendant physician, and the corresponding liability of the hospital for failure to complete its duty of care to the client, was partially demonstrated by the strength of the nurse's notes in the client's chart.

The impact and significance of written records related to client care should never be underestimated. The best guide to the construction of written records is to include exactly what happened, as soon after it happened and as objectively as possible. Nurses' errors in recording are of two kinds—either too little or too much. It is neither necessary to compose a novel when describing the client's morning bath, nor is it wise to dismiss an episode of client-reported pain as "apparent gas." Both examples, though ludicrous, do happen.

Good record keeping is a simple and almost automatic process of noting observations, actions, and responses of the client in relation to health status and care regimen. Many legal issues have been generated over less.

Jeopardy

We use the term *jeopardy* to refer to a state of risk or the threat of risk when speaking of client health. The term is equally applicable to the relationship of health professionals to professional liability (malpractice). Jeopardy is a state or risk or the threat of risk faced by the health professional. It is as perceptible as any human interaction. Perception is a factor of the severity of the situation and of the skills of the observer. Just as one meets nurses and physicians who are particularly adept at diagnosing a client's health problem, one meets people who seem to have a sense for when a situation offers jeopardy for legal consequences. There are logical steps one can take to recognize the symptoms of jeopardy-laden situations and the actions that can be taken to relieve or minimize the consequences of such jeopardy.

Situations that contain the potential for involving professional liability arise in a variety of ways. It is possible to arrange these situations into three nice, neat, little categories, which, upon investigation, refuse to stay so neat and tidy. We will explore the situations of jeopardy according to: (1) actions involving oneself; (2) actions involving subordinates or colleagues; and (3) actions involving superior personnel or physicians. We will examine these situations with regard to what can occur, what one's personal responsibility in the situation may be, and what can be done to prevent or minimize the legal ramifications.

Legal Jeopardy—Self. Just as in war and football, when one is attempting to minimize legal jeopardy resulting from one's own actions the best defense is a good offense. In this instance, a good offense involves a few simple concepts relating to practice. First, the knowledge of one's own strengths and limitations; second, the ability to act on knowledge of limitations by seeking either assistance or self-development; and third, the ability to act as one's own advocate when needing representation to correct a situation in which the potential for jeopardy is apparent.

Knowledge of one's own strengths and limitations is perhaps the most advantageous yet most difficult of attributes to acquire. This skill is a direct function of ability in self-evaluation. A realistic appraisal of where talents and knowledge exist, and where there may be deficiencies in capabilities, is a requisite bit of information for the task of avoiding legal jeopardy arising from one's own actions. An appraisal of oneself is not lightly undertaken, but the information gained is well worth the process. The simplest way of assessing one's own strengths and limitations is to view the environment in which one is attempting to function, and compare its requirements with his knowledge and skills. A mismatch, in which one is expected to function at a level of sophistication beyond his abilities, is a situation ripe with the potential for legal jeopardy. Recall that one of the methods for legally evaluating conduct is the standard of the "reasonable and prudent person." The reasonable and prudent nurse does not attempt to function within situations that demand skill beyond his or her abilities. The new graduate who accepts assignment as a staff nurse in intensive care without further preparation may be found as liable for damaging conduct as the supervisor or institution that made the assignment. It would not be reasonable to expect the beginning practitioner of nursing to possess the knowledge and skill requisite to functioning in the complex and demanding environment of intensive care, and the assignment of the new graduate to such an environment, without first assessing abilities and providing further assurances that such abilities meet the needs of the environment, is a foolish misjudgment on the part of all involved. It is in the best interests of nurse, client, and sponsoring institution that one be able to clearly articulate strengths and limitations in relation to professional role expectations.

Legal Jeopardy—Subordinates and Colleagues. The principles of law are quite clear on the issue of one's responsibility for the conduct and actions of subordinate personnel. It is expected that the prudent supervisor be able to assess and utilize staff according to their capabilities. The supervisor who knowingly assigns an attendant to a client requiring care beyond the attendant's capabilities is responsible for any damages that might result from the gap between needs and services provided. Ignorance of an attendant's limitations is not considered a defense for incorrect assignment, for the prudent and reasonable supervisor is aware of her subordinate's limitations. The supervisor has the ongoing responsibility to evaluate subordinates and to attempt to develop potential, while maintaining cognizance of limitations.

The law specifically mandates the superior's responsibility for the actions of subordinates through the doctrine of *respondeat superior*, which is roughly interpreted as the master's responsibility for the conduct of the servant.

This doctrine obligates a hospital to be responsible for the conduct of its employees, and provides much of the legal motivation for institutional efforts to maintain and upgrade the knowledge and skills of employees; it also provides an incentive to institute systems of evaluation that permit assignment of staff according to abilities. It is this doctrine that obligates a supervising nurse to be cognizant of, and act according to, the abilities of her subordinates.

The only exemption a superior may successfully plead to this doctrine is that the conduct of a subordinate was such that it could not have been anticipated. For example, an attendant is confronted by an angry patient. The attendant is attacked and responds by brutally striking the disoriented client. The supervising nurse and the employing institution may be able to demonstrate that the attendant's behavior was so inappropriate as to be unanticipatable. The defense of both the institution and the supervising nurse would be destroyed if it could be demonstrated that either had any reason to expect such behavior from the attendant, such as previous incidents of inappropriate behavior. Should previous indications of the attendant's behavioral control deficiencies exist, the interpretation of *respondeat superior* might find that the reasonable and prudent superior or institution would not have continued to assign that person to client care.

The issue of individual responsibility for the inappropriate practice of professional colleagues is more difficult to resolve. The practitioner who regularly criticizes and questions the judgments of fellow workers is not easily tolerated and may find her own practice coming under close, painful scrutiny. Yet the unsafe actions of colleagues can have legal, as well as ethical, consequences for companion practitioners.

The development of the ability to differentiate between care that is simply less than excellent and care that is actually unsafe or harmful is necessary. It is one matter to observe a nurse who is rude and unfriendly, and do nothing; it is another to observe a nurse administer an incorrect medication or perform a procedure in a threatening manner, and not take appropriate action. The former might be seen as a situation requiring mental notation for action at a later time, or may not require action at all, depending on the relationship between staff and the goals and aspirations of the observing nurse. The latter situation, however, requires some form of intervention, for many reasons.

The nurse who knowingly allows another to endanger or threaten the safety or health of a client has failed to complete her responsibility to the employer, the client, and possibly to her colleague nurse. An employer may expect staff to attempt to assure the competence of colleagues in certain situations. A nurse who fails to report the consistent incompetence of a peer is simply not meeting her responsibilities to her employer. The nurse would be most wise to briefly report her observations to her supervisor, who is then obligated to act to verify this information. The nurse who fails to intervene in a situation where intervention may prevent damage, and where failure to intervene assures harm or the threat of harm, has simply not completed her responsibility to her employer. The legal ramifications of the failure to intervene are unclear. In most instances, one would anticipate few legal consequences from the omission, particularly if the observing nurse were in no way responsible either for the client's care or for the supervision or evaluation of the peer's performance.

The duty to attempt to assure that care given is at least not harmful is more an ethical responsibility than a legal duty in the situation where the prime actors are colleagues. However, if the employer has clearly established an expectation of peer review and evaluation, the failure to act may result in employment consequences for the observer.

Certainly the entire issue of what to do when aware of the incompetent practice of others would be incompletely discussed if we did not give some attention to the need to establish channels of communication between colleagues and to the need to use these channels to relay one's observations to her peers. The first and most appropriate action for the observing nurse to take when aware of the limitations of a colleague is to attempt to share this perception with the colleague. There may be circumstances or mitigating factors that affect the situation, of which the observer is unaware; or the peer may not be aware of the observed problem and may be able to correct it. The necessity for sharing such observations with the individuals involved is twofold. It may prevent the inaccurate, and later embarrassing, reporting of the colleague to a superior, and it may prevent or rectify the difficulty for the future. It would be unfair for all concerned to act on information without having first consulted the person on whom the information focuses. The only exception would be if the failure to take immediate and drastic action would result in irreparable harm and injury to the client, or if the attempts at sharing such observations have been made in the past and have not met with modified behaviors.

The entire problem of evaluating and acting on evaluations of peers is quite thorny. We are always concerned with our ability to withstand similar scrutiny. We also don't like to make waves, stir up trouble for others, or be the focus of unwanted or unpleasant attention. Yet we must also examine the obligation extended to all clients, and the responsibility owed an employer and supervisor, not to tolerate and accept peer behavior that harms clients and jeopardizes the institution. Moreover, appropriately handled peer evaluation and counseling can lead to personal growth and professional development for all concerned. The important factors are an attitude of mutual trust and acknowledged motivations based on desire for quality of care and personal growth.

Jeopardy—Superiors and Physicians. One would like to believe that the actions and behaviors of one's superiors and of physicians are totally unrelated, in a legal sense, to one's own responsibility for care. Unfortunately this is not true. The behavior of any individual that threatens or harms the safety or health of a client affects the responsibility of all who are aware of it. Nurses who are aware of the irresponsible behavior of a superior staff member are obligated both by ethical responsibility and the duty owed to the employer to report such behavior to the appropriate person. This situation is similar to that experienced in relation to observation of the behavior of a colleague or peer. The fact that one may not be directly responsible for the behavior of another does not relieve the obligation to report such behavior when it endangers client welfare.

Nowhere is the topic of reporting unacceptable behavior more delicate and touchy for nurses than in relation to physician practice. For many years the nurse was considered a subordinate of the physician. Under certain circumstances, this legal relationship still exists. Moreover, the power and control most physicians have within hospitals and other health care institutions is such that the nurse who dares to criticize medical care does so at considerable risk. Physicians call the shots in most situations. Their economic, educational, and practice base is broader than that of the nurse. The physician can control the environment in which she practices; the nurse may not be as fortunate. Yet the nurse who observes and tolerates dangerous care of clients by physicians is placing himself in legal jeopardy. The observation of care or failure to render care that places a client in risk of impairment of safety or health must be recorded and shared with one's appropriate supervisor. The legal consequences of a failure to do so are complex and devastating.

The classic case demonstrating the degree to which an institution can be found liable for the actions of a physician, and the importance of the nursing staff's involvement in the documentation of the physician's incompetence, is the Darling case. Darling was an eighteen-year-old, injured in a football game and transported to a small community hospital in Charleston, Illinois.[3] The physician on call treated the boy's injury by applying a cast, even though the physician had not treated this type of fracture in three years. The physician failed to obtain any consultation. After applying the cast, the boy was consistently complaining of pain. After a few days, the physician split the cast, again not requesting consultation. Later, the boy was transferred to another, larger hospital, where it was found that his condition was sufficiently dire to require

---

3.Holder, p. 214.

amputation of the leg because of impaired circulation caused by the improperly applied cast. The legal action that resulted found the physician responsible for his negligent treatment of the injury, but was more monumental in that it established the legal precedent of holding the hospital responsible for the physician's actions, even though the physician was not a salaried employee of the hospital. The court stated that the hospital had a duty of care to the client to assure that medical staff affiliating and acquiring clients through the on-call procedure in the emergency room were competent to render care. Furthermore, it held the hospital responsible because the floor nurses, hospital employees on salary, failed to recognize and act upon the boy's deteriorating condition.

The reasonable and prudent nurse is expected not only to assure that her own care and that the care of her subordinates is minimally safe and competent; she is expected to observe and take appropriate action when the care by superiors or physicians is negligent or potentially harmful. Failure to complete this responsibility can result in the hospital's liability for resultant damages. In turn, the hospital, particularly if it has clearly delineated the responsibilities of staff to include the obligation to report negligent care of others, can expect employees to fulfill this obligation to the employer. The hospital may even attempt to pursue the extent of the employee's legal responsibility for failure to meet this duty to the employer.

One can imagine a situation in which the staff nurses observe a physician administer an inappropriate medication, after which the client expires. The client's family brings suit against the hospital and physician, and is successful in obtaining award of damages. The hospital could, in turn, bring suit against the nurses for having failed to meet their duty to their employer by not reporting the alleged incompetent care. Although I am unaware of such action having yet occurred, I can well imagine that it might.

Finally, what should you do if you see or participate in a situation that suggests litigation? Each practicing nurse, in moments of complete candor, will admit to having observed incidents during professional practice that almost cried out for litigation.

We sometimes are privy to facts and information that lead us to make the observation, "if it were me, I'd sue." This observation is occasionally founded on incomplete or inaccurate information and should not be lightly uttered. Rarely is anyone in complete possession of all pertinent facts in any given situation. We often observe the actions of others and are critical, neither knowing the underlying motivations for actions nor all of the possible alternatives. Thus the judgment that an action was or was not correct is frequently unfair and not really ours to make.

Occasionally the situation is such that one is very informed about the facts and circumstances of a particular situation and believes that the client's rights or health were endangered or impaired by another's error. Here is a serious dilemma for even the most mature and experienced of health professionals. Where is our ethical/legal allegiance, and what are the consequences of various actions for the persons involved?

Certainly the professional nurse who has defined an ethical system that places priority of decision-making on the client's welfare, and is informed concerning the legal ramifications of her actions, will be most confused and confounded by the dilemma. Failure to share the significance or a potentially harmful action of another with the client can be assessed as a breach of the nurse-client obligation, if one perceives the nursing role as that of client advocate. The consequences of sharing such information with the client, however, can be drastic. It is possible, for example, that the nurse's information is incorrect. False reporting can place one in a legally complex situation. What does one do?

The nurse who shares observations, opinions, and judgments concerning the care rendered by others is courting dangerous risks, and thus must be cognizant both of risks and the factual nature of the information transmitted. Transmission of information that is incorrect is damaging to the client's welfare in that it impinges upon and potentially destroys client trust in professional judgment. It is a grave legal risk in that the failure of the information to be validated by whatever litigation ensues can result in the reporting nurse's liability for having communicated incorrect information; this can result in litigation for slander, libel, and/or defamation of character. The most obvious consequence of sharing such information with clients is the risk to continued employment. Even if such data are later verified, employers are hardly enthusiastic about the prospect of their shortcomings being publicized by someone on the company payroll.

The decision to share opinions critical of the professional competence of others is a delicate, yet important, one. The ramifications of the decision are profound and pervasive. It is advisable not to undertake such actions without first engaging in intense contemplation and having sought collaboration with an uninvolved professional colleague. The decision arrived at will be important for all concerned. Certainly one of the factors that must be weighed is the benefit that possession of such knowledge will have for the client. If the central focus of the health system is client welfare, any course of action that does not benefit the client will not be a viable alternative.

GETTING HELP

The prudent practitioner will tend to be successful in preventing the legal entanglements that so frequently and needlessly frighten health professionals. However, even the best planning, foresight, and contemplation are known to be less than successful under some circumstances. Assuming that your care is well founded on the best that is nursing, your practice can still be endangered by the unsafe practice or actions of others. Health care is a team effort, even when all members of the team may not perceive it as such. As in team sports, the efforts of a proficient team can be jeopardized by the inactivity or incompetence of one member, even a member far removed from the playing field. The efforts of the most conscientious of nurses can be undermined by a split second of thoughtless behavior by a nurse's aide or orderly, or by the offhand remark of a passing physician. We can control our practice, supervise the practice of others, and attempt to influence the practice of still other actors in the delivery system. But in the final analysis, the system is far from predictable and controlled. So the most conscientious of practitioners is prudent to understand the mechanisms for obtaining assistance and advice in circumstances where legal ramifications are potentially great.

Note the use of the word potential. In the practice of health care, we continually urge our clientele to avail themselves of service whenever the situation warrants intervention—as soon in the process as possible. We much prefer the person with mild chest pains to seek medical consultation rather than waiting until a full blown myocardial infarct is in progress. The same concept applies to the availability and wisdom of getting assistance with possible legal problems in health care. It is both prudent and efficient to attempt to get information and assistance as soon as one is aware that a potential problem exists. Just as in our medical example, there is frequently much that can be done to prevent or minimize the entanglements of the situation, if action and advice are sought early enough in the process. This does not, of course, mean that each health practitioner must have a practicing medical liability attorney under constant retainer. It does mean that the wise practitioner is aware of the lines of communication within the health system in which practice is delivered, and avails himself of these lines when issues relative to legal or professional problems arise.

Action after the fact is never as efficient or as effective as action in prevention. Reaction is less controllable than action. Too frequently we ignore or tolerate a situation until its impact is beyond our control. Such activity is foolish from the view of the interests of the professional person involved, and certainly questionable in light of the client's welfare.

What to Do

If one should suspect that a situation bears potential for legal ramifications, it is wise to act on this information as soon as possible. The first step in the process is sharing one's observations with one's immediate superior. It is important to relay information factually, accurately, quickly, and calmly. Thus, it is advisable to organize thoughts and observations in the form of brief notes. These can be retained for one's own record in case the situation should develop further. Regardless of the source of the perceived problem, the supervisor needs to be involved as soon as possible (unless it is the supervisor's conduct that concerns one; then, if attempts to meet with the supervisor are unacceptable or unsuccessful, the next individual in the line of supervision is the appropriate recipient of information).

It is unprofessional and legally dangerous to share observations concerning another's potentially negligent behavior with other than appropriate supervisory personnel. The nurse who freely shares his negative opinion of a physician's, or other colleague's, behavior with people not involved in the situation is courting danger. The sharing of information that later proves to be inaccurate can be interpreted as defamation of character, particularly if it calls a professional's competence into question. It is appropriate for an employee discreetly to share observations of import with a supervisor, but inappropriate to gossip with peers and colleagues or subordinates.

Regardless of the source of the potential problem, whether one's own mistakes, the mistakes of subordinates, those of superiors, or no one's mistake at all—rather the unfortunate happenstance of nature— the perception of a situation that may later involve legal ramifications should initiate some automatic actions on the part of the prudent nurse. The first of these actions is to attempt to minimize or prevent any actual harm.

Observation of an aide using unsafe body mechanics in the transfer of a client from a wheelchair to a bed should motivate immediate, appropriate intervention by the nurse to prevent any injury to the client. Should the nurse be too late to prevent the incident from occurring, she should provide whatever immediate assistance is required to minimize harm and risk incurred.

Once the incident is complete or prevention of further harm or injury is no longer possible, the prudent nurse attempts briefly to record observations and actions of all concerned. This record is not a part of the client's chart, although later one may want to refer to these notes for completing charting responsibilities. The existence of anecdotal notes can greatly assist one in accurately recalling and reporting the incident to the appropriate supervisory personnel.

It is also necessary carefully to observe and complete all institutional procedural requirements under the circumstances. If hospital policy mandates that an incident form be completed and forwarded, then it is a good idea to do so immediately. This both fulfills one's obligations to the institution and demonstrates his willingness to comply with the duty to his employers. If institutional procedure mandates that the physician or another designated person be involved, it is wise also to inform the supervisor prior to informing the physician of record.

In order to observe accurately, it is very important not to panic. The ability to remain calm when a situation is as frightening as those which promise legal complications is crucial. Most dilemmas are resolved in manners which benefit both client and staff. Rarely does a situation develop to the point that actual litigation results. Yet the complications that are created by panic, inappropriate communications, and a generally hectic, unorganized approach can be mammoth.

Should one be assured that a situation is grave enough to warrant legal complications and if she is suspicious that she will be involved, it is wise to notify immediately her insurance carrier. This statement assumes that all practitioners are prudent enough to acquire professional liability insurance immediately upon entry into practice!

Professional liability insurance (malpractice insurance) is maintained by contractual arrangements through employment at many institutions. Because of the presence of such institutional insurance, many nurses mistakenly believe that they are individually covered and do not attempt to acquire their own professional liability insurance. Such behavior is foolhardy, and risks both financial and professional disaster. Institutional insurance is designed to protect the institution first and foremost. Should the carrier (insurance company) in any way be able to transfer liability from the institution to the practitioner, they will attempt to do so. Moreover, such institutional insurance covers the practitioner only while in the employ of the institution and only when on duty. Coverage does not extend to off-hours or to other environments. The nurse who assists a neighbor with a health problem and later incurs a law suit will not receive any assistance from the insurance carrier of her employing institution.

Professional liability insurance for professional nurses is obtained either through membership in one of the professional associations, such as the Federation of Nurses and Health Professionals or the American

Nurses Association, or through private insurance carriers independent of association membership. The premiums for professional liability insurance are quite small, particularly if one compares the cost to the expense of defending a liability suit or paying damages in a finding of negligence. Whether one is found responsible or not, the legal fees alone are hefty and are well worth years of money spent on liability premiums.

Notification of one's insurance carrier of a potential legal problem usually brings a most predictable reaction—help and advice. It is in the best interests of the insurance carrier to see that you are kept out of trouble and they are acutely aware of the advantage to be gained from early intervention in a potential liability occurrence. Most carriers will immediately avail themselves of professional legal assistance and advice, and provide this service directly to the insured party. It is most comforting to have the opinion of an expert whenever one perceives herself to be in jeopardy.

. . . And What Not to Do.

Should the unfortunate occur, and you find yourself in the midst of a legal entanglement despite your own prudent, professional, practice, there are distinct actions to avoid. After fulfilling one's obligations to one's employers and obtaining whatever advice is appropriate, it is wise to keep discussion of the situation to a minimum. Sharing one's plight with peers and friends might prove cathartic at the time, but may become, in retrospect, a mark on one's professional credibility and reputation. Further, one is never assured of another's discretion and certainly there is no need to fuel the fires of the litigation by providing additional information to the various parties involved. Keep the details of the situation to yourself and maintain professional decorum.

Summary

It is easy to become paralyzed at the maze of legal entanglements that confront health care delivery. The effect of legal influences on health care is pervasive and continuing. Yet the individual practitioner of care, if able to maintain safe standards of care and practice within an ethically derived framework, is not likely to face many of these legal disasters. The individual's awareness of the potential of legal consequences of his own actions, and appreciation of the ways in which one can prevent or modify the risks faced, is sufficient to ensure a high degree of legally safe practice. The professional who is motivated by concern for quality client care, maintains currency of competence, and establishes valid avenues of communication has minimized the risks of legal jeopardy in all but the most extreme circumstances.

Legal Concepts and Applications

Evaluate each of the following cases according to the principles and concepts of law and health care as presented in Chapter 4. Are you able to readily affix responsibility for the actions taken? Or are there questions concerning the outcome of each case from a legal perspective? Are you able to name the concepts that would be most applicable in each situation?

Case A. The Careless Patient Ms. Ashley was admitted via the emergency room to a general hospital complaining of chest pain and disorientation, and displaying aphasia, hemiplegia and sensory impairment. Routine medical evaluation disclosed a suspected cerebral aneurysm, and appropriate medical treatment was begun. Her family physician said that she had been treated for hypertension and advised to lose some of her significant bulk. The physician's office nurse had initiated a weight-loss teaching plan with Ms. Ashley, who chose not to comply.

Ms. Ashley's family sought legal advice, claiming that her family physician and his office nurse had failed to institute proper and appropriate preventive health measures, and furthermore, that they had failed to apprise her of the gravity of her condition.

Case B. The Uninformed Nurse Nancy Nurse is a full-time evening staff nurse in a general hospital intensive care unit. A new respirator filter attachment was delivered during the day. Ms. Nurse attempted to affix the attachment to a functioning respirator in treatment of a comatose patient. The patient later suffered cerebral damage due to anoxia. The family sued claiming negligent use of equipment by untrained staff.

Case C. The Uncooperative Child Johnnie Fast, a three-year-old male, was admitted to the hospital for treatment of an upper respiratory infection. His hospital recovery was uneventful except that he refused to stay in bed. Two days prior to his planned discharge, Johnnie's physician ordered application of pediatric restraints to ensure Johnnie's bedrest. Restraints were applied and appropriately evaluated by the day charge nurse. The evening nurse, a float named Ms. Golden, relieved the day staff and proceeded with 3 p.m. rounds. Upon entering Johnnie's room she found his lifeless body dangling from the bed, the restraint positioned as a noose. She immediately initiated appropriate emergency procedures. Johnnie could not be revived. His parents eventually brought suit claiming damages from the hospital, physician, and staff.

Case D. The Reluctant Physician Ms. Gray, a seventy-five-year-old female, was admitted to the hospital for the treatment of a fractured femur. A cast was routinely applied and Ms. Gray was sent to the orthopedic unit for care. The night nurse found Ms. Gray's protruding foot on the casted leg to be cold, blue and swollen in appearance. She noted these observations in the chart and relayed her findings in the morning report. The day nurse again checked Ms. Gray, observing similar findings. She contacted the patient's physician. He received the nurse's report without concern. He gave no further orders and instructed the staff not to bother him unless it was an absolute emergency. Later in the day Ms. Gray became agitated, complained of excruciating pain in her affected leg and finally became uncontrollably hysterical. Only prompt intervention prevented her death. Removal of the cast disclosed an extensive circulatory impairment that was not responsive to treatment and eventually resulted in the amputation of the leg. Ms. Gray's family brought suit against the hospital, staff, and physician.

Case E. The Authoritarian Nurse Ann Ross, R.N., is evening charge nurse on a large Medicare unit of a community hospital. The evening of the following incident she is chagrined to learn that the scheduled practical nurse has called in ill. Ms. Ross assigns the practical nurse's duties, including the application of a heat lamp treatment, to an experienced nurse's aide. The aide's protests are waived aside by Ms. Ross. In the course of completing the heat lamp treatment, the aide knocks over the lamp, burning the treated patient. The patient, a diabetic, suffers a small burn which will not heal. He later sues the hospital which in turn, attempts to shift the legal responsibility for the incident to Ms. Ross.

Suggestions for Further Reading

George J. Annas, "After Saikewicz: No-Fault Death." *The Hastings Center Report,* Vol. 8, No. 3 (June 1978), pp. 16–18.
    Discusses question of who is permitted to make life and death decisions with legal immunity. Refers to case of Saikewicz (Massachusetts Supreme Judicial Court). Offers legal advice to hospitals.

Bertram Bandman and Elsie Bandman. "Do Nurses Have Rights?" *American Journal of Nursing,* Vol. 78, No. 1 (January 1978), pp. 84–86.

Briefly depicts issue of nurses' rights in professional context. Focuses on nurses' "privileges," and the actual legal/ethical rights of the nurse.

Gregory Bruce and Ruth L. Gouge. "Disfigured by a Violent Patient: A Case . . . and Comment." *RN*, Vol. 42, No. 3 (March 1979), pp. 61–62, 65, 72.

Discusses case of nurse's rights when attacked by patients. Examines compensation and courses of action to be taken.

Bonnie Bullough and Vern Bullough, eds. *Expanding Horizons for Nurses.* New York: Springer Publishing Co., 1977.

Examines recent legislative enactments and ethical problems involved in controversial clinical issues—abortion, homosexuality, and euthanasia—and the nursing profession's inherent need to stay abreast of change.

Claire M. Fagin. "Nurses' Rights." *American Journal of Nursing,* Vol. 75, No. 1 (January 1975), pp. 82–85.

Examines the model of rights in resolution established by the Michigan State Nurses' Association, exploring "responsibility," human rights, women's rights, and nurses' rights and how to keep them.

Samuel Gorovetz et al., editors. *Moral Problems in Medicine.* Englewood Cliffs, N.J.: Prentice-Hall, 1976.

Medical reference reviewing moral philosophy, physician encountered dilemmas, legal concepts and contemporary social problems. Collection of articles by leading scholars in each discipline. Advanced comprehension required.

Mary Dolores Hemelt and Mary Ellen Mackert. *Dynamics of Law in Nursing and Health Care.* Reston: Reston Pub. Co., 1978.

Examines dynamic law as applied to health care, legal doctrines and principles, defenses and damages, contracts, contemporary legal-medical issues; presents a variety of vignettes involving such issues as forcible restraint.

James M. Humber and Robert F. Almeder, eds. *Biomedical Ethics and the Law.* New York: Plenum Press, 1977.

Introductory anthology viewing biomedical ethics as a discipline utilized in such decision-making areas as abortion, mental illness, human experimentation, human genetics, and dying; each is examined with regard to legal influence.

Lucie Young Kelly. *Dimensions of Professional Nursing,* 3rd Ed. New York: MacMillan Publishing Company, Inc., 1975.

Overview of non-clinical aspects of nursing, including nursing history, growth of practice in U.S., and current status with religious and legal aspects, and an overview of organizations, publications, and career opportunities.

Lucie Young Kelly. "Nursing Practice Acts." *American Journal of Nursing,* Vol. 74, No. 7 (July 1974), pp. 1310–1319.

> Defines and depicts certain nurse practice acts and practitioner roles in a changing profession. Requirements for licensure, exemption from licensure, fees and renewals, State Board powers, and educational standards are all reviewed.

Marguerite Mancini."Nursing, Minors, and the Law."*American Journal of Nursing,* Vol. 78, No. 1 (January 1978), pp. 124, 126.

> Discusses basic concepts used in law when caring for persons who have not reached legal adulthood. Defines terms and concludes that minors have rights to make decisions regarding their own health care.

Ronald W. McNeur, ed. *The Changing Roles and Education of Health Care Personnel Worldwide in View of the Increase of Basic Health Services.* Philadelphia: Society for Health and Human Values, 1978.

> In a period of changing practice, redefines role of nurse and doctor in a consumer-based health care system. Considers health services related to health manpower and functions worldwide.

Dorothea E. Orem. *Nursing: Concepts of Practice.* New York: McGraw-Hill Book Company, 1971.

> Provides a basis for organized nursing knowledge. Proposes structural frameworks of nursing relevant to concepts and principles involving ethics, values, legalities, and nursing as a human service.

William Andrew Regan, ed. "Professional Nurses *vs.* Hospital Regulations." *The Regan Report on Nursing Law,* Vol. 19, No. 9 (February 1979).

> Depicts not a single incident or violation of a rule, but rather a continuous disregard of important rules and regulations established by hospital. Employer terminated operating room nurse, courts affirmed.

Daniel A. Rothman and Nancy Lloyd Rothman. *The Professional Nurse and the Law.* Boston: Little, Brown & Co., 1977.

> Comprehensive text discussing a broad spectrum of legal topics relating to health care, including: rights fundamental to all human beings, how legislation is enacted, and its influence on the changing role of the nurse, a description of the various Nurse Practice Acts, and a discussion of contemporary issues such as consumerism.

5

Social Issues

"The hottest places in hell are reserved for those who in time of great moral crises maintain their neutrality."
DANTE ALIGHIERI

IMPACT OF SOCIAL ISSUES ON HEALTH CARE

Social issues are topics of general controversy within society. They are problems with multiple solution alternatives: alternatives each of which depends on different support groups and bears different consequences. One of the most emotionally charged contemporary social issues is that of abortion. The controversy involves many complex problems, including respect for human life, control over one's own body, theological influence on legal constructs, and many other factors. Many of the issues involved seem to bear little or no relationship to health care. Yet resolution of the controversy will certainly have a pervasive effect on health care. The importance of the involvement of health professionals in the legal and social debate is obvious.

Many other social issues bear either directly or indirectly on health care delivery. For example, the debate over the right of public employees to engage in collective bargaining may not seem to be important to health care. But if the issue is resolved in favor of the employee's rights to withhold service it will certainly influence patient care. If, on the other hand, resolution leads to recognition of the inherent obligation of health professionals to deliver service regardless of employment conditions, what will happen to the inalienable rights of employees faced with intolerable working conditions and unacceptable wages? The resolution of this issue will have a great impact on the future structure of health care delivery, hence it merits the attention of the health professional.

Scrutiny of the debate over most current social issues reveals that they bear significant potential for impact on the health care delivery system, its providers, and its consumers. Whether one considers euthanasia, the distribution of scarce medical resources, payment and responsibility for control of health services, or the contemporary evolution of sex roles, one can see the potential for bringing about change in health care. The entrance of women into the professions traditionally denied them will change the delivery of health care. The decisions that must be made regarding when to terminate extraordinary life support efforts will change critical and long-term care. The responsibility for allocating scarce medical resources will have legal and ethical consequences for all whose lives are touched. It is difficult to think of a topic of current debate that does not bear some potential impact for health care.

Thus it is imperative for health professionals to be informed in matters of current debate. We must become familiar with the major issues of the day.

ORIGIN OF SOCIAL ISSUES

Many of the topics that will be reviewed in this chapter stem from a common source: the success and concomitant failures of science and technology. Science has been a revered discipline since the Renaissance, and the growth of science has brought with it the growth of technology—technology being the application of scientific discovery. The rapidity of scientific progress can best be appreciated by comparing the American lifestyle of today with that of a mere fifty years ago. The revolutionary changes in living have been due to scientific discoveries and inventions, such as the use of electricity, the internal combustion engine, and the theory of sound waves, all of which have had related technological applications. These everyday features of our lives would have looked like miracles only a few generations ago. Much of the ebb and flow of our daily lives is dependent upon the technological advance of science.

The miracle of scientific inquiry has not been without concomitant problems. With each major technological innovation has come social change and new technological problems. As labor-saving devices and birth control technology became available to millions of women, changes in the traditional role of women were stimulated. Because women no longer are required to spend the majority of their adult years in child-rearing and homemaking, many are pursuing careers and questioning the roles and restrictions traditionally placed upon women by society. Would the feminist movement have been possible without the advent of the "pill"? Scientific inquiry generated a multitude of social changes in an attempt to resolve the problem of population control.

Many of the social changes generated by this scientific inquiry are desirable, such as the liberation of women from unwanted pregnancies and the infusion of talented, yet hitherto unknown, labor into the workplace. But some of the less positive social changes of the recent past are also partially attributable to birth control technology. The alteration in risk of pregnancy is thought by some to be responsible for the alteration in sexual attitudes and behaviors, and society's new-found acceptance of sexual expression. The rising number of teenage pregnancies may be one result of this new sexual openness. The revolution in sexual attitudes has failed to provide for the use and understanding of the technology of population control, creating a new tragic social problem. Thus science gave society both a boon and a problem. This is typical of many of the great scientific discoveries. Each carries some important consequences that are only recognized later.

ON THE NATURE OF CONTROVERSY

Many of the issues that will be reviewed in this text are both emotionally charged and highly important. The nature of controversy is such that these issues would not be debated if their outcomes were not of such importance. But how does one evaluate the significance of an issue? What fuels a debate?

The essence of controversy is conflict. Whether a conflict in judgment or a conflict of values, difference of opinion generates differing solutions for common problems. Just as the heterogeneity of society leads to the need for laws and legal systems to govern the conduct of participants, the heterogeneity of society leads different people to different positions on similar problems. It is central to a free society to debate issues of importance to that society.

Tumultuous debate is indicative of the heterogeneity of society and the degree of freedom it allows. The abortion controversy, so vigorous in the Western democracies, could probably never have occurred in the Eastern European countries, where the decision to legalize abortion was perceived as a state right and was not opened to discussion or participation by citizens.

It is precisely this freedom and heterogeneity that mandate the obligation of informed participation in the debates over the major issues by as many members of the society as possible. Thus another rationale for the interest and involvement of health professionals is apparent. Health professionals have a unique contribution to make to the process of discussion, because they represent an informed constituency with a unique perspective. It should also be noted that an essential precondition to free choice is information. Without knowledge of the alternatives, choice is neither free nor wise.

In the following review of significant social issues that affect health care, the attempt will be made to furnish you with a brief discussion of the essence of the controversy, a summary of the alternative positions, the rationale undergirding each point of view, the legal entanglements inherent in most of the issues, and a projection of the impact of issue resolution on health care delivery. The review is neither complete nor comprehensive. Many difficulties attend an undertaking of this sort. Not the least of these is the susceptibility of the review to the values, beliefs, and prejudices of the author. This problem is pointed out in advance because it is one of the purposes of this text to allow the reader to develop personal positions on the issues indicated, not necessarily to adopt the view of the author. The need for participation of health professionals in the debate over these issues is erased if participation reflects rote learning rather than real thought. In diversity of input lies the strength of the process. The more informed minds become involved, the higher the potential for acceptable problem resolution.

ABORTION

Abortion is defined as the termination of fetal life. The legal parameters of the current debate were established with the United States Supreme Court's decision (*Roe v. Wade*) in January, 1973, that determined that the state did not have the right to prohibit intentional (therapeutic) abortion during the first trimester of pregnancy. Furthermore, the decision stated that the state's right to regulate abortion during the second trimester was only within the bounds of setting standards for the environment in which the abortion would be performed. Later court rulings expanded the implications of the 1973 ruling by limiting consent authority of parents over abortions for minors and by eliminating the requirement of some states that the husband consent or have input into the decision to abort. Thus abortions may be legally performed within the requirements of public health statutes of all states. This development fueled an already heated debate over the topic.

The degree of emotion over the resolution of this issue can be assessed by reviewing the number of altercations generated during demonstrations outside of abortion clinics and the amount of money contributed to the pro-life movement. The controversy is steadily increasing, without promise of subsiding in the foreseeable future. The debate has become so intense as to preclude reasoned discussion and discourse. Both sides treat anyone without a position as a proponent of the opposing view. The degree of emotion and rhetoric defies explanation until one evaluates the substantive issues involved. The abortion debate touches the most central of human questions: definition of the nature of human life.

The Arguments

Pro-life forces base their objection to abortion on a respect for human life in any form. The basic assumption is that fetal life is, indeed, human life and as such carries the rights inherent in the social mandate to respect and preserve human life. These forces are unwilling to accept any position other than the view of the absolute humanity of the fetus from the moment of conception. Their position is also founded on a belief that the state has an ultimate responsibility to protect the right to life over all other rights. Thus they view the prohibition of abortion as the only reasonable and ethical stance the state can take.

The rationale for their philosophy is quite sophisticated. The state does have an obligation to its citizens, and a responsibility to itself, to preserve the social fabric by protecting the lives of its constituents. The determination of human life is also a difficult, if not impossible, task. Where does the attribute of humanity begin and end? If the fetus is not human, is the grotesquely malformed child human? The hopelessly senile patient? The insane mass murderer? At what point does the permission to discontinue life begin and end? Pro-life adherents would ask, "Who makes these crucial decisions?" If the decision to terminate fetal life is a state right, then possibly the decision to exterminate the retarded is also a state right. They extrapolate the outcome of legalized abortion to the extent that they view this step as the first in a series of diminutions in valuing the sanctity of human life that could eventually lead to a Hitlerian approach to assessment of fitness for living and procreation.

These are excellent questions, and the answers are not easily forthcoming. The impact of abortion as a legal and moral precedent in valuing life and in sanctioning euthanasia is unpredictable. The question of awarding dignity to unborn humanity is also quite thorny. Society is sensitized to the obligation of citizens and the state to maximize respect for human life, regardless of the beliefs, attributes, or quality of that life. This sensitivity is heightened by remembrance of Hitler's plans for a master race, which first resulted in the active euthanasia of thousands of physically handicapped and retarded German citizens, laid the basis for the extermination of additional "undesirable" elements, and ultimately resulted in one of the most hideous crimes in history: the Holocaust. No sane citizen would want to lay the groundwork for any movement that resembled Nazism. This fear alone is sufficient to motivate close scrutiny of the morality of abortion.

The belief that all human life requires safeguarding and that fetal life is human life is emotionally appealing, and has gained great support. The "pro-life" movement enjoys a diversity of membership unusual in modern times. Representation includes clergy from Jewish and Catholic faiths, political conservatives who view the movement as potentially beneficial in controlling government regulation of private affairs, academicians who focus on ethical imperatives, and suburban homemakers enraged at the perceived threat to family life.

The stance of the pro-choice forces is equally appealing. Their position rests on the dual bases of respect for privacy and the obligation to provide a measure of quality of life. The respect for privacy is the basis for the concern that the pregnant woman maintain control over her own body. Pro-choice people would recall that neither the state nor any other party should have the right to mandate the course of one's bodily functions. They compare the prohibition of abortion with forced pregnancy, and cite the Hitlerian breeding of concentration camp inmates as an example of the moral outrage that can result from the prohibition of abortion.

Pro-choice advocates note that respect for life should include a respect for the quality of life, and point out that the quality of life available to an unwanted child is likely to be minimal—not to mention the dim hope for any quality of life for a fetus that can be predicted to be malformed. They would have us recall that human life implies dignity. To mandate pregnancy robs woman of the dignity of control of her own body, and to mandate life for an unwanted or malformed fetus robs the child of life with a chance of dignity. The concern for privacy, control over personal matters, and the dignity of life is central to the pro-choice position. There are other, equally compelling, rationales that are also put forward by pro-abortion groups. Not the least of these is the concern for population control. Although abortion is not offered as a means of contraception, it is noted as an alternative to unplanned pregnancy, particularly when pregnancy is the result of a contraceptive failure. Given the acute problem of worldwide population and resource consumption, who would add to the problem with unwanted children?

The pro-choice groups would point out that the state should not interfere in private matters, and that the separation of church and state is fundamental to our society. They view the prohibition of abortion by legal statute as a threatening opening that tempts the state to interfere in other personal matters. They discount the state's interest in the fetus, and ask that the government not be given license to interfere in matters that do not directly influence the future of the state. Pro-abortion forces point to the predominance of religious alliances in the pro-life movement as evidence of the threat that the movement holds for separation of church and state. Because many of the prime movers behind the pro-life movement are clergy, and because much of the money given to anti-abortion groups is derived from church sources, the pro-choice people are alarmed at the influence of a theological position on political affairs. They ask whether, by tolerating the intrusion of religion in the legal system, we are not opening the door to further intrusions by religious groups.

The pro-choice position is also attractive. The notion that abortion should be a matter of free choice, and that abortion may be desirable when the fetus is unwanted as this might ensure a higher quality of life to children born, is compelling. Furthermore, the argument that religious beliefs should not be imposed on the general populace is also powerful. There are many historical instances of states that allowed religious groups to affect their citizens adversely.

Both pro-life and pro-choice forces have strong cases. Yet both sides cannot be right. Which side is accurate in its predictions of the dire consequences of the adoption of the opposing view, and which is a false prophet?

Possibly there is no right or wrong answer, except the answer one arrives at for herself. The legal entanglements are already complex, and are becoming even more involved with each new court decision. The legal web reflects the diversity of public opinion that is the result of our pluralistic society. But ultimately there appears to be no ground for compromise: either abortion is legal or illegal. Even conservative criteria for determining the legality of abortion (when the mother's life is endangered, or when pregnancy is the result of rape or incest) compromise the sanctity of fetal life. On the other hand, the flat prohibition of abortion compromises a woman's right to control over her own body, her right to privacy, and the right of all humans to a reasonably high quality of life. There is no simple answer.

So far the debate has generated tremendous heat, but little light. The high degree of emotion that accompanies any discussion of the subject clouds the issue and prevents clear thought. The typical debate rapidly deteriorates to a shouting match between "baby killers" and "woman oppressors." Such invective does little to forward the march of reason.

The Arguments Refuted

Actually, the stances of both parties can be viewed as quite unreasoned when examining their position from their own rationale. If human life is always to be sanctified, then doesn't the life of the mother bear the same degree of respect as that of the fetus? Which life bears the greatest degree of eligibility for respect? Who is to decide the value of either? When the decision to complete an unwanted or dangerous pregnancy is made, the individuals involved fail to offer assistance in meeting the resulting financial and social responsibilities.

On the other hand, pro-choice advocates insist that the mother's right to the privacy of her own body be respected. Yet at the same time they propose that the fetus's similar rights be ignored. Thus neither side in the abortion debate has a fully logical position. However, if the ethical dilemma seems confusing, the legal implications are positively mind-boggling.

The United States Supreme Court decision, *Roe vs. Wade,* set the precedent for the abolition of abortion restrictions that had existed in most states. The decision did not set firm guidelines for the regulation of abortion. The Court simply ruled on the constitutionality of a Texas law prohibiting abortions except where the mother's life was in danger. The Court's decision set judicial precedent; it did not set interpretive rules. Specifically, the Court's ruling stated the following general principles: (1) the decision to complete a first trimester abortion is a private matter—the responsibility of the patient and her physician; (2) the state may regulate second trimester abortion in ways relating to its interest in promoting the health of the mother; and (3) the state may, because of its interest in the viable fetus, regulate and even prohibit third trimester abortions. These guidelines are intentionally vague and have resulted in a host of states' attempts to interpret, set regulations, and even circumvent the intent of the Court. Thus, the activity of anti-abortion groups has been much concerned with influencing state legislatures to construct rigid regulations that would effectively prohibit abortions by making the process difficult. Conversely, the "pro-choice" advocates have expended much effort in persuading legislatures to maintain flexible, permissive statutes. The political struggle has been tremendous. Its extent can be demonstrated by the fact that anti-abortion forces succeeded in forming a powerful, single-issue political party in the State of New York in 1978. Pro-life forces are mounting an impressive drive to launch a constitutional amendment protecting the life of all unborn humans. The pro-choice forces are equally active, if not so well financed.

State and local governments continue to attempt to come to grips with the legal ramifications of the 1973 decision. Attempts at control range from the simple establishment of minimum qualifications and licensing standards in most locales to intentionally restrictive ordinances. A statute recently enacted in Akron, Ohio, for example, requires that a physician thoroughly review the nuances of fetal development, including potential for life, with each abortion candidate prior to completing any procedure, regardless of the stage of gestation of the fetus at the time of the requested abortion. The legal struggle shows no sign of abating. As recently as January, 1979, the Supreme Court reviewed a Pennsylvania statute and struck down its restrictive provisions, which required that an attending physician take all possible steps to ensure life in an aborted fetus that held any potential for viability.

Clarifying a Personal View

The ethical debate is furious. The legal situation is tangled. The future potential for definitive resolution of the thorny issue of abortion seems dim. The debate will continue for many years to come. Where does the health professional stand legally, ethically, and functionally? These questions must be answered from several perspectives, the most significant of which is personal.

One's personal values should be the major factor in deciding how one stands in the abortion controversy. The influence of legal and professional regulations governing abortion is also quite significant. Yet one's own conscience can be one's harshest critic or loyal advocate, and thus it is in the process of introspection that the assessment of the issue of abortion must begin.

Probably the greatest influence on many people who oppose abortion is that of religion. An individual with strong religious beliefs, or who experienced significant exposure to a particular religious philosophy during formative years, is likely to reflect that philosophical stance when evaluating abortion. Major western religious denominations have taken a position on the issue. The Catholic, Orthodox Jewish, and fundamentalist Christian faiths have uniformly denied the option of abortion. Reform Judaism and many Protestant faiths have defended the stance of the "pro-choice" advocates on moral and religious grounds.

The impact of religion in this issue is generally indirect (the effect of a philosophical attitude toward life) rather than direct imposition of a "party line." The pervasive effect of early education on one's life values is well documented, and thus the impact of early religious training on the adult cannot be underestimated.

One's experiences with pregnancy, childbirth, and related parenting responsibilities will also affect attitudes toward abortion. Frequently one hears of an experienced mother of several children who is either a strong pro-lifer or a strong supporter of the pro-choice movement. Experiences, both positive and negative, that the individual has in life are used to reflect on and judge the experiences of others. Similarly, life experiences become guides to future actions.

The stance that one assumes is a reflection of personal values and attitudes, which in turn are the product of life experiences and teachings. Abortion is an emotional topic with no easy solutions. The alternatives are many and complex. A sane approach mandates that one probe values and attitudes to preclude the possibility of accepting a position and promoting a point of view or participating in a process which may be contrary to personal standards and which would result in diminution of self-esteem.

One way to deal with controversial matters is to remain open and flexible and able to assimilate new data with changing situations. By doing so, it is possible to weigh each situation as unique and deliberate each decision anew. This model is philosophically appealing in that it requires that each person bring to each situation a well-developed sense of trust and well-honed logical skills. It is, however, cumbersome and legally precarious. Imagine the attending surgical nurse in a hospital surgical service debating and weighing the pros and cons of each abortion case assigned!

The reasonable and open-minded professional adopts a moderately flexible attitude. One can neither focus continually on issue resolution, nor simply arrive at a stance and hold firm regardless of alterations in the facts or discovery of new information. Rather, one assumes a position based on the facts and information at hand—a position congruent with personal values and intrinsic attitudes. But one also understands the need to remain open to the re-examination of that position based upon the availability of new and different information or altered circumstances. The sane compromise on the issue of abortion is to assess personal values, weigh attitudes, come to a conclusion, and commit oneself to periodic re-examination of the conclusion as new data are available, or as the situation mandates. The decision and decision style are a personal choice; the impact of the decision is a personal consequence.

Impact of Abortion on Health Care

The potential impact of the resolution of the issue of abortion on the structure and delivery of health care services is tremendous. Each possible solution will alter the nature of health care and change the roles of health care professionals. Health care is a reflection of the surrounding society. As society resolves its abortion dilemma, health care will reflect the alternative chosen. Several alterations in health care can be predicted for each of the alternative resolutions to the abortion dilemma.

Should pro-life advocates succeed in their quest to eliminate abortion as a legally sanctioned medical procedure, many current features of health care will change. The closing of the many clinics and services devoted to abortions will be the most obvious result. Also, the alteration of the services offered through surgical departments in many communities will be curtailed. This will mean that women, particularly poor women, will be faced with an increased number of unwanted pregnancies. Poorer women will more likely be affected than affluent women, because they have less access to family planning services and less money to spend on family planning devices or procedures, and are more likely to experience gaps in health care knowledge. Also, women from more affluent backgrounds will be able to afford the luxury of the inevitable criminal abortion services that will undoubtedly abound. The result of the growth of illegal, unsupervised abortion services is usually a corresponding increase in the need for emergency medical intervention for victims of mishandled abortions. One can predict changes in maternal and child care, outpatient services, emergency and acute care trauma intervention, and other health care services, as the result of restrictions on the performance of abortions.

If abortion remains legal in America, health care will see a different set of developments. The issue of public financing of abortions and the related problem of whether hospitals that receive public funds may refuse to perform abortions would require clarification. Currently, many hospitals, usually religiously affiliated, refuse to perform therapeutic abortions. They do so despite the fact that most receive a majority of their fiscal support through reimbursement from public welfare, third party insurance, and federal construction grants. The issue of public funds supporting a private point of view would require resolution. Should the liberalized abortion requirements result in compelling these facilities to perform abortion, a whole new set of moral dilemmas would arise, possibly including massive resistance to the law. The debate would bring chaos and confusion and the threat of curtailment of service to many hospitals that are religiously affiliated. What would replace these venerable institutions? Also, what would be the effect of liberal abortion statutes on the birth rate? On the number of handicapped or congenitally disabled children, and the corresponding effect on the design and delivery of services for this population? Would it be possible to deliver abortion services effectively to the medically disadvantaged and medically indigent, lessening the disparity in services that now exists? The continuation and expansion of abortion as a legal option would indicate many changes for the structure and delivery of health care.

On the other hand, if pro-life advocates succeed in their quest to eliminate abortion, we will witness the dissolution of current abortion services and a possible increase in the birthrate for certain segments of the population, namely those for whom public funds support abortion, and who are unable to avail themselves of opportunities for effective family planning.

Summary

The problem of abortion involves many opposing points of view, legal and moral implications, and potential threats of change for health care. The health professions have a distinct interest in participating in the process of resolving this highly emotional social issue. The solution will speak not only to the legality of a simple medical procedure, but also to the extent of society's commitment to life, the quality of life, personal privacy, governmental interference in personal matters, the distinction between church and state, and the extension of health services to the poor and disadvantaged. The tangential issues of population control and utilization of diminishing natural resources will also be addressed in the manner by which this issue is resolved. Health care will be inextricably affected by these decisions, and therefore must participate in this great national debate.

COLLECTIVE BARGAINING

Collective bargaining is the process by which individuals with common vocational skills or common employment conditions band together to negotiate with employers or employing agents. It is a historically proud movement in America, a movement marking the recognition of the rights and responsibilities of the individual, as opposed to the rights and responsibilities of the corporate entity. Collective bargaining takes many forms, from unionism to the less easily defined, yet equally effective, professional associations—such as the American Nurses' Association.

Prior to the emergence of the union movement in the United States in the late 1800s and early 1900s, the employee was virtually at the mercy of the good will of the employer. Working conditions, wages, and hours of employment were established by the rule of supply and demand, with labor usually in good supply and thus having little control over determination of the terms of employment. The union movement was born with great strife and some violence. Employers did not welcome the advent of any organization that would diminish their absolute control over the work environment. The degree of control afforded ownership prior to the development of unionization can best be understood by examining the structure and operation of the mining industry. Appalachian miners were probably the last of the large exploited labor pools in the United States. The extent of control of mine ownership over the lives of mine employees was almost total. Miners and their families lived, worked, played, and worshipped within communities located entirely on mine-controlled property. Stores, homes, and even schools were built and owned by the mine operators. A benevolent management could do much to improve or sustain the quality of life under such circumstances. But a less-than-benevolent management could do much to exploit unskilled and powerless people, given this degree of control. Unionization, frequently a bloody process, did much to contribute to the acquisition of better working conditions, humane living standards, and a degree of autonomy and dignity for the mining population. Unions were a way of gaining power through the clout of collectivism. The history of the development of the United Mine Workers serves as a model for understanding of the growth and development of unions in America—from their infancy to their current state of power.

The unionization movement has come full circle in contemporary times. From a movement that was met first with disdain and later with active opposition by a government susceptible to the influence of the established powers of private property, unions have developed into an arm of the same establishment, and are effective political organizations that carry their own political clout. Organized labor has gone from a phenomenon of controversy to an element of the social *status quo*.

When the term collective bargaining is used, it represents more than the usually acknowledged forces of unionism. Collective bargaining may also represent the political and economic power of a group of individuals with a common vocation, attempting to ensure the preservation or prosperity of that vocation within the larger economic system. The American Medical Association is, in many ways, a union of physicians, although the majority of its members and its officials do not see it as such. The American Nurses' Association is also a union, in that the ANA represents nurses in collective negotiations for economic security. Both associations exist to support their respective professions. The objectives of each organization consist of promoting the image of the profession, establishing professional standards of conduct, providing avenues of communication among members of the profession, and representing the interests of the profession to outside powers and influences. Through a largely informal but effective mechanism, the AMA also has established a tight control over entry into and maintenance of credentiality in medicine. Their control of accreditation of medical schools, coupled with their extensive influence over licensure boards, gives the AMA significant influence over the determination of physician supply. Of course, control over supply equals influence of demand, an economic benefit afforded to physicians belonging to the AMA. This, more than any other feature, establishes the AMA as a union.

Until recently the effects of collective bargaining were largely confined to the private sector of the economy. The tools of power of unionization are negotiations and, when negotiations fail, the withholding of service—a strike. These tools have recently been utilized by employees in the public sector, those workers whose salaries come from public funds such as taxes. Previously the phenomenon of public servants striking was unknown; now, however, the message that unionization is an effective means of gaining power has reached segments of the population virtually untouched by the union movement in the past. Police, fire, and municipal employees are discovering that the threat of withholding service can bring recognition of otherwise unheard concerns. The union movement has gained entry to the health professions and institutions. Nurses, auxiliary personnel, and physicians have used the process of collective bargaining and occasionally the threat or actuality of a strike to gain recognition of their interests by health institution administrations.

The advent of collective bargaining and service withdrawal by public employees has generated a discussion concerning the entire process of collective bargaining and the right of public employees to unionize. Concurrently, the strength held by unions on a national scale is coming into recognition. It is becoming apparent that the right combination of union alliances in a cooperative strike can easily cripple the economic system. The authority of unions is such that they have virtual control over the labor of many strategic industries and services, including heavy industry, transportation, communications, and food processing. The potential impact of a coordinated national strike has generated public debate over the rights and responsibilities of participants in collective bargaining.

Health care is an essential service. Increasingly, Americans have come to regard health care as a fundamental right. The threat of unionization of health care employees is not lightly regarded. The scrutiny of this option for workers is underway, and is certainly of utmost significance to health professionals.

The Arguments

Health care employees would point to the fundamental right to control one's own life as the foundation of the right to organize in collective bargaining efforts. The traditional and continuing undervaluing of the work of health professionals in terms of reimbursement for services is a strong indication of the need for unionization efforts. True, any physician can anticipate an income befitting a member of the upper middle class; but what of other health care workers?

The December, 1978, issue of the *American Journal of Nursing* listed advertisements for registered nurses, quoting a salary range of $1206 to $1466 per month. The annual equivalent of this salary is $14,472 to $17,592. In 1977, the *after-tax* income of plumbers, as computed by the Tax Foundation, Inc., was $22,360! The after-tax income of steelworkers was $20,923. It is easy to see why members of the health professions have suddenly become interested in unionizing. The value of the work, the degree of difficulty, the amount of preparation, and the extent of responsibility associated with the role of the registered nurse, if compared with the role of the steelworker or the plumber, underlines the discrepancy between job function and job compensation that most nurses perceive. This is not to undervalue the jobs performed by plumbers or steelworkers, but to point out the discrepancy in compensation between their vocations and that of the nurse.

Collective bargaining advocates would also point to the recent efforts of the professional organizations to negotiate better patient care standards and other conditions contributing to quality of care. The nurses' strike at Cook County Hospital in 1976 focused on issues of compensation and staffing, as well as coverage and patient load for nursing staff. The nurses' union contended that prevailing staffing patterns, including the understaffing of critical care units, failed to provide for specialized preparation for staff assigned to critical care areas—a major issue in assuring quality of patient care.

Union advocates would also remind the public that they represent thousands of people who, were it not for unions, would be at a great disadvantage in negotiating with management. Local and national management associations, such as the American Hospital Association, provide hospital and agency management with information and support in dealing with employee problems. Are not the employees entitled to the same benefits accorded to their peers? Alone, the employee is almost at the mercy of the employer. In numbers there is strength, and that is the basic power of collective bargaining.

Opponents of collective bargaining rights for health care employees also present compelling arguments. Their primary objection is the potential danger inherent in withholding a crucial service such as health care. The harm that is done in a hospital strike is not as keenly felt by management as in an industrial strike where owner profits are curtailed. Rather, in a health care employee's strike, the adverse effects of the job action most keenly affect the recipient of service, the patient. As hospitals are not generally profit-oriented operations, management is not particularly discomfited by work stoppages. It is the middle level supervisory personnel who may be inconvenienced, by having to staff for the missing employees, and it is the patients or potential patients whose comfort and safety are jeopardized. Thus, the negative impact of unionization is felt by precisely the population the employees claim to be striking to protect—the patients.

"Management rights" advocates would also remind us that health care workers are accorded a high social status and derive other social benefits by virtue of their vocation. The assumption of a professional occupation carries certain ethical responsibilities that workers in the trades and in non-professional vocations do not bear: it is inappropriate for anyone who has taken the oath of Hippocrates, Maïmonides, or Nightingale to deny her services to the patient.

The Arguments Refuted

The proponents and opponents of collective bargaining in the health professions are both able to mount reasonable, sound arguments for their respective points of view. Yet neither group is able to refute entirely the point of view of the other—possibly because neither argument is entirely sound.

It is illogical to claim that withholding service to patients can be beneficial to patient care. Only under the most extreme of circumstances would this be the case.

On the other hand, the cry that unionization undermines or denies the ethical commitment of professionals to service is equally faulty. The assumption of the mantle of professionalism does not abrogate fundamental rights. The registered nurse does, indeed, benefit from the social esteem in which nurses are held; however, becoming a nurse does not strip one of her rights as a citizen—including the right of free association.

Clarifying a Personal View

The individuals on either side of the collective bargaining issue hold persuasive, rational views. The health professional who finds herself in an environment where the issue is current, or has the potential of arising, has an obligation to analyze both views and decide which arguments and courses of action she believes in. There are several considerations that the individual should contemplate in the decision-making process.

The primary determinant of the necessity of collective bargaining in any situation is the extent to which the strategy will be effective. This judgment can only be arrived at after other alternatives have been exhausted. It is also important to decide the degree to which one's value systems jibe with unionization. Both factors merit detailed examination.

Collective bargaining involves two factors: general dissatisfaction with the *status quo,* and leadership in organization of the collective group. Employees who feel that they are integral to an organization's accomplishment of its objectives, and who believe that they are valued and that their value is rewarded on a fair and consistent basis, are seldom motivated to unionize. Personnel who feel disenfranchised from the decision-making process, feel undervalued, or think they are exploited are more open to the unionization process—particularly if they do not see other alternatives to the resolution of their concerns, or if experience with other alternatives have met with frustration.

You will have noted that such terms as "exploitation" and "disenfranchisement" are largely subjective, rather than objective, in nature. What one group of people finds satisfactory, another will judge to be insufficient or even insulting. It is the perception of disadvantage that leads to collective bargaining, not necessarily disadvantage itself. Successful unionization drives are often due more to perceptions of exploitation than to actual inequities in compensation.

Dissatisfaction does not always revolve around such issues as salary, staffing, or fringe benefits. Frequently the major impetus towards unionization, particularly when the effort is aimed at organizing professionals, is a professional concern, such as the alteration of staffing patterns or care procedures without the involvement of the "rank and file" staff. Particularly when unionization is the strategy of professionals, it is often seen as the last resort in a series of efforts to correct grievances. A discussion of the factors that encourage collective bargaining efforts would be incomplete without mention of the concept of communications, for it is frequently because of miscommunications that the dissatisfaction leading to unionization occurs. In any institution or organization, there are many people involved in many different roles. The people drawn to the organization come from different backgrounds and bring different experiences and educations to the work environment. When these different types of people attempt to interact, there can be missed messages, misinterpreted messages, and blocked cues that lead to misunderstandings and bitterness.

In any hospital, there are a multiplicity of people and types of work performed. Any small unit within a facility will demonstrate this fact in microcosm. For example, a small medical unit in a community hospital is staffed by registered nurses, nurses' aides, ward secretaries, occasionally dietary and housekeeping staff, visiting physicians, and ancillary personnel, not to mention the presence of patients, visitors, and possibly hospital volunteers. Each of these people has a unique and valuable role to fill in meeting the institution's objective: patient care and health promotion. Yet each of the individuals brings a different background and a different set of objectives to the unit. The registered nurse may be motivated by concerns for patient care and financial security; the aide may be working to gain money to put a child through college; the ward clerk may be here because this was the only employment available at hours convenient to her schedule; the physician may be here only to serve the patients assigned through an on-call procedure, and may be upset at missing a strategic golf date with a potential office partner. Hospital volunteers are usually motivated by a desire to give comfort to someone less fortunate than themselves (although membership in a hospital auxiliary has also been known to be motivated by social considerations).

Given this diversity of backgrounds, preparations, and motivations, it is easy to picture the disagreements, missed communications, and other interpersonal relationship problems that can develop in such a highly charged atmosphere. If these difficulties are met with understanding, elementary communications skills, and patience, they can be resolved. But without good communication skills on all sides, employees might well feel the dissatisfaction and frustration which spark the unionization process.

The decision to unionize in order to gain power through collective bargaining is undertaken in a variety of circumstances. It begins with the existence of unacceptable employment conditions, coupled with deficiencies in communication. Much of the turmoil that leads to perceptions of grievances is founded in poor communications; problems are more readily resolved when individuals are able to communicate effectively.

When one is confronted with an employment situation in which the effective resolution of grievances seems impossible, the decision to participate in some form of collective activity is attractive. The decision should be made only after attempts at resolving communications problems have been unsuccessful. The process of unionization is such that relationships between staff and management are permanently altered, becoming more formal and less friendly. Thus, the decision to unionize is not lightly made or easily reversed. But if a collegial relationship exists between staff and management, there is usually little sense of frustration and thus few motivations for the collective bargaining strategies. Dissatisfaction is a necessary prerequisite to the process, and miscommunication is a first step towards dissatisfaction. It is best said that poor management plus poor communication are the vital ingredients to unionization process, not necessarily poor working conditions or inadequate compensation.

The intolerable employment situation leads to three options. The first is adaptation to the situation, attempting change where possible, but accepting the *status quo* where change cannot occur. The second alternative is unionization. The third alternative is to look for another job. The appropriate alternative for any given person is entirely dependent upon individual values, preferences, options, and skills.

BEHAVIOR CONTROL

Each individual possesses inherent rights, including the right to life, liberty, and the pursuit of happiness. Few people would disagree with the tenets of the Declaration of Independence. Yet we are witnessing an increasing involvement of society in the setting and maintenance of behavioral standards and prohibitions. Most people would claim adherence to a philosophy that deems any behavior acceptable, so long as that behavior does not adversely affect the lives of others. Should someone choose to smoke, that decision, although physiologically unwise, is hers alone. Should that person choose to smoke in a public area, thereby inflicting a hazard on others, then their rights are compromised by the behavior of one individual, and they may attempt to regulate such behavior.

On first examination, behavior control seems a simple issue to understand. Behavior is a personal choice, and any behavior is tolerable as long as the rights of others are not compromised. If only it were so simple! The issue of mental illness presents this simple problem in its most complex form. The severely depressed individual may choose suicide—an alternative to what may be, for that person, an intolerable existence. But the act of suicide is strongly prohibited, even to the extent that in many states the act of attempted suicide is a crime that is prosecuted.

Thus the issue of behavior control is really quite complex. Where do we decide that individual rights to self-determination and control end and group interests and rights begin? Our society answers this question in many difficult and conflicting ways. We allow anyone over the age of eighteen or twenty-one to consume alcoholic beverages without limit, thus inducing less-than-logical, sometimes even homicidal, behavior. Yet we regulate marijuana with great vigor, even though the behavior-altering effects of this drug are less drastic than those of alcohol.

In many states it is illegal for consenting adults of the same gender to have sexual relations. Yet in those same states it is not illegal for a man to rape his wife. Our determinations of acceptable and unacceptable behavior occasionally seem to reflect our prejudices rather than our intellect. When is it appropriate for society to attempt to regulate personal behavior? When do the social costs outweigh the benefits of individual freedom? How do we measure the costs of attempting to control personal freedom in a free society?

It is probably most efficient to subdivide the issue of behavior control into smaller, more manageable groups of material. In the following pages, a number of aspects of this issue will be discussed.

The Question of Sanity

The definition of sanity has been debated for over a hundred years, since Alfred Pinel instituted the first modern measures for dealing with the insane, and Freud made his historic discoveries concerning the human mind. Society is no closer to an acceptable universal definition of mental health than it was many years ago. But the debate has generated many interesting observations concerning human behavior and, just as in many other endeavors, the observations frequently speak more eloquently about the characteristics of the observer than of the observed.

Nowhere are the issues of behavior control, the rights of society versus the rights of the individual, and the uses of behavioral control mechanisms more hotly contested than in the area of mental health and psychiatric services. Thomas Szasz, a Boston psychiatrist and author, was one of the first in his field to point out the shortcomings of many of the practices of the psychiatric establishment. Throughout *The Manufacture of Madness* and *The Myth of Mental Illness*, Szasz attempted to explore the uses of psychiatry as a weapon of the state against socially different persons.[1] He theorized that the concept of mental illness was created as a disease entity to justify the confinement of socially subversive personalities—society's "humane" way of sweeping a problem under the rug. According to Szasz, the real problem is with society, not with the supposedly mentally ill. He challenged the moral and legal rights of society to detain "mentally ill" persons under the guise of protecting them from themselves. Szasz's controversial approach to the issue of behavioral control began a new chapter in the history of the study of this issue.

The crucial question in the issue of behavior control is not what is normal or abnormal, but rather, *who determines* what is normal and abnormal. The issue focuses on the question of power and influence in the social structure. Thus Szasz, in *The Second Sin*, defines perversion as a sexual practice disapproved by the speaker.[2] This summarizes his conception of the issue of behavior control: behavior control usually reflects the attitudes and values of the controlling group, rather than adhering to any particularly logical standard for determining the potential harm or good resulting from the behavior in question.

Currently we claim to institute therapeutic modalities without client consent only when client behavior is such that it holds a potential threat of harm to the client or to others. Behavior that is simply strange, a variant from the norm, is not affected unless the client voluntarily seeks change. But is this an accurate reflection of the *status quo* of mental health care? I think not. Many voluntary clients, particularly in state-run care systems, volunteer only in the sense that it was made clear to them that if they did not cooperate they would not be allowed to remain free.

---

1. Szasz, Thomas. *The Manufacture of Madness*. New York: Harper and Row, 1970, and *The Myth of Mental Illness*. New York: Hoeber Harper, 1961.

2. Szasz, Thomas. *The Second Sin*. Garden City: Anchor Books, 1974, p. 12.

Moreover, many of these so-called voluntary clients are institutionalized for having exhibited behavior that, although possibly not normal, was certainly not threatening the life or well-being of anyone. Simply put, the state is able to coerce clients into hospitalization even when their behavior may not require it.

What is normal? What constitutes an acceptable deviation from the norm? And what constitutes unacceptable behavior? The answers to these questions are not easy. It is not comforting to realize that Richard Speck, prior to the murderous rampage that resulted in the death of seven people, had been examined by court-appointed psychiatrists and pronounced capable of functioning within the social milieu. It is simply impossible to predict dangerous behavior.

There is a dangerous tendency to regard the behavioral sciences as capable of offering definitive statements regarding the behavior of individuals. This is to misunderstand the nature of these disciplines. Should a physicist announce that she has discovered a new principle of motion, it is possible to evaluate and criticize the research she has done. The truth or falsehood of the theory can be definitively determined by the processes of scientific problem-solving through research replication and verification.

Unfortunately, the behavioral sciences are not nearly so valid, reliable, or testable. If a psychologist announces that he has discovered a new and wonderful way of treating homosexuals by punishing them with painful responses to homoerotic stimuli, the scientific world is much less able to verify the theories promulgated. Yet much of the professional world, and a good portion of the lay public, is swept up in waves of enthusiasm for just such announcements. We seem to trust psychology as if it were a predictable science—which it is not. In actuality it is greatly a matter of chance, magic, and faith that anything in the way of change or discovery occurs in the area of human behavior prediction and therapy. (In this instance, the implicit societal assumption is also made that it is desirable to rid society of homosexuality.)

Misplaced faith in the social sciences has generated many misconceptions in the public mind. A prime example is the faith placed in the expert testimony of psychologists and psychiatrists in the judicial process. Although even the amateur student of the human mind is aware of its complexity and variability, we continue to place an inordinate trust in the pronouncements of the experts concerning the sanity or insanity of a criminal mind. The Speck case, and the more recent "Son of Sam" case, demonstrate the influence of the psychiatric sciences in legal proceedings.

This is not to denigrate the importance of the study of human behavior for the future of humankind. The last great frontier is undoubtedly the human mind, and we have a desperate need to see to it that the best talents and greatest resources are brought to bear on this field of inquiry. My purpose here is to point out the danger of viewing this area as a field of scientific inquiry with predictable and testable results. Man's greatest threat is from himself. We know far too little about this animal that has dominion over the earth. The need for greater insight and understanding of the workings of the mind is pressing. The current state of the art leaves much to be desired.

The health professions, particularly nursing, are caught in an ethical bind in the issue of sane/insane. We are asked to participate in the therapeutic regimens, and thus tacitly to agree that they are scientifically valid methods of treatment. Staff in care institutions are often assigned to the support and assistance of regimens of care whose scientific, even ethical, bases are ambiguous. Modalities ranging from the relatively innocuous group therapy to the physically violent technique of electro-convulsion therapy can only be carried out with the assistance of an army of health professionals. We participate in and contribute to systems of care that reflect the values and attitudes of the designers of the systems, and rarely reflect the values and attitudes of those on the receiving end of therapy. In his text, *Readings On Ethical and Social Issues In Biomedicine,* Richard W. Wertz asks two important questions: "1. For whose benefit is the control obtained? 2. Is it likely that the 'ruled' will have access to the techniques the 'rulers' would apply to control him?"[3] Anyone who has witnessed aversion therapy or electroconvulsive therapy knows that those who apply the therapy would be less than enthusiastic in sub-mitting to their own devices.

Thus we are participants in a health care system that insists on applying a medical model of wellness/illness to human behavior. Well-ness is socially acceptable behavior. Illness is socially unacceptable be-havior. The system has promulgated and continues to support treatment modalities that are coercive, occasionally cruel, and usually less than effective. The recipient of care is rarely a voluntary participant in the process. And—the ultimate problem—therapy is applied with a view to attaining health, a state that has never yet been adequately defined, and which simply reflects the idealized version of what is normal as held by the controllers of the system.

It is a difficult problem that requires the participation of the vast majority of society in its resolution. We need to examine our reverence of the high priests of psychiatry, the new religion. We need to critique the predominant concepts of sane and insane behavior, and to strive for

---

3. Wertz, Richard W., ed. *Readings on Ethical and Social Issues in Biomedicine.* New Jersey: Prentice-Hall, Inc., 1973, p. 161.

truly voluntary systems of care based on recipient dissatisfaction with lifestyle and/or behavioral outcomes. We need to define proper limits for the uses of psychiatry by the government and the legal system. And we need to examine the use of inhuman therapies for supposedly humane purposes.

Controlled Substances

Nowhere is the strange problem of determining the value of public welfare over private rights more graphically illustrated than in government control of certain substances. Alcohol and many medications are subject to remarkable attempts at regulation and control. The philosophical position represented is that it is in the public's best interests to have the government control these substances. In effect, the government has been charged with the responsibility of protecting us from ourselves. The difficulty encountered is compounded when one considers which substances are controlled, to what degree they are controlled, and the rationale behind the control.

The controls placed on alcohol and drugs reflect quite accurately the issue of who controls, as opposed to what is controlled. The adverse effects of alcohol on judgment and motor coordination are quite well documented. The minimal effects of marijuana on the same functions are generally accepted by researchers. Yet alcohol may be freely obtained by those over the legal minimum age, while marijuana use continues to provide ample opportunities for young people to obtain a criminal record. The difference between the control of these substances is not their effect, but who decides their effect. Alcohol provides a socially acceptable form of substance abuse to most of the adult, decision-making population of the United States. Attempts to prohibit alcohol provided a historic comedy. Prohibition statutes were in effect while wine was served at the White House.

The need to protect the public from drug abuse is keenly felt where the substances abused are those routinely handled by the young, lower socioeconomic groups, and minorities. When the abused substance is routinely used by members of the rule-setting majority, as is alcohol, the regulations are much more flexible and usually amenable to the ruling majority's tastes.

Part of the difficulty encountered whenever government attempts to regulate a behavior (for the use of controlled substances is simply a behavioral option) lies in the inability of government to legislate moral behavior. This problem is compounded by criminal trafficking in the prohibited substance. Were marijuana to be legalized, a substantial amount of currently illegal profits would dry up. There are even some wags who claim that part of the effort to control marijuana and other drugs originates in organized crime, which, like any other business, doesn't want its profits diminished. When Prohibition was repealed, many criminals found themselves suddenly unemployed.

Thus, when government decides to exert mandatory controls on any substance, it invites criminal activity. It also faces the difficult problem of enforcing private morality.

Currently, some substances are controlled, but permitted under certain circumstances (attainment of legal majority for the use of alcohol, prescription by a licensed physician for the use of other controlled drugs), while other substances (heroin, for example) are prohibited under all conditions. The use or abuse of the substances is supported in large part by criminal organizations, which profit directly both from substance abuse and substance regulation (were drugs legally available in the stores, where would the profits from illegal drug sales be?). Tacit approval of some forms of drug use is common (Betty Ford's acknowledgement that her children may have sampled marijuana provides an example of the gap between what is approved formally and what is acknowledged informally). The situation breeds tremendous amounts of controversy and conflict. Just where does society's right to protect itself from the deleterious effects of abused substances end and where do personal rights to freedom of control begin? How much of the current legal structure devoted to the regulation and control of substances is founded upon a criminal effort not to have the market for illegal drugs eliminated and profits from drug trafficking reduced? Where does the need to be one's brother's keeper stop? How are health professionals involved in this controversy? What is our role in the resolution of the issue of substance abuse?

Health professionals frequently observe and must attempt to deal with the results of the use and abuse of controlled substances in therapeutic environments. This is the case when clients are admitted for the therapeutic management of addictive disease, such as alcoholism; it also happens when clients come into the system for care of other conditions that may be related to, affected by, or masking addictive disease, such as chronic liver disease. The impact that substance abuse has on the clients of health care is affected by legal and social attempts to control these substances and thus also affects the health practitioners working for and with these clients. If heroin use is illegal and we are confronted with a client who is using this drug, what are our legal and ethical obligations to the client and to society?

Some practitioners would remind us that the professional's role is ideally that of client advocate, and that it would be inappropriate for the client advocate to bring any form of additional stress to bear on the client's already impaired health state—including stresses incurred by the legal processes entailed in drug abuse.

Others would remind us of our larger obligation to the society that supports and approves of our profession. They would point out that the rationale behind many of the substance control ordinances is to shield society from the presence of drug abusers. To conceal instances of such abuse contributes to the potential harm that might be done to the social system.

In considering these questions, one does well to keep in mind the legal principle involving confidentiality of client information. The exception to this principle is action or information that, if withheld, would endanger the health or well-being of others (certain infectious diseases, suspected child abuse, and client threats of violence to others are examples of information that may legally be reported to appropriate persons).

The underlying problems that lead to the use or abuse of any substance are diverse and complicated. Both sociological and psychological causes have been suggested by research. There is even some evidence to suggest that some forms of alcoholism may have a physiologic basis through a genetic predisposition. Nonetheless, clear-cut causes cannot be outlined, and completely effective therapeutic modalities are not available. The health professional is often asked to participate in chancy therapies with minimal potential for long-term remediation of addictive disease. In addition to this frustrating state of affairs, the fact is that even if the addictive condition is effectively dealt with, the underlying causative factors may not be approachable and may lead to other, equally debilitating conditions.

Current media attention has been drawn to an impressive new awareness of suburban, middle-class alcoholism. For years, many people in the health professions have assumed that alcoholism is a problem of the down-and-out. Suddenly we are confronted with the realization that affluence is no insurance against alcohol or drug abuse. In fact, given the expense of either of these addictive conditions, affluence may prepare the necessary financial base for acquisition of the raw materials of abuse. The sight of the suburban mother admitted for treatment of acute alcoholism is no longer rare. Yet we treat these victims of addictive disease as if the alcoholism itself were the substantial problem, when frequently the difficulty is the lifestyle and social conditions that brought the individual's self-esteem to the level where a psychological crutch became necessary. It is extremely frustrating to treat such addictive clients, only to return them to the environment that spawned the original addiction.

We rarely address the problem of abuse of controlled substances by health professionals themselves. Who has greater access to, and control of, prescription medications than physicians and nurses? It is a frequent occurrence to observe a physician giving herself medication for a variety of illnesses and conditions. We who have founded much of our professional existence on the belief that medication can cure whatever ails one are most likely to take our own philosophy too seriously, and attempt to deal with many of life's stresses and strains with chemical assistance. Sidney Willig, in "Nursing And The Law,"[4] cites an American Nurses' Association study of the most frequent violations by nurses of various codes. Of the six violations cited by Willig, three were the mishandling, prescribing, or use of prescription medications and alcohol. The problem of health professionals' misuse of controlled substances is huge and growing. Why is this so, and what can be done to remedy the situation?

Our faith in medication and our ease of access are probably two reasons why substance abuse is so frequent among practitioners of health care. A critical examination of the ways in which we have been educated to view a pill as the solution to many problems would assist us in coming to grips with our own misuse syndrome. Medications provide avenues to solutions, but are infrequently the final solution to any problem, whether physiological or psychological. Even the prescription of an antibiotic to combat infection is simply the assisting of the body's own defense mechanisms, and not a solution by itself.

So much of health professions education focuses on illness education that we tend to lose sight of the essential wholeness and integrity of the human body when left alone. Many of the cures that are attributed to medical intervention may, in fact, be the unaided work of nature. Our reliance on intervention has led to the belief that assistance is always required, when frequently the best of therapies is to allow the client to heal himself. Given this interventionist education, with its emphasis on pathology and cure, it is little wonder that health professionals turn to medication at times when its use is inappropriate and counterproductive. We simply have bought our own sales pitch!

It behooves health professionals to become involved in the social movements and debates that examine the ways in which substance use and abuse can be addressed more effectively. We need also to involve ourselves in the examination of the roles of government in the control of substances.

A final note of caution is necessary. We have a tendency to view some of our assumptions as if they were fact, and some of our facts as if they were unchallengeable. The issue of controlled substances is replete with assumptions and facts that desperately need scrutiny. It is the obligation of the health professions to provide such scrutiny. The illogical

---

4. Willig, Sidney in Dorothea Orem's *Nursing: Concepts of Practice.* New York: McGraw-Hill, 1971, p. 212.

nature of many of the assumptions underlying treatment of addictions is capsulized by Thomas Szasz when he states, "Treating addiction to heroin with methadone is like treating addiction to scotch with bourbon." We need to take a fresh approach to this whole problem.

Legal and Illegal Behavior

A host of behaviors are prohibited in some geographical locations and permitted in others. These are behaviors that do not indicate either wellness or illness, do not necessarily affect others adversely, and pose little or no potential threat to the social system. I refer to the range of sexual behaviors that are legally regulated in contemporary society. Homosexual conduct today is illegal in all but thirteen states. Prostitution is illegal in all but one state of the United States, and in that one state (Nevada), it is controlled or prohibited on a county-to-county basis. Even the conduct of married heterosexual couples is subject to control in many areas. Why this perceived need of the state to control the behavior of consenting adults?

Many of the current legal statutes prohibiting or controlling sexual behavior are the result of the attempts of conservative governments to reflect the mores and morals of their constituents. Recalling the Puritan influence on the origins of American society, one can see how the government came to see its role as that of protector of the values of the ruling groups. The continued presence of these legal mandates and their current attempts at enforcement are testimony to the time lag between changes in social mores and changes in the law.

Most of us would acknowledge that social attitudes towards many of the forms of sexual expression mentioned above have been greatly modified during the past twenty years. Our ability to accept members of the social group who choose to explore alternative sexual lifestyles has increased and expanded. The news that a friend or professional colleague is involved in a "living together" relationship is no longer automatic cause for great gossip and potential professional jeopardy. We are increasingly able to accept clients with alternative sexual orientations. The dropping of homosexuality as a disorder classification by the American Psychiatric Association was a landmark in medicine's discovery that humans vary in sexual dimensions and that variance does not necessarily mean disease.

When much of the sexual behavior that is prohibited can be shown to have minimal adverse effects on others or society as a whole, why does society continue to seek to control this behavior? Possibly more than a reflection of our deeply conservative religious origins as a nation, it may indeed indicate that most Americans still feel uncomfortable with behaviors and individuals who are different in some way. We are most comfortable with things familiar. Since the vast majority of individuals are unfamiliar with many of the forms of sexual behavior that are outlawed (or at least would be most reluctant to admit familiarity), it stands to reason that they would prefer to eliminate these behaviors from the immediate environment. The unknown conjures many images, most of which reflect fear. Such fear is the seed of prejudice, and it can result in efforts to remove the object of prejudice from sight. As we become more aware of the number and normalcy of persons with sexually variant lifestyles in our midst, we will be more able to accept and understand this behavior and less tempted to seek to extinguish it.

Health professionals are exposed to sexually variant behavior by virtue of their access to private and privileged information concerning client lifestyle and health history, and through their proximity to clients in vulnerable, controlled states. The power of health professionals, particularly nurses, over the client's ability to attain sexual expression is tremendous.

Hospital confinement assures a drastically limited, if not completely curtailed, sexual expression for most clients. Nursing home or extended care facility residents are equally deprived of normal sexual outlets, even if married and residing together. We undervalue the sexual dimension of human existence, and underestimate both the impact of health and illness states on sexual expression and the impact of sexual adaptation on health.

The need for health professionals to attain and maintain a sensitive, accepting attitude toward client sexual lifestyle is great. But health professionals are the product of the society around them, and can only be expected to reflect the larger society's values and attitudes. As society grows more able to cope with sexual variance and to accept the extent to which all human beings have needs for various forms of intimacy and gratification, the health professions will begin to come to grips with their need to understand and make provision for the sexual dimension of human existence.

Summary

Behavior control is a diverse and complex subject. It extends from the issue of mental health and illness determination, through the subjects of substance abuse, to human sexual behavior. Central to the topic is the question of the government's right to protect individuals from themselves. The participation of health professionals in the dialogue concerning these topics could be enormously beneficial. The impact of the resolution of these issues on health professionals in both their personal and their professional worlds will be great, and thus they have a strong rationale for involvement.

DEATH AND DYING

The topic of death and dying, once taboo, is suddenly in vogue. It is as if we have discovered death's existence, or acknowledged that it is a feature of all life. Even after it was considered enlightened and in good taste to educate one's children about sex, death was a forbidden topic. Now parents are giving attention to this universal phenomenon, and acknowledging that death, as well as life, is a concept that must be relayed to one's offspring.

Though we should all expect to die, few of us have given serious thought to this assured experience. We are mirrors of our society, which has made valiant attempts to shield itself from the reality of death. At long last, the topic has been approved for public discussion and a flood of newly discovered information is being published to meet the demand. This universal experience is now a universal topic.

As we become more aware of the fact of death, we are beginning to expect the institutions and professionals who care for us as we approach death to be adequately prepared to deal with the requirements of the dying process. Health professionals are drawn into the topic, if not by personal interest, then by consumer demand. Death has long been the unacknowledged enemy of the health professions. Suddenly to attempt to understand, and at times cooperate with, the enemy is a feat that many are unable to accomplish. So, at a time when more consumers are demanding the right to die with dignity, the health professions must learn new ways to cope.

Much of the public awareness of and sensitivity to death and the dying process is due to the contributions of a few brave risk-takers who first explored this territory and shed light on the topic. Elizabeth Kübler-Ross is the pioneer educator in this field, and the person who first began to criticize the health professions' inability to deal with psychological preparation for final stages of life.[5]

Her work was the result of observations of the unmet needs of dying patients. Her sensitive interviews with dying patients, which were used as educational experiences for staff attending terminal clients, were in-

5.Kübler-Ross, Elizabeth. *On Death and Dying.* New York: Macmillan Publishing Company, 1974.

strumental in illustrating most poignantly the failure of the helping professions to render service at a time when competent professional care could be so significant.

Death is a stage of life. It is the last portion of a series of developmental experiences. As in most of life's experiences, no two deaths are identical; there are no final rules or protocols for how each of us must die, except the rule that each of us *will* die. The exact nature of death, beyond its physiological manifestations, remains a mystery. The adventure that may await us after death likewise remains a matter of belief or speculation.

Death, the end of life, conjures many images and arouses many of our most fundamental fears and hopes. It is the end, and possibly the beginning, or maybe simply a transition. Death remains the final frontier for human exploration, and this is one trip for which each of us is guaranteed passage. Funerals, caskets, last rites, embalming, corpse, immortality, grave: each of these is a powerful word connoting images and visions. Much of what we feel about death and dying is the product of our culture. The way we say goodbye, or don't, is an expression of how we view this last phase of acknowledged human existence.

For health professionals, the approach of death is often seen as the acknowledgement of our failure. We are educated to promote and maintain life. Many of us will undergo ceremonies in which we take a pledge to promote life and prevent death at all times. But how foolish it is to expend such effort forestalling the one universal. For as each of us is born, surely each of us will die.

Hospitals are woefully inadequate in their preparation for death. Nurses, who deal frequently with dying clients, are unable to withstand the emotion that the presence of death evokes. Physicians scurry away from patient and family alike, frequently leaving them at a time when they desperately require some form of understanding companionship.

Contemporary mourning has become quite a commercial venture. We bundle the dead body off to a funeral home, where it is restored to a cosmetic semblance of life and then displayed in a bedlike coffin intended to make the onlooker believe that his loved one has not died, but has simply entered that long night's sleep. We embalm, encase, entomb, and enshrine the remains in memorials of sandstone, marble, or granite. After spending a fortune for a few hours of public ceremony, we are alone again with our grief. The support systems of the extended family and close community no longer exist.

The topic of death has not always been regarded with the fear and awe it currently inspires in Western civilization. Our forebears regarded death as a natural event. A death, no matter how tragic, would bring together the extended family into a network of mutual support. The family of the early 1900s was able to cope with death in this way. A death in the family was regarded as a natural event. A wake was often held: a simple custom of readying the body for display in the home and then having relatives and friends visit the corpse, recite prayers, extend sympathy and support to survivors and generally have an opportunity to exchange information and greetings with people not often visited. The occasion was marked with lengthy religious services, which gave to survivors the succor of hope for heavenly repose of the "departed loved one." Then the entire family was off to the cemetery or family plot to bury their dead.

Contemporary death customs attempt to minimize the reality of death's occurrence. Social and religious structures no longer provide the undergirding support of previous times. Death no longer is likely to occur at home. More likely, dying will be done within a health institution, where staff are ill-prepared to cope with the needs of the client or family. How can we assist ourselves, our clients, and their families to cope with this inevitable phase of life?

Current death education efforts for health professionals provide reassurance that change is underway. The attempts to increase professional sensitivity and skill need to be given the priority of attention so desperately deserved if significant change is to be accomplished. Nurses, more than members of any other health profession, can make significant contributions to support dying clients and their families. We have the proximity, access, and role appropriate to such a therapeutic thrust. The only unmet skills are those of understanding and coping with our own feelings about death and acquiring facility in supporting others through this process. As more people choose to die at home, and more families undertake this gesture of love and support involved in this choice, more assistance from community health nurses and independent practitioners will be sought. The potential for nursing's contribution to this, the last of human life changes, is enormous.

GENETIC ENGINEERING

The term *genetic engineering* refers to any activity that results in the intentional alteration of a specific human gene pool. The human gene pool is that storehouse of hereditary blueprints—chromosomes and genes—which lay the groundwork for determination of each characteristic, from eye color to gender. The human gene pool is the combined hereditary information of the species, which has, until contemporary times, evolved in a more or less random fashion as programmed by the forces of natural selection and Darwinian evolution.

Medical technology and its applications now give humanity the tools with which to affect the content of the gene pool by either selecting or rejecting hereditary information. The techniques vary from the exotic and not yet perfected methodology of deprogramming and reprogramming human genetic information, to altering or substituting genetic information, to controversial gene transfer techniques (currently under close scrutiny by the federal government), to the relatively harmless-sounding procedure of genetic counseling.

Whether one considers the impact of the exotic or the mundane, the concept of humanity altering its own biological future conjures Orwellian images and reminds us of Hitler's psychotic dreams of a master race. Who is to control the transmission of genetic information in the human gene pool? What are the potential benefits and detriments of such activities? How is the practitioner involved in such processes? What are the fundamental questions that must be answered before humanity attempts to imitate nature?

There are several current techniques that alter and subtly affect the gene pool. Some appear rather harmless; others are quite impressive, if not frightening. Each represents an exercise of man's recently-acquired capacity to affect the transfer and duplication of hereditary information.

Genetic screening. The process of evaluating individual genetic makeup for the presence or absence of particular genetic information (such as sickle cell trait).

Genetic counseling. Providing clients with information and knowledge of alternative courses of action available, based upon evaluation of their genetic potential to produce offspring with such hereditary diseases as sickle cell anemia.

Sickle cell anemia, a hereditary hemolytic anemia, is detectable both in victims of the disease and in carriers of the genetic trait. The procedure for ruling out or determining the presence of the disease is relatively simple, and is available to masses of individuals throughout the United States. If the trait's presence is ascertained, the typical procedure is to inform the client and to offer an opportunity to decide whether the risks and possible consequences are acceptable. The disease is prevalent among blacks. The dissemination of counseling information thus has potential for racist overtones if not adequately controlled. No one would argue that the prevention of the duplication of this trait is indeed a noble and lofty goal. But what if the trait is the forebearer to an evolutionary advantage, if the presence of the sickling phenomenon poses a survival possibility when allowed to evolve in the population? Would we be then eliminating from the gene pool an advantageous trait that might ensure the potential evolution and survival supremacy of the black population? The possibility that sickle cell anemia represents nature's attempt at finding a future advantage is remote, but certainly real. Who are we to meddle in the process of evolution, particularly when doing so may result in the elimination of a potentially advantageous strain? Of course, one also is reluctant to advocate the continued presence of sickle cell anemia in the black population; the physiological and psychological results of this crippling and sometimes fatal disease are dreadful. So what is the acceptable alternative?

Contraception (The exercise of control over reproductive functions that allows sexual activity without resultant parenthood).

Contraception, a seemingly harmless activity of birth control, also represents a means of effecting genetic engineering. The intentional control of population through the application of contraceptive devices is subtly and slowly changing the demographics of world humanity. The availability of contraceptive devices in developed and industrialized countries is much higher than in less developed countries. Thus, western cultures are approaching zero population growth while many of the emerging nations are still struggling with the problems of accelerating overpopulation. The change in a balance of world population will certainly affect the allocation and utilization of natural resources and the dissemination and use of technology. But what of the effect on the hereditary future of humankind? As western cultures control population, they reduce the duplication and contribution of their genetic descendants to the world-wide gene pool, at the same time that the contribution of other cultures is increased. The effect on the world-wide gene pool— and thus on humankind's racial and ethnic characteristics—can only be guessed. Whether this effect is harmless or helpful can also only be surmised. But the potential for providing the basis for the dominance or extinction from the gene pool of some potentially harmful or helpful attribute in evolutionary terms must be considered. For example, Tay-Sach's disease, a genetic disease prevalent in Jews, may represent a potentially beneficial mutation of the human hereditary cycle. As the replication of this genetic information is curtailed by the declining birth rate of contemporary Jews, the potential contribution of this information to the human gene pool is also diminished.

Amniocentesis (The withdrawal of a sample of amniotic fluid to permit evaluation for the presence or absence of deleterious chromosomal formations).

Amniocentesis presents many complex problems. It represents the ability of technology to outstrip moral and ethical development. The procedure was researched and implemented long before either the potential impact of its use or the ethical considerations of the dilemmas imposed were clear. The technological sophistication that is required for the successful completion of amniocentesis is considerable. But the preparation both of clients and practitioners to adequately deal with the information gleaned is even more crucial.

The knowledge of defects in the genetic construction of the fetus permits the decision to abort or maintain pregnancy on the basis of the viability or acceptability of the fetal potential by the parents. It is all well and good to desire to prevent unnecessary grief for parents and pain and suffering for children by terminating an unsuccessful pregnancy. But what of the parents who choose to terminate pregnancy simply because the amniotic fluid reveals the fetus to be of an undesired gender, though healthy? Still more confounding is the difficulty encountered when the information obtained reveals a defective fetus and the parents are unable, for whatever reason, to sanction termination of the pregnancy. Many ethical dilemmas were engendered by the development and implementation of this technological breakthrough.

The legal issues involved are also complex. What is the responsibility of the attending staff to reveal information obtained? Should the procedure (which is not always reliable) fail to detect an aberrant fetus, is the health care institution responsible? And what if the technique predicts a defective fetus, and abortion is performed—only to discover that a normal child was aborted? The responsibilities and liabilities of health professionals and clients alike are tremendous.

The greatest threat amniocentesis holds is its potential for genetic evaluation on a prenatal basis. Currently we have to wait until birth to unwrap the package and discover whether the babe has blue or green eyes, red or black hair, and a host of other attributes. As genetic information reveals more and more indices of its power to determine who and what we are, and as amniocentesis permits increased knowledge of genetic content, what is the potential for pregnancy termination or continuation decisions to be made on arbitrary and capricious grounds, such as eye color, height, or intellect?

When is the fine line between use and abuse of information crossed? Certainly the world has witnessed many examples of man's ability to control, and even exterminate, his fellow man. It would be unwise to risk initiating further means of manipulating the species without first establishing rules for using those means morally.

Eugenics (The intentional breeding of certain humans, with the objective of promoting the presence of their hereditary characteristics in the gene pool).

The concept of eugenics is particularly repugnant to our free-will-valuing society. The idea that humans might be encouraged to reproduce on the basis of their genetic desirability smacks of cattle-breeding. We would like to see ourselves as having progressed beyond this moral level—as having advanced to recognition of the value of self-determination and free will. Yet such diverse groups as Orthodox Jews, militant black activists, and arch-conservative political parties (John Birch Society) have all urged their members, in recent years, to examine the effects of large versus small families on the promulgation of the group's existence and survival in society. How is this subtle hinting different from the process of eugenics?

Euthenics (The support and maintenance of humans who would not, because of the presence of disease or disability, otherwise have survived to have an opportunity to contribute their progeny to the gene pool).

Euthenics is a result of the efficiency of our health technologies, and of our humane intentions. We have gone far in the battle to care for the least among us: those who, because of disease or disability, would not have survived unaided. Because of this effectiveness and humaneness, these disabled or diseased people are able to contribute their genetic information to the collective pool. For example, we are now able to maintain victims of cystic fibrosis to ages when these disease-trait carriers are able to produce their own offspring, thus increasing the presence of this deleterious gene in the collective genetic storehouse. Conceivably, we are, by dint of our own good intentions and excellent health care, providing the fuel for potential hereditary catastrophe. But who is to decide who may and who may not bear children? Is it appropriate for anyone to deprive his brethren of the right to experience parenthood? Could these presently deleterious genes later prove to be an evolutionary fortune for the survival of humankind? A multitude of problems and difficulties are presented.

Each of the methods of genetic engineering mentioned above is currently in effect. As opposed to recombinant DNA transfer or gene transplantation, these methods offer real evidence of man's ability to influence the evolutionary future. How these methods will be used, and what the long-term effects will be, is yet to be determined.

GERIATRICS AND AGING

Nowhere is the success of our standard of living more apparent than in the statistical analysis of population patterns over the past several decades. The life span of humankind is greatly expanded over the expectation of just one century ago. The white male child born in 1976 can be expected to live to the age of 69.7. This figure compares with a life expectancy of 48.23 only 80 years ago. The white female child has a current life expectancy of 77.3 years.

These changes in predictable patterns of aging have had profound impact on the characteristic makeup of society. As our population includes more people in their sixties, seventies, and eighties, we are beginning to examine the roles allocated to seniors. As more of us recognize the impending reality that we too, if lucky, will see this mature period of life, the motivation to once again include the older citizen as a fully enfranchised member of society will be greater. Yet contemporary society seems to have little use for the aging adult. We are singularly insensitive to the fate of a group of people whose ranks we all hope to join—the healthy aged.

Roles for older people are well defined, circumscribed, and not very realistic. Until contemporary society relegated the aged to shelter care, senior members of the family had an integral role to play. When agrarian culture was common, or families lived in an extended (as opposed to nuclear) fashion, the older members of the family were accorded respect and a rank of some merit within the system. Grandmothers were considered the experts on birthing and childcare, and their assistance was sought after. Grandfathers were the acknowledged patriarchs and, as such, had the ultimate authority on a host of familial decisions. The achievement of survival was accorded respect and stature.

Contemporary family models require high degrees of mobility and flexibility. There is little room for the luxury of supporting an aging member, much less motivation for according this person a rank of distinction and respect. Sometimes people are even forced to retire from productive roles in industry and commerce at arbitrary ages not related to measures of competence, but simply based on the accumulation of chronological years. The role expectation placed upon the elderly is one of helplessness, senility, passivity, and inaction. We provide few, if any, constructive work opportunities even for the aged who have managed to ignore the directives of society to deteriorate. It is astounding that a future that many of us hope to attain is relegated such a low priority on our social action agenda.

What is *age*? What is *geriatrics*? How do the concepts differ? *Age* is a physiologic process, the result of survival success. The mature period of life is one of many developmental stages of human growth. People entering the age range of sixty through eighty are simply sixty to eighty years old. The accumulation of chronological years may connote some physiologic and maturational changes, but does not predict inactivity and incompetence. Age is a process of nature. It is also a state of mind. Many twenty-year-olds display a senile attitude towards life, while many octogenarians display the vigor and enthusiasm of youth. The achievement of years does not necessitate the loss either of function or of intellect. In fact, the achievement of years can accord the opportunity for insight and wisdom that the sheer accomplishment of either education or material success alone can never bring. People who surmount life's crises, and survive, are recipients of experience and knowledge that only survival can teach. The achievement of advanced age should be accorded stature and respect, for it denotes the ability to meet life's challenges and overcome them.

Geriatrics is the health specialty concerned with the care of the aged. All geriatric clients are aged; all aged people are not geriatric clients. Aging itself is a normal physiologic process, not a disease. As a normal process in the human developmental trajectory, it does not require health intervention, but simply health maintenance. Geriatrics deals with those health impairments that interfere with the enjoyment of a normal, productive life during the advanced years. Geriatrics is the health discipline concerned with prevention and cure of debilitating and confining conditions, such as arthritis, arteriosclerosis, and atherosclerosis. Age is a stage of development; geriatrics is a stage of impaired health. The terms are not interchangeable, any more than the term pediatrics means that all children are ill and require medical attention. The achievement of advanced age is not a disability, but an asset in the opportunities accorded and the wisdom achieved. The sooner society understands the necessity to utilize this achievement and this wisdom, the sooner we will have recognized another resource that has long gone ignored.

THE ENVIRONMENTAL CRISIS

More people, more consumption, fewer resources, and steady state space availability: this sums up the problem of the environmental crisis. We have developed social and cultural systems without parallel in human history, attained a standard of living unequalled in the world, and, in the process, placed ourselves squarely in the path of environmental disaster.

The production/consumption orientation that is largely the motivating force behind current technological development has been instrumental in the attainment of our sophisticated lifestyle. It is also a counterproductive approach to resolution of the new problems this lifestyle has created. The drive for exploration, consumption, and new development must be modified to include recognition that all of what we produce and consume is part of the larger ecological system. The laws of ecology need recognition.

The laws of ecology state: (1) everything is connected to everything else; (2) there is no "away"; (3) Mother Nature knows best; and (4) there ain't no such thing as a free lunch (TANSTAAFL). These principles should not be surprising to students of the health professions, for as we explore the human body, we have learned that its systems are beautifully integrated and interdependent, exhibiting natural balance and wholeness when all is functioning well. Thus, we know that in humans, everything is connected to everything else; if one part of the system experiences a change, the entire system is affected.

The notion that there is no "away" also should be logical to health professionals. We know that once physiologic or psychic waste is accumulated, the process of throwing it away incurs a cost on the system. Should a substantial amount of alcohol be consumed, the liver and its attendant systems must cope with the detoxification problem and will demonstrate considerable change if taxed too heavily. There is no away.

The concept that Mother Nature knows best should also be familiar from our study of health and illness. We know that, except under drastic circumstances, the body's own mechanisms will seek to correct imbalances in any physiologic system, that the natural pattern of life is towards health, and that Mother Nature attempts to achieve wholeness and health in the human physiologic systems.

Finally, there is no such thing as a free lunch: everything has its costs and benefits. Human health is an excellent demonstration of this principle. Stressful behavior, chronic fatigue, smoking, and obesity are all activities that extract physiologic payment from the body. We receive nothing without having to pay for it in some fashion; the mere progress of surviving the onslaught of life is filled with costs.

The principles of ecology are well understood by health professionals who witness their demonstration in the course of each practice day. The application of these principles to the environment in which we exist certainly doesn't take much in the way of imagination. We can observe the effects of neglect of these principles in our daily existence. Once-clean air is now fouled with effluents; water requires extensive purification prior to consumption; the natural habitat, and hence the existence of hundreds of species of animals and plants, is threatened with extinction. Human progress has exacted a heavy toll from the environment. More people require more space and more food. The higher the standard of living, the more resources are required to support it. The consumption of a forest of trees to manufacture wrappers for bubblegum and hamburgers is beyond the imagination, yet an actual, everyday occurrence.

It is no longer possible to ignore these environmental threats. We are faced with the realization that the easy production/consumption lifestyle is over. New gains will be harder to achieve and will be won at much higher costs. We are approaching the exhaustion of finite natural resources, particularly the fossil fuels. We are facing the problems inherent in overcrowding, overpopulation, and overconsumption. Having created expectations of the good life for all, and established a model consumerist behavior for the rest of the world to emulate, we suddenly are confronted with the need to pay the piper and may, indeed, be short of funds.

The faith that human beings have placed in private enterprise, technological invention, and scientific inquiry has been well rewarded until current times. There is little doubt that if an appropriate reorientation and increased sensitivity to the ecological systems of which we are a part can be accomplished, this same effort can solve much of the environmental crisis it has created.

The need is for a mass public awakening to the costs of progress, an awakening that is slowly occurring due to the energy crisis. As people become more sensitized to the personal costs that such consumer behavior extracts, conservationist attitudes must begin to prevail. It is a matter of survival.

Garrett Hardin,[6] in his essay, "The Tragedy of the Commons," speaks most clearly of the human tendency not to give priority to a problem or need until it hits close to home. He points out that until the costs of overcrowding and pollution are personalized, individual actions to solve these problems will be minimal. Certainly we appreciate this principle more when we recall how blasé most Americans were toward the mass executions in Cambodia in the late 1970s, yet how anguished each of us was by the murders of some twenty to thirty Chicago-area youths reputedly committed by John Gacy during those same years. Tragedy far from home is hard to realize; tragedy at home can be devastating. Hardin would remind us that the time to take preventive steps is before the tragedy hits home. The question remains: Are we capable of such foresight when it entails changes that would cramp our lifestyles?

It is quite easy to become angry, shake our fists, and demand action when we learn that the XYZ Conglomerate Paper Company has been poisoning a local stream with its by-products. It is more difficult for us to see our own ecologically unwise behaviors, such as insisting on automobiles that meet ego needs instead of transportation needs, or buying "disposable" convenience products that may constitute a dangerous environmental hazard. It is easier to ask the other guy to clean up his act then to clean up our own.

---

6. Hardin, Garrett, "The Tragedy of the Commons," Appendix B in *Exploring New Ethics for Survival*, Baltimore: Penguin, 1972, p. 250.

The environmental crisis will result in changes in lifestyle for most Americans. The constraints placed upon consumption of energy, the economics involved in increasing acquisition of goods and services, and the penalties associated with inefficient living will soon become too heavy a burden and will force change. Such change will affect health care extensively.

Energy-efficiency criteria will cause reappraisal of the ways in which we deliver health care services. What are we currently doing in hospitals and clinics that can be safely accomplished on outpatient or even over-the-telephone basis? How can the goods and services we consume be used more efficiently? Will we begin to demand reusable supplies and end our consumption of disposable items? Will the demand for health care drop as people experience increasingly tight economics? Will health care become a luxury item, priced beyond the family budget?

The health professions can also learn other messages from the environmental crisis. The late E. F. Schumacher's thesis that "small is beautiful" needs to be applied to health care delivery. We are currently obsessed with the notion that all of the latest in medical gadgetry must be available at every facility, without regard to the unnecessary duplication of services, and the added expense and waste this attitude creates. Better inter- and intra-institutional planning and cooperation can result in the conservation of vast amounts of monies and other resources, and can result in more equitable care.

The fact that everything is connected to everything else, along with the realization of TANSTAAFL, should help us to examine the techniques and approaches we bring to individual client care. We know that every therapeutic modality has a planned effect, and most have many undesired and frequently unplanned effects. The rapid acceptance and utilization of oral contraceptives brought with it a welcome relief from unplanned pregnancies. It was only after the fact that many women learned of the unanticipated and frequently detrimental side effects of this therapy. Many other remedies have similarly been welcomed at first and later discovered to have unexpected drawbacks. When will we finally learn that interference in any natural system affects all the parts of that system, and should therefore be introduced only when absolutely necessary?

The lessons of the environmental crisis for the health professions are twofold. The first is to attempt to apply the ecological principles to our own discipline in the hopes of preventing further destruction of the natural systems we work with so closely. The second is a message to us as citizens of this Spaceship Earth, that we are involved, and have an investment in, the efficient, effective management of the spaceship by her crew. To fail to respond to the lessons of the environment is to court further disaster and eventual destruction.

ALLOCATION OF SCARCE MEDICAL RESOURCES

On first examination, the problem of allocation of scarce medical resources would appear to involve only those directly concerned in the delivery of health care. However, in order to resolve the problem, fundamental social and ethical priorities must be clarified. These decisions will affect the entire social system served. Given a situation in which both economic and environmental constraints dictate that society conserve resources and place priority on developing only those goods and services that are fundamental to continued survival, it is possible to forecast an increasing limitation on the expansion of health care facilities and manpower. No longer can the costs of sophisticated health care and exotic health professions education be easily borne by the social system. The benefit received from continued infusion of massive amounts of resources into the health care system is decreasing. The ability of society to support continued expansion of the health professions and the services they render is much diminished by other pressing fiscal priorities. The boom in health professions education and health facility construction is coming to a close.

Given an increasing population (whose expectations of health care are constantly growing) plus the prospect of steady state existence of health resources to meet these expectations, how will decisions regarding who gets what, for how long, and how much, be made? This problem, although it sounds as if it were a distant prospect, already exists.

The technological capacity to perform exotic life-saving procedures exists, yet the availability and distribution of this capacity is quite limited. For example, the effectiveness of kidney transplantation is now beyond question. But the availability of donor kidneys and transplantation facilities is quite limited. How are decisions to allocate these resources made? Currently much is left to chance (first come, first served) and nebulous notions of which candidates would be the best risks for transplantation. Are we willing to live with such vague and potentially unfair selection criteria?

There are many examples of widespread disparities in resource allocation. The variation between the quality of care obtainable at one institution and that of another, located a short distance away, can be considerable. Each hospital seems to have its own strengths and weaknesses, depending on the orientation and philosophy of its board of trustees and the specialties and influences of its medical staff. One may have a sophisticated cardiac care unit, while another may specialize in pediatric intensive care. Yet the allocation of these resources is such that each facility purports to offer care to all who come, regardless of the ability to match client needs with institutional resources. Moreover, it would be economically impossible to duplicate each of the myriad specialty facilities in each institution; nor would demand for specialty care be sufficient to justify these resources, if provided. How do we attempt to match client needs with institutional resources? Only in the most severe of cases do we have adequate procedures for transfer of clients to specialty centers. It would appear that hospitals view each other in a competitive light, since they are all vying for the consumer's economic resources. But the laws of the marketplace, which allow the consumer to compare suppliers and channel business to the source most compatible with needs, do not apply in the world of health care. Hospital selection is more a matter of chance and physician choice than client preference. Thus two clients with similar conditions and a similar prognosis may in fact experience far different results, simply because one was more fortunate in the hospital care game than the other.

We are able to deliver extremely sophisticated care to those who are able to pay for it. But what of those who are not able to finance care? We would like to believe that they have access to the same quality of care, but this is not so. The case of Howard B. Smith illustrates the gap between technological capacity and availability. Mr. Smith was injured in an auto accident and taken to Capitol Hill Hospital in Washington, D.C. Unfortunately for Mr. Smith, he had no insurance and had little money with him at the time of the accident. After examination, Mr. Smith was dismissed from the hospital by the emergency room nurse, who called police and told them that he "only has three cracked ribs and we don't normally admit patients like that." Smith died later the same day. An autopsy demonstrated the presence of severe damage to the liver and adrenal glands, ten fractured ribs, and various other internal injuries.

According to the columnist Carl T. Rowan,[7] Mr. Smith was the victim of his lack of financial ability and the chance that he was taken to a private hospital, rather than a public institution equipped to admit charity patients. The unfortunate death of Mr. Smith provides lessons in the gap between what is available to some, and what is available to others. How can this gap be bridged?

The quick answer is to suggest infusion of massive amounts of economic resources into the health care delivery system to ensure the availability of quality care to all. But this is not necessarily the most productive use of these resources. The economic law of diminishing returns dictates that, after the first few billion dollars, the return from

---

7.Rowan, Carl T. "Health-Care Inhumanity." *Chicago Sun-Times,* 22 March 1979, p. 64, cols. 1–2.

the investment gradually decreases in terms of the efficiency of investment to outcome. There is a point beyond which it is foolish to expand health resources further, a point at which the number of people served becomes smaller, and the needs of these people more exotic. Eventually, the economic resources are diverted from other priorities that might more effectively contribute to health and well-being. For example, coronary bypass surgery may cost $50,000 per patient. This money may buy the client a few additional years of limited life. What would the same amount of money do if applied to health education in prevention of coronary disease?

The fact of the matter is that our resources are limited; we cannot extend quality care at any cost to all people. Decisions as to who gets what must be made. The fundamental issues are how one decides, how to maximize benefit from resources allocated, and, when conflict arises, what criteria to use in resolution.

The solutions to these questions involve the entire social system, because the answers will touch everyone in the system. The current decisional framework favors the needs of the affluent and the established. This may not prove to be the most equitable method. We must all examine the structure of the *status quo,* and the relationship of economics to health care, and decide what changes, if any, are warranted.

"ISMS"

Everyone knows blacks have rhythm, Jews have money, the Irish are gregarious, and American Indians are drunks. These inflammatory statements represent the essential nature of what I choose to call the "isms" of life—racism, sexism, anti-Semitism, and any other ism. Isms are prejudices, unfair assumptions about people. Difficult to define and more difficult to erase, prejudice remains the fundamental obstacle to human cooperation in the process of each of us getting through life in a satisfactory manner. Our assumptions about others, based on race, sex, religion, ethnic group, or sexual preferences, are rooted in fear and misconception. Much of what passes as knowledge about other, different people is actually the accumulation of years of misunderstanding and ignorance. The problem of intolerance creeps into, and poisons much of, everday life for many of our fellow humans.

I will discuss racism briefly, and sexism more fully, in the following pages. My purpose is to illustrate both how pervasive and how similar most prejudices are. Whether I am fearful of you because of skin color, gender, or religion, the effect my fear has on your well-being is similar.

Racism

Racism is the assumption of characteristics about people based on their racial heritage. It takes various forms, from that experienced by the vast majority of American blacks to that experienced by Mediterranean peoples in northern Europe. It is the sneer of disapproval on the face of the observer who watches an integrated couple walking their child to school. It is the equally destructive notion that all whites are devils, all blacks are welfare cheaters, and Hispanics are lazy. Racism is a worldwide negative force in contemporary society. The presence of racial prejudice is universal, though the objects of fear and loathing change with the location. Arab distrusts Jew (although they probably share a common racial heritage), black hates white, Polynesian is loath to associate with Oriental, and nobody likes everybody. It's an endless chain of fear based on ignorance and superstition.

The fact remains that there are simply no data to validate differences between groups of people when compared by race, other than the obvious differences of appearance. The experience of treatment based on race was most poignantly conveyed by John Howard Griffin in his book *Black Like Me*,[8] which is the account of a white man who learned what it is like to live as a black in the South. The prejudice to which Griffin was treated is not confined to the American South, nor has it changed drastically since his experience in the mid-1960s. Our society continues to stereotype people on the basis of racial category, stifling human expression and preventing the full participation and contribution of vast numbers of people.

We each are reared with the presence of many messages regarding the stereotypical images of others. Like all other values and attitudes, racism is acquired, not inborn. It stands to reason that what is learned can be modified. We are able to examine the belief systems with which we are familiar and attempt to validate or expunge information on the basis of experience and fact, as opposed to the acceptance of whatever our culture has chosen to impart. But this task is not easily accomplished; it is in fact beyond the reach of many.

Given that we are health professionals and that most of us would cleave to an ethical stance requiring uniformly high-quality health care to all consumers, regardless of their racial background, how do we prevent these prejudices from affecting the quality of the care we give?

The first step is to acknowledge the reality and impact of prejudice. The second is to realize that we all have some assumptions about others. These assumptions may not be valid, we may actually know them to be

---

8. Griffin, John Howard. *Black Like Me*. New York: Signet Books, 1964.

less than objective, but nonetheless they continue to be a part of our personalities. When these assumptions interfere with our ability to render competent, compassionate care, it is only appropriate that we should remove ourselves from the arena of service.

One final, disquieting notion. All of us are members of a group that is hated somewhere. The fact of racism is universal, its particulars unique. It is helpful to recall that, given different circumstances, we might each be on the outside looking in. This knowledge makes it a bit easier to empathize with those whom we may not understand.

Sexism

Sexism is the label applied to the pervasive force of prejudice that assumes certain characteristics or roles are appropriate to an individual or group of individuals solely on the basis of gender. Sexism affects men, women, and children in all aspects of the normal conduct of life.

A biologist will explain that in the human species there are more differences *among* the sexes than *between* them. Yet, even while the physical and mental attributes that comprise the human race are represented in fairly equal proportions in each sex, many false assumptions are made regarding roles and behaviors appropriate to a gender. Many of the roles imposed by sex-role stereotyping have little or no validity in contemporary society, but stem from periods in human development when such role-appropriate behavior may have been justified by concern for survival. These stereotypes can no longer be biologically justifiable. Nevertheless, such assumptions continue to prescribe and proscribe behavior both for women and men.

Prehistoric humans had two distinct biological mandates: to perpetuate the species through reproduction, and to maintain the species through provision for food and safety. The distinct roles of the male and female in this primitive society were determined by the female's high value as the mother, nurturer, and tender of the young. Men were assigned, by circumstance, the role of hunter, gatherer, and protector of the nurturing family unit. Possibly it was not the greater strength of the male that decided this role for him, but the simple fact that the female was bound by pregnancy and nursing, and was thus unable to participate in the other activities of preservation and survival.

Regardless, the role of the male as the breadwinner and of the mother as the nurturer were established around simple biological mandates to survive. Quite possibly, men and women who selected alternative patterns—such as women who chose to attempt both to gather food and to provide nurturance to the young—were unsuccessful and thus were not able to perpetuate alternative lifestyles simply because they were unable to survive. The dominance of the male in the family system is thought to have been established by his ability to provide food, and to have been perpetuated through evolution to more sophisticated social structures. Perhaps the necessity of male dominance over female family members was later emphasized by the need to identify heirs for the purpose of establishing inheritance rights. The expression "mother's baby, father's maybe" takes on real meaning if the paternity of a child is open to question. If the conduct of females is controlled by the male head of the household, paternity is more readily guaranteed—a necessity when social systems include the ownership and inheritance of property.

Speculation about the origins of current male-dominant/female-submissive social patterns is a fascinating exploration. But the pattern makes little sense in our current state of social evolution. The requirement of physical strength to protect the species through perpetual warfare no longer exists. In fact, the aggression that is culturally associated with the attribute of maleness may be counterproductive and actually destructive in a world whose greatest need is peace, and where survival is an exercise in human cooperation. We have possibly reached a point in the evolution of human societies that mandates the supremacy of the female-associated attributes of passivity and nurturance to ensure the perpetuation of the species.

The assumption that aggression or passivity are inescapably linked with gender is erroneous. There is little physiological evidence to support the assumption that men are by nature more aggressive, or that women are by nature more passive. Characteristics associated with gender are primarily expressions of sex-role-appropriate behavior that are learned through the processes of socialization. Early in life we teach little boys not to cry, for fear of compromising their masculinity; we teach little girls not to play competitively, for fear of destroying their "femininity." Both behaviors—aggression and passivity—are within the realm of possible behaviors open to all humans. The elimination of either in the process of socialization creates a deficiency for the child as well as for society as a whole.

The notion that men must be strong, aggressive, and stoic, places on the male a tremendous burden. The stress of continuous responsibility, real or imagined, without the relief that can be gained by expressing anxiety of grief, is a toll exacted from the "masculine" man as the price of constant superiority. The physiological cost in terms of ulcers, heart disease, and related stress diseases has been well documented by Ashley Montague, Hans Selye, and others.[9] The burden of playing the

---

9.Montague, Ashley. *The Natural Superiority of Women*. New York: Macmillan, 1968; Selye, Hans. *The Stress of Life*. New York: 1966.

male role is costly, both emotionally and socially. What has society lost by excluding men from the role of nurturer and homemaker? What contributions to the family structure and to the rearing of children have been blocked by the sex-role stereotyping that excludes men from these roles?

Equally, the concept that women, by their very biological structure, are weaker and more passive than men is also a loss both for the individuals who are trapped in this role and for society as a whole. The exclusion of more than fifty percent of humankind from the upper echelons of power and decision-making roles has resulted in the loss of a perspective and a pool of intellectual talent that is crucially important. In the face of monumental economic, environmental, and political problems it is foolish to believe that we can afford such a waste of human talent. Sexism in the selection of leadership is a luxury that human survival can no longer afford or tolerate. Undoubtedly the most significant resource for continued survival of the human species is intellect and imagination. Can the future continue to squander this resource?

The female caught within the socialized roles of femininity also pays a price. Women are more likely to experience low self-esteem, and have a higher frequency of physical complaints and psychological impairments, than their male counterparts—particularly at the time that a woman finds her traditional role as mother and homemaker threatened by the maturity of offspring and the lessening of domestic responsibility. The plight of the middle-aged woman is recorded in such articles as Pauline Bart's "Depression in Middle Aged Women."[10] Women face the loss of their primary role of mother and the physiological alterations imposed by menopause, including the attendant myths purporting that menopause initiates a loss of femininity and sexuality. Given the value that society places upon women's sexuality and the significance of youth and good appearance in determining self-esteem for the female, menopause presents a traumatic change for most women trapped within the feminine mystique.

The dimensions of sexism in contemporary society are frightening. Although women comprise fifty-two percent of the adult population (21 years of age or older) of the United States, they represent fewer than ten percent of the licensed physicians, fewer than ten percent of practicing attorneys, and less than twenty percent of the total blue collar workers. A woman with a college education can now hope to make as much money as a man with a grade-school education. Even in the United States Congress, author of recent equal-pay-for-equal-work statutes, a female congressional aide can expect to be paid about thirty percent less

---

10. Bart, Pauline. "Depression in Middle Aged Women," *Woman in Sexist Society*. Gornick & Moran, editors, New York: Basic, 1971, p. 163.

than her male counterpart. Women receive one-fifth as many earned doctorates as men. Currently there is only one woman United States Senator, and no female Supreme Court Justices. Women face significantly lower pension benefits than men for an identical number of years employed. Medical insurance benefits for pregnancy, abortion, and sterilization procedures for women are typically either absent or insufficient. Working women can expect to work as hard, for less pay and fewer retirement and fringe benefits, in more of the menial occupations, than men.

But what of the cost to men? The death rate for men at forty in the United States is approximately twice that for women at the same age. A wife attains rights to her husband's social security benefits after his death; a husband, unless his wife was the sole support of the family, does not receive his wife's benefits at her death. Men represent less than seven percent of the registered nurses in the United States. They represent fewer than forty percent of the teachers at the high school and grade school levels. The cost to men in emotional terms of the deprivation of the role as nurturer to children, and the cost in physical terms of having to bear the weight of masculine stoicism in the face of stress, can only be imagined.

The effects of assumptions derived from gender identity begin almost at birth and carry on until death. A newborn baby is swaddled in a blanket of the appropriate hue of pink or blue, given the appropriate name, and then subjected to a stream of sex-role stereotyping that ranges from the early admonition, "big boys don't cry," to the inability of the newly-retired male to find a meaningful role for himself because his social identity and gratification were based on the rewards of his job. Men and women pay dearly for the privileges of gender identity. Women must be foolish and helpless and need to be protected. In return for her services as a wife and mother, the woman can expect life-long economic security, even if her role as wife is terminated. Men must, in return for the privilege of being king of the manse, display continued strength and fortitude, never weakening, certainly never crying. How weary these roles become, and how wasteful.

The Feminist Perspective. The ardent feminist would point to the thousands of years of discrimination and exploitation that women have endured. The need to reorganize social structures around less paternalistic lines is emphasized. The value that society places on mothering and nurturing must be increased. Likewise, the obstacles that prevent women from gaining access to the realms of power and prestige need to be removed. The basic argument of the feminists is that the current sexist *status quo* is based upon the false assumption that women are weaker and less capable than men.

The argument that women are subject to the hormonal storms associated with menstruation and menopause can be answered by the equally compelling fact that men experience similar hormonal cycles associated with androgen production, and that these cycles may even be dangerous to the future of human survival if, as some physiologists have posited, increases in androgen flow correspond with increased needs for aggression on the part of the male. One old objection to a woman President was, "Who would want her to make a decision on whether or not to go to war when she has her period?" The feminist could reply that past wars may have been the result of excess androgen meeting insufficient intellect, and that the power decisions are more safely placed in the hands of the female of the species, as she is not subject to the whims of hormonally-induced aggression!

The assertion that the nurturance women have provided has been a viable force in maintaining human life, and that it has gone undervalued and unrecognized, is correct. The thought that "the hand that rocks the cradle rules the world" takes on new significance when considered in light of developmental theory that postulates the first few years of life as the most significant for a child's psychological formation. The powerful influence of women from behind the scenes has long been recognized. Feminists would simply point out that society should remove the façade and allow the ladies into the forefront of authority.

The state of human existence is such that the most pressing problems facing humankind are *man*made. Whether we review the impact of industrialization on the environment, the problems of overpopulation, hunger, and overcrowding, or the burgeoning threat of global conflict, the hand of man can be seen as most destructive. Perhaps it is time that the hand of woman be given a shot at running things. Can it be that the heart that rears children will be less likely to allow their eventual destruction through war?

Feminists would also point out that the probable motivation for much of the discrimination against women has deep historical roots in man's ignorance and fears of women. To the prehistoric man the woman's mystical monthly flow and her ability to produce offspring must have evoked a bit of awe and fear. Can it be that men needed to subdue women because of this fear? Or was it simply envy of women's creative and nurturing role? Speculation on the topic can lead to many interesting observations.

The origins and motivations for the historical evolution of the current pervasive discrimination against women will always remain open to speculation. The result, however, is irrefutable: women have less power and money than men; women derive the majority of their economic and social status from their association with men; and women are likely to be defined as someone's daughter, wife, or mother, and to have their income and social position attached to this role. From the acquisition of name to the recognition of title, women have the second place option only. How do you address a female physician and her non-physician husband? As Doctor and Mr. Smith? At marriage a woman even loses the right to her first name, becoming Mrs. Masculine Surname. The message of social posturing is quite clear: the value is attached to the male, and the female is relegated to the status of chattel; the change of name represents a change of ownership.

Feminism calls for the redressing of these myriad grievances by the enactment of legal and social reforms that would seek to liberate men and women from the stereotyped gender roles to which they have been assigned. It seeks to dismantle employment and educational barriers, and to restructure current laws and regulations to allow women an equal opportunity to work. A new look at family roles, with increased emphasis on the mutuality of responsibility for domestic tasks and the reciprocal rewards of parenthood, is urged. The liberation of men from the lifelong responsibility of financial support of women simply because a women is or was a wife is also sought. And concommitantly, if women are to release their stranglehold on the earnings of men, they must be allowed to pursue their own professions and working roles.

The changes sought by the proponents of a more androgenous social structure are sweeping. The benefits promised are enticing. The cost of adherence to the old *status quo* of sexism is disastrous. Feminists would remind us of the dire plight in which most of the world now exists and would offer their alterations in gender roles and social structure as a viable alternative to more of the same strategies that brought us to the brink of the abyss. Examination of a feminist perspective leads to the realization that certainly gender has a pervasive influence on one's lifestyle. Whether or not that influence is good, bad, or indifferent is a matter of experience and perspective.

The Opposition's Arguments. The supporter of the *status quo* must also be heard and evaluated. Sweeping changes in the social system carry threats of undetermined origin. Each of the great developments of human history, regardless of value, have exacted a price for the progress made. Air pollution was the result of industrialization. Improved and efficient health care is giving us overpopulation and geriatric problems. Even the benefits derived from aerosol deodorants and hairsprays are having an environmental impact. So for all the purported benefits espoused by feminists who seek to restructure the current social system, what are the costs to be exacted from our beleaguered social systems? Will an influx of women into the professions and trades deprive others of their livelihood? Will changes in the traditional structure of the family adversely affect the growth and development of children and give us a generation of psychotics? Can women indeed bear up under the stress of the real world that men have so valiantly endured? What will be the quality of decision-making when decisions are made by a female brain? Life as we know it is founded on the nuclear family. Do we want to tamper with the very essence of modern society, a society that despite its faults is still the most accomplished and comfortable in the annals of human history? In short, why tamper with a good thing when the results are so unpredictable?

Keeping An Open Mind. The feminist perspective is appealing. It does seem unfair and unwise to deny an individual the opportunity to make significant contributions to any realm of life solely on the basis of gender. The waste of human talent is deplorable and offends one's sense of fair play. But will an alteration in the traditional gender roles assigned to men and women create unseen destructive side effects in the social fabric? And is it fair to ask contemporary men to redress the grievances of women that are attributable to the acts of our ancestors? The professor who is denied tenure because of a quota system that seeks to promote the advancement of women is no less offended than the female professor who is denied tenure on the basis of gender. In either case, the experience can be bitter.

The assertion by the advocates of the *status quo* that women are in some way less capable than men is patently ridiculous. Yet the notion that society must take drastic and immediate steps to redress thousands of years of discrimination is equally foolhardy. Change is always too rapid for some and much too slow for others.

This is a topic upon which it is difficult to stay neutral. The adage, "if you're not part of the solution, you're part of the problem," is most appropriate. Your personal experiences, life aspirations, and familial relationships will shape the way in which you approach this topic of controversy. There are neither easy questions nor easy answers, just the need to explore.

Impact of Sexism on Health Care. The effect of sexism on health care must be examined from two perspectives: that of the providers of care and that of the consumers of care. Each experiences a unique and noteworthy effect of sexism within the health care arena.

Consumer Perspective. The female patient is confronted with a health care system in which the majority of the care givers are female, but in which the ultimate decisions about rendering care are made by males. The perceptions that the male health professionals have about the innate attributes of males and of females color the decisions that are made about health care. It is frequently assumed that women are less tolerant of pain than men, that women are more prone to psychosomatic illness, and that female patients are more likely to exaggerate the extent or severity of their symptoms. Thus the complaints of female patients are less realistically evaluated than the complaints of male patients. Women are more likely to be referred for psychiatric assistance before the physiological basis of symptoms is completely explored. Female patients are more likely to have their requests for assistance postponed. Thus female patients are more likely to pay for their gender through postponement of care, inadequate care, underevaluation of their personal accounts of symptoms, and a host of other factors that can be summarized as less-than-equal care. The problems encountered by women patients are compounded by the fact that they are most frequently dealing with male physicians. The usual communications patterns between men and women find women in an inequitable role. The rare female patient who is able to meet her male physician as an equal is likely to be viewed by him as aggressive and pushy, and modification in care tendered can be expected.

The problems encountered by women patients are no less great when dealing with other women health professionals. The professionals are educated along the male model of stereotypic behavior. Thus the female nurse is as likely to perceive the female patient as a malingerer as is the male physician. Added to the stereotypic expectations of female patients by female and male health professionals are the difficulties encountered in relationships among women—whether professional to patient, or professional to professional. Women are socialized to value youth and beauty, and to promote these attributes in an effort to win the hand in marriage of an economically prosperous male; thus, competitiveness is naturally induced between women. Each woman can see in another the potential rival for the attention of surrounding males. Age, marriage, and education do not seem to fully block the effect of this bit of early childhood learning. Women patients are likely to be perceived as, and perceive others as, rivals for the attention of male health professionals. The nursing staff of a hospital, whose communication with physicians follows closely the prevalent stereotypical pattern, are not likely to perceive the attention given to female patients as anything less than a threat to their own status as females. The competition among women encouraged by society in general spills over into the health care realm and adversely affects patient care.

Validation of the discriminatory effect of sexism on the quality of health care given to female patients can be accomplished in several ways. Select a medical textbook on gynecology and review passages dealing with reproduction and childrearing. Most contain blatantly sexist assumptions promulgated as fact, such as assertions that women are by their mothering nature more passive, or that women naturally assume a more submissive role in sexuality. Leafing through the pages of almost any medical journal will illustrate the degree to which women have been depicted as more prone to psychoneurotic symptoms and complaints. Advertisements for tranquilizers and sedatives are much more likely to depict an overwrought or menopausal female seeking the assistance of an omnipotent male physician. Rarely does one view a drug ad depicting a male executive soliciting medical assistance from a competent female physician.

Even the mass media emphasize the appropriate roles of males and females in the health care system. Television depicts the competent, cool doctor as male, and frequently depicts the hysterical and neurotic patient as female. Magazines demonstrate the need for all methods of control and remedy for the natural functions of the female body—from the requirement that women use "personal hygiene deodorant sprays," to the creation of a need for special vitamins and pain relievers "because you're a woman." The message that women are more frail, less tolerant of illness and pain, and in need of more medical intervention is carried wherever one surveys mass media.

Male patients are not much more fortunate in their encounters with the health care system. True, their complaints of discomfort and pain are more likely to be seriously evaluated, and the communications between male patient and male physician are not hindered by the stereotypical assumptions relating to women. Yet male patients labor under the belief that somehow they are stronger and more stoic, and thus should not be sick in the first place! The socialized gender-appropriate role for men requires that they be strong, active breadwinners. Expressions of weakness are relegated to women. When ill, one must assume a passive lifestyle, accept the assistance of others, and admit vulnerability to illness. None of the characteristics of this role are compatible with male gender role-appropriate behavior. The ill male is forced either to suffer in silence, or to disclaim the normal male role and accept a less masculine alternative. Even the simple act of admitting pain and requesting pain relief is fraught with emasculating effects. The male patient is already relegated to a role diminished from that of the usual male; add to this the insult of acceptance of the ministrations and directions of the female nursing staff, and the degree of humiliation afforded the male patient is great indeed. Man bears a heavy burden when fulfilling the masculine role mandates.

Provider Prospective. Women health care professionals are faced with a unique set of problems generated by the effect of sexism on the health care system. They are effectively placed in a no-win situation.

They must choose either to be an autonomous professional with the concommitant loss of feminity, or to accept the traditional female role and decline the mantle of professionalism. The characteristics of professionalism and the attributes of the gender-appropriate role for women are mutually exclusive; they cannot coexist. Women are to be passive, dependent, and weak. Professionals are accountable, competent, and strong. Attainment of one role precludes successful fulfillment of the other. What a trap! Failure in one or the other is assured.

L. I. Stein, in an article, "The Doctor-Nurse Game," nicely summarizes the degree of deception and subterfuge that normally undergirds physician/nurse communications.[11] The nurse, although possibly more knowledgeable about some aspects of patient care than the physician, must feign ignorance to prevent the possibility of her threatening the physician's self-concept of autonomy. Nurses who fail to learn or play this game are penalized by either unfavorable reports by physicians to nurse supervisors or by the inability to obtain physician cooperation in meeting patient care requirements—a result that also penalizes and perhaps even endangers patient care.

Nurses learn early and well not to appear to be more knowledgeable or competent than physicians, their acknowledged superiors in the hierarchy of health care. Conversely, nurses soon learn that urine flows downhill, and that there are a host of downhill occupants beneath the stature of the nurse, one of whom is the patient. Thus the nurse who is made to feel incompetent and frustrated in her interactions with the superior, more knowledgeable physician may play the game of one-upmanship on the unsuspecting patient or on subordinate nursing personnel. It becomes a long, unhappy chain of frustration, as each party to the system seeks to regain self-image through the diminution of the person one step down. Unfortunately, the patient is too often the last rung on the ladder; hence, the target of health care also becomes the target of health practitioners' frustration.

Female physicians, few though they may be, pay a dear price for their entrance to the heady atmosphere of power play. The process of medical education requires allegiance to the form and content of the medical school curriculum, including the acceptance as truth of the assumptions concerning the inherent weakness and vulnerability of the female. The woman doctor survives an education loaded with messages about her own inferiority. The system is also replete with institutionalized prejudice. Until recent federal regulations were enacted, many medical schools maintained a quota for women of five percent of any

11. Stein, L. I. "The Doctor-Nurse Game," *Archives of General Psychiatry*, Vol. 16, 1967, pp. 699–703.

one medical class. The thought was to not squander this precious education on too many women, because most women would shortly marry, leave the profession for motherhood, and let their medical skills atrophy. Even with the effect of equal educational opportunity legislation, women still comprise less than twenty percent of most medical school classes. Once inside the halls of ivy, women are the focus of a barrage of subtle and obvious forms of discrimination. From the exhausting student clinical schedule that precludes attention to family responsibilities to the actual refusal of some senior medical mentors to instruct female physicians, women face a host of obstacles to the completion of their education which are not experienced by their male colleagues.

Women who are able to survive the barrage of ammunition intentionally and unintentionally thrown at them in their pursuit of a medical education are forced to make a series of sacrifices and adjustments. Frequently, the first attribute to go is that of any semblance of allegiance to feelings of feminism. It is difficult to survive any form of professional education without modeling oneself after one's teachers. The term *professor* is derived from the verb *profess*, to proselytize a position or philosophy. If medical textbooks and curricula assert the vulnerability and weakness of women, and women students are placed in positions that reward modeling of the educational stance presented, then it is natural that the female medical student will be forced either to accept the authority of her mentors on the subject, or to rebel and accept the consequences of confronting authority. The role of student is loaded with messages about authority and power. Medical school, a rarified atmosphere when one finally gains admittance, is not easily abandoned once entered. Neither the rewards accrued to those who graduate and practice, nor the efforts that admission to medical school indicate in terms of academic achievement and financial sacrifice, are to be easily discarded. The motivation to succeed by copying the symbols of success is great; the risks of rebellion are equally great. Women in medical school unconsciously modify both personal behavior and self-image to align their entrance to the medical realm and its sexist, stereotypical view of femininity. The sacrifice may be great for a woman who is sensitive to the plight of others.

Once the female medical student has learned to live with the *status quo*, subverting femininity to meet male role model requisites, and viewing female patients from the same frame of reference as male professorial authorities, the die is cast for future behavior and attitudes. It is not uncommon to hear the complaints of nurses that female physicians are more demanding and degrading than their male colleagues. It is permissible for a male physician to excuse the female nurse for her shortcomings, to try to protect and lead her through the maze of medical miracles. Such a protective, paternalistic behavior on the part of a female physician would be inappropriate and might even be misread as symbolic of masculinization, with lesbian overtones.

If a physician is a feminist, the difficulties of surviving the rigors of medical education are multiplied. If she accepts the sexist view that medical education purveys, she must acknowledge her own inferiority to her male colleagues. Once graduated and licensed, she must choose between the role of authoritarian medical doctor with no option for paternalistic relationships with subordinate staff, or she may attempt to establish colleagial relationships with female health professionals—with the attendant risk of perception as a weak sister, probably better suited to nursing, in the eyes of her male peers.

It is simply impossible to be both a feminist and a physician without expending an enormous amount of personal energy and risking professional repercussions. Such a waste of time and talent is indeed unfortunate.

But what of the male caught in this sexist system of medical education? We've examined a medical education system that presents an image of women as weaker, more vulnerable, and less physiologically sound. The structure of such education presents the male medical student with reinforcement for all previous learning presenting sexist stereotypes. Alternative models of feminine existence are simply not available. The male student soon learns to perpetuate the traditional view of women, and to treat the patient on the basis of stereotype, rather than individual characteristics. This form of medical care cannot be very gratifying to deliver, much less to receive.

The male medical student and doctor are put in a role of double jeopardy. Not only are they male in a system that requires that men be stoic, strong, and decisive, but they are physicians, another role that demands that its occupant be a paragon of strength and authority. It must be debilitating to constantly shoulder the burdens of total omnipotence. The male physician is frequently caught in the role of requiring information from subordinate female medical personnel, yet is ill-equipped to ask for help or information when schooled to demand consistent perfection of himself. It is hard to ask the nurse's opinion, if both one's self-image and one's education have ingrained an attitude that the role and intellect of the nurse must be inferior to the role and intellect of the physician. The cost in crucial information to the physician is sometimes disastrous for patient care. The wear and tear on the psyche and physiology of the male physician from the maintenance of a continuous facade of complete competence and coolness must also be phenomenal. Yet will we allow our physicians to turn to other health professionals for advice, support, or even companionship in the delivery of health care?

If the male physician pays a price for sexism, the male nurse is twice the casualty. Male nurses are confronted with continuous questions regarding their ability to assume the "role of nurse" and, when they successfully achieve this role, are confronted with aspersions upon their masculinity. For if the female physician is viewed with a jaundiced eye, the male nurse is even more suspect.

I recall a conversation with an extremely well-respected hospital administrator regarding the clinical placement of nursing students. He assured me that there would be ample opportunity for students to rotate through all of the services provided by the hospital, particularly for the male nurses to experience emergency room care and for the female students to affiliate in labor, delivery, and postpartum care. When questioned about his placement concepts, he responded that any male in nursing is a frustrated physician, and thus would enjoy the decisive atmosphere of emergency nursing, whereas women were drawn to nursing because of their innate motherly qualities. Furthermore, he stated his belief that all male nurses were homosexuals. This represents, in an extreme degree, many of the assumptions and beliefs about men who enter nursing. Medical technologists, physical therapists, and other allied health professionals are only slightly less suspect. The question is always, "Why would a man choose a nurturing career if the attributes of nurturance are only naturally found in the female?"

Men who do succeed in challenging and surmounting the sexist barriers confronting them when entering the career of nursing are rewarded for their gender in one way in which their female colleagues are not. A man in nursing is much more likely to be perceived as a leader or teacher, or in other authoritarian roles, than is a woman. Although men comprise less than seven percent of all registered nurses, it is estimated that they comprise fifteen percent of registered nurse administrators. When gaining entrance to the profession, they are advanced along assumptions of maleness even in the female world! Their colleagues are more likely to tolerate assertive behavior and the attributes of leadership from a male than from a female; thus, men in nursing are able to move up the supervisory ladder more rapidly than their female peers of equal education and competence.

Analysis

The cost of sexism to health care is great. It detracts from the individualization and quality of client care. It limits and stunts the potential contribution of health care providers. The assumption of appropriate behavior and attributes on the basis of gender prevents health consumers and health professionals alike from realizing their true roles and contributions to and benefits from the health care system. From the preponderance of one gender over another in the different professions, to the view that men must be stoic and bear pain and women must be fragile and may receive pain relief, the effects of sexist stereotyping are persuasive and unacceptable.

Summary. We have taken a rather close look at the issue of sexism and its impact on health care and health professionals. Yet the issue of sexism, although possibly more closely related to health care than some of the other isms, is no different from any other form of prejudice. The limitation of a person by pigeonholing according to characteristics other than capabilities and capacities is not only unfair: it's wasteful.

We are at a time in human existence when neither society nor the individual can afford the luxury that prejudice and discrimination represent. We require the full participation of all human potential if the huge problems which face the whole of humanity are to be effectively resolved. Eliminating or reducing the contribution of one or more groups of people is a mistake and a moral outrage.

EXOTIC TO MUNDANE: A SHORT TRIP

Talk of genetic engineering, cryogenics, and behavior programming stimulates images appropriate to science fiction novels. Our contemporary world seems to be a far cry from these technologies of the imagination. However, it is an extremely short trip from today to tomorrow, and the speed with which the distance is traversed is always increasing.

Pacemakers, amniocentesis, psychoactive medications, and transplants were all, at one time, figments of imagination. Today they are commonplace medical technology. The process of transforming the idea to the reality occurred within the last quarter-century.

When scientists first postulated the possibility of detecting fetal abnormalities well before term of pregnancy, little public or professional discussion ensued. Blind acceptance of this latest of medical miracles was the rule. People welcomed the theoretical postulate in the misdirected belief that widespread implementation capability was not within the grasp of the immediate future. So the technological capability was developed without much scrutiny of the ethical or social ramifications. There was a false sense of security that such a procedure would be a long time in coming. Suddenly the research was complete, the capacity for implementation widespread, and the eagerness of every medical center to add this procedure to its laundry list of services was tremendous. Abortion laws were drastically revised concomitantly with the development of amniocentesis (although law revision was certainly not a result of the development of the procedure). Suddenly a complex ethical dilemma burst upon the medical world. We had the capacity to predict and to preclude the birth of a child with certain detectable genetic anomalies.

The discovery that the information gleaned from amniotic fluid could provide a base for the decision to terminate a pregnancy created a crisis in the realm of health care. Tremendous debates grew around such issues as revealing the gender of the fetus to parents. The concern focused on the possible decision to abort a pregnancy if the fetus were not of the desired sex. Additional debate centered on the implications of informing parents of a malformed fetus in cases where elective abortion was not a moral or economic option. Should parents be given time to prepare or is this placing another stress on an already stressed life stage? The degree of liability of personnel completing amniotic withdrawal for procedural safety and the implication of results were also examined. Some attention was even focused on the legal ramifications inherent in revealing genetic disease probability, should the fetus/infant not display the defect upon abortion/birth.

All of these complex ethical and legal questions were debated by the health professions and the general public after the technological capacity and widespread capability to perform amniocentesis were developed. Very few of these issues were broached during the research phase of the technology. While the scientific and technological problems were resolved, the social, moral, and legal issues were largely ignored. Why?

Alvin Toffler in his classic book, *Future Shock,* discusses the concept of cultural lag.[12] Cultural lag is the gap between technological development and society's ability to cope with development in ethical and legal dimensions.

Nowhere is the reality of cultural lag more evident than in the implementation of medical wizardry. The ability to research, design, and institute new mechanically exotic medical regimens far outstrips the readiness to examine the ethical and legal implications of such regimens. The result is that we leap without looking.

Enthusiastic, unquestioning acceptance and institutionalization of the results of medical research is the result of our reluctance to examine the ethical and legal dimensions of such research. The product is a harvest of legal problems and ethical dilemmas experienced after implementation, and attempts are made to repair the system after the damage is done.

---

12. Toffler, Alvin. *Future Shock.* New York: Random House, 1970.

We fail to realize the irresistible force of change, the inevitable development of tomorrow's technology from today's dreaming, and the need to *plan* change, evaluate alternatives, predict impact, and attempt to orient our thinking towards the future. We are a society of pragmatists in terms of ethics and law; we merely react to change. But we are a society of futurists in terms of research and technology, seeking new directions and placing fiscal and intellectual priority on these endeavors. The mismatch of today's ethical and legal codes with tomorrow's technology is discordant, and produces legal, ethical, and social Gordian knots such as currently experienced in abortion and euthanasia.

Certainly it would be foolish to lower the priority given to research and application. The mismatch is *not* productively resolved by diminishing one set of efforts. Rather, a new effort to examine the social and ethical ramifications of research trends and proposed innovations is needed. Much of what will be real in the world of medicine tomorrow is already predictable today. Now is the time for audiences that these technologies will influence to engage in the debate.

After-the-fact shock, disbelief, or moral outrage are counterproductive and inefficient, and lead to a general societal questioning of the role of science and the trustworthiness of the health professions. Much of the discord could be prevented by active scrutiny of research and predictions of such dilemmas before the fact.

Subduing or controlling scientific inquiry will merely compound current human problems. The headlong rush to develop and implement new technologies will only create new and unforeseen problems while attempting to ameliorate old ones. A reasoned scrutiny of research thrusts in an attempt to predict concomitant ethical, legal, and social impacts will help direct change in more controlled directions.

What does this mean to the practitioner of nursing, or, for that matter, to any other health professional? Certainly nurses, medical technologists, respiratory therapists, and the other allied health practitioners have little input or control over the research thrusts of science. Yet the latest in research efforts are announced and accorded grand publicity well before they are ready for implementation and widespread distribution.

Professional and lay journals continually report news of scientific discoveries and inventions. What is required is the practitioner's increased sensitivity to such news and awareness of the implications such inventions carry. Each of us is able to define our own role and function. When we have done this, we can decide the impact of a given change on our practice, and then predict problems, concerns, and dilemmas arising from the conflict of technology with legal and ethical standards. We must then try to share our concerns with our professional colleagues and the general public. Free debate and close scrutiny can help prepare us for the impact of change and help us take steps to prevent conflicts.

For example, it is predictable that current scientific inquiry will lead to sophisticated techniques of behavior control. Pharmaceutical and possibly microelectronic agents will make directed personality change possible. The chronically depressed, suicidal, or aggressive individual will be accorded opportunities to exhibit more socially acceptable and personally gratifying behaviors. Currently available mood elevants, antidepressants, and even refined electroconvulsive therapy are simple forerunners of coming psychopharmaceutical and electronic advances. Such developments are predictable and certainly desirable in light of the personal tragedy and social cost of depressive or aggressive behavior.

However, sophisticated behavior control options will also initiate social, legal, and ethical problems. Moreover, the opportunity for abuse of such power will be readily available if sufficient control mechanisms are not concurrently implemented with technology development. The benefits of the advance may well be offset by costs in terms of freedom, control, and morality.

Now is the time to dream, postulate, plan, and speculate about the impact of this technology on the real world. Moreover, such speculation should derive not only from ethicists, theoreticians, and researchers, but also from the rank and file of the health professionals whose efforts and skills will implement behavior control technologies.

The practicing psychiatric nurses can assess the impact of behavior control technology for practice within this realm. The ethical and legal questions that arise are multiple and complex. For instance, who is legally and ethically responsible for the failure of the technology when such failure produces personal or social damage—the physician who prescribed it, the nurse who administered it, or the company who developed it? If a sophisticated anti-depressant were to be developed that inhibits suicidal behavior, and if this medication were administered to a suicidal patient who is pronounced cured, but then commits suicide—who is liable? Who is responsible? Who bears the financial and professional consequences of this failure? Do we, indeed, have an ethical or legal right to thwart suicide? Do the health professions have either ethical or legal jurisdiction over interferences in this person's life? These are complex issues that derive directly from the practice application of technological innovation.

Because many of the complications, dilemmas, and implications of research innovation derive from practical application of theoretical discovery, it is mandatory that practitioners involve themselves in scrutiny of the future. Scientists equipped with experimental machinery and theoretical knowledge are prepared to do what they do best—research.

Practitioners are also prepared to do what they do best—practice. How can we demand practice sensitivity from theoreticians and researchers, any more than we expect theoretical research from practitioners?

The prediction and prevention of ethical/legal disasters from research application in health care is a mutual responsibility for all involved. Each participant in the health care industry has an obligation to evaluate potential change and prepare to meet change-induced challenges. The failure to fulfill this obligation will result in two potentially catastrophic results.

First, the poverty of planning in the implementation of change produces incalculable stress and strain on the economic and social capacity of health care providers and consumers. The impact of innovation is not predicted, and is therefore relatively uncontrolled and comes as an after-effect or shock wave. Much of the energy expended reacting to the shock wave could be conserved for more constructive tasks. The headlong rush for each and every hospital to own a CAT (computerized axial tomography) scanner resulted in great economic waste, duplication of services, and misdirection of personnel and monetary resources from other equally justifiable priorities. Such waste has resulted in public outcry and renewed attempts at government intervention aimed at health care cost containment. The planning gap wasted precious professional resources.

Secondly, such planning failure also results in loss of professional reputation and public trust in the health care system. Each time innovation is greeted with enthusiasm and then confusion, the public sees another reason to view the health care industry and its band of professionals with a jaundiced eye. Our seeming inability to manage planned change invites intervention, regulation, and additional bureaucratic overlays on the already complex administrative network of health care. Duplication of services with resultant gaps in other priority need areas was one of the motivational rationales for the drafting and implementation of the current Health Systems Agency statutes (composed of both provider and consumer representatives). These organizations are empowered to review and approve proposals for health facility expansion, development, major equipment acquisition, and remodeling.

The implementation of HSA regulation activities, although possibly not an adverse influence, puts into effect another time-, energy-, and resource-consuming process to hamper the ability of the health system to respond to perceived change needs. This step exists because the health system itself was incapable of coping effectively with change. Remember, too, that the health system is not some brick and mortar entity. It is all health care providers—from technician to neurosurgeon, administrator to admitting clerk. The quality of health care and the profession's capacity to predict and cope with change is directly dependent upon the abilities of the rank and file practitioner to predict and cope with change.

It is an exceedingly short time before tomorrow is today. Coping with change, predicting ethical, legal, and social consequences of innovation—these are the responsibilities of all members of the health professions. Failure to meet this responsibility can only result in renewed efforts at public control of health care and increased mistrust of professional credibility. The competence of health care professionals, I believe, is sufficient to meet this challenge.

Group Grope

In this exercise you are to assemble a small group of fellow learners (10–15) and complete the role-playing situations as given. The objective of the role-playing situations is for each of the participants to view the variety of perspectives that abound when evaluating any of the complex legal/ethical dilemmas that currently confront health care delivery. The individual assuming an assigned role is to defend the position of that character in the scenario. The moderator informs the observers of the situation presented and at the close of the role playing, leads a general group discussion.

Case I. Profit *The moderator presents the following scenario to the group:*

A young nursing student is having low back pain and seeks assistance from a young, struggling family practice physician; the resultant fee for his services is $50.00. Both the student and the physician are caught by the economics of the times. Also caught is a young registered nurse in the same community, the sole support of two children, who receives notification that her insurance premiums have been increased due to the rising medical costs in her area. All three are justified in complaining, or aren't they?

Nursing student: You are a financially struggling, academically successful nursing student in your last semester of studies. You have been experiencing low back pain and some leg numbness. As the sensations have worsened you have sought assistance from your new family physician. After a brief examination he has diagnosed your ailment as muscle strain and prescribed muscle relaxants and bedrest. Upon leaving the office you are presented with a bill of $50.00 for the office visit. You are aghast, make a feeble excuse concerning future payment and stagger out the door. How do you feel about this fee for the service rendered? Will you pay the bill? If not, why not? What are your rationale?

Physician: You are a young struggling family physician. You completed medical school by virtue of a series of loans, family assistance and frugal living. The cost of initiating your fledgling practice was born through a high interest bank loan that you are currently attempting to pay off, along with school-related debts. Your years of internship and residency were spent supporting your wife and young children on the meager salary afforded to house staff. Now you've succeeded in opening the small office you had hoped for. The cost of maintaining the office—including receptionist, nurse, liability insurance, medical equipment, and supplies—is approximately $75,000 per year. In addition to your current financial obligations and the reimbursement of past educational debts, you are now ready; and acknowledge that you feel yourself deserving, for some of the amenities which have been previously denied to you and your family. How do you view your rights to financial compensation for your services? What will you do when a patient who apparently can pay doesn't pay? Who is responsible for the expensive commodity health care has become? What do you believe can be done to more equitably distribute the costs of health care, including the costs of medical education?

Nurse: You are the honest, hard-working breadwinner of a small family. Your salary of $15,000 per year as a registered nurse supports you and your two small children in modest comfort but without luxury. In your mail you received notification that your family's health insurance, already a hefty monthly fee of $75.00, has been increased to $90.00 per month. The rationale included with the notification states that the increase is necessitated by the increased cost of health care services in your area. How do you feel about the increment? Is it justified? Who should bear the cost of health care? Are you carrying an unfair burden in comparison with other consumers? What are you going to do about the situation?

Discussion Questions There are many viewpoints to be considered in an attempt to analyze the current high cost of health care. Which of these participants is most responsible for increasing the cost of care? Is anyone responsible? What can be done to alleviate the dilemma presented for the nursing student, for the physician, for the young nurse? If federally funded supports are provided to any of these actors, who will ultimately foot this bill? If no federal controls or assistance is supplied what will the effect on health care costs and quality be? Are there any solutions to this dilemma?

Case II. Sane/Insane Moderator: Present the following scenario to the group. Sue is a premed student in a highly competitive college class; she is leading all other students in the race to earn entrance to the medical school. Several students, hoping to thwart her success, have arranged to pass an erroneous rumor to her concerning a report of suspected cheating to be filed by a professor. Sue is extremely competitive and very high strung concerning her academic standing. Upon hearing of the alleged report she runs to the professor's office, threatens him and begins to behave violently. The shocked professor, oblivious to the circumstances surrounding Sue's outburst, contacts the campus police who remove Sue to a psychiatric facility for observation while notifying her parents of her status.

Sue: You are a young college student enrolled in premed studies. You are a high achiever having received excellent grades until this time. You recognize that entrance to your chosen medical school is dependent upon your continued achievement of excellent marks. You are notified by another student that your chemistry professor suspects you of cheating and intends to report you for this alleged offense, having you dismissed from the college. In a fit of rage, you confront the professor, threaten to "tear him limb from limb" and proceed to violently pound his desktop and scatter papers around his office. The campus police are called and you are removed to the local psychiatric facility where you are kept waiting pending the notification of the campus authorities and your family. What is your response to the episode? What does this mean to your future, even if the cheating allegations aren't substantiated? What do you think of the label you now wear of having received psychiatric treatment in an emergency situation?

Professor: You are a professor of chemistry, quietly seated at your desk grading papers when one of your better students in the organic chemistry class approaches your office. She enters the office and begins to threaten you, pounding her fists on your desk, and shoving the papers from your desk to the floor. You contact the campus police saying "a student has gone berserk in my office! Please come remove her before she hurts either herself or me!" The police respond, removing the girl to a psychiatric facility for the care she so obviously needs. What is your response to the situation? To the knowledge that the student's hospitalization for psychiatric care may adversely affect her later medical school admissability?

Roommate: You are roommate to a highly successful premed student. You become aware that some of her companion students are attempting to dupe her into believing that her academic future is in jeopardy. The ruse works and you later learn of her hospitalization for the results of her outburst in the chemistry professor's office. Knowing that the hoax was deliberately perpetrated with the intent of eliminating your roommate from grade competition, and knowing who the participating students are, what do you do and why?

Discussion Questions: There are many viewpoints in attempting to analyze the given scenario. The issue of honesty among the classmates arranging for this bit of academic subterfuge is a central question, not only from the simple assessment of whether or not the competition is sufficient rationale to explain the undue pressure that might bring lucid students to the point of committing an irresponsible act but also from the perspective of evaluating the decision-making base of these students when faced with later pressure situations in their medical careers. One must also evaluate the degree to which psychiatric care represents a stigma in contemporary society. The admission of the student to a psych unit may preclude her successful medical school enrollment. What point does this make about the social view of those who may require some form of psychiatric services? Are there any strategies that may redress the grievance done this student, or did this episode reveal an underlying unstable personality, thus giving support to her later unsuitability for the medical profession?

Case III. Abortion The moderator presents the following scenario to the group: A young female college student is currently completing the third year of her four-year radiologic technology curriculum. She lives with her fiancé, a fourth-year premed student. They plan to marry after she is able to support the expense of his medical education with her professional employment in health care. She has conscientiously avoided the problem of pregnancy by using a variety of contraceptive devices—except oral contraceptives which are contraindicated by her familial history of breast cancer. Lately, she is feeling quite tired, occasionally nauseous, and has experienced amenorrhea. A visit to the health center confirms her suspicions of pregnancy. The clinic physician attempts to discuss her alternatives, including abortion, marriage and motherhood, unwed motherhood, completing the pregnancy, and placing the child for adoption.

Woman Student: After learning that you are pregnant with the child of your fiancé you must consider your options. Financial and educational complications make this a most difficult time to consider motherhood, but you are also aware of the moral implications involved in aborting a pregnancy. You are also aware that during the last semester, not knowing of your pregnancy, you were in many radiological clinics as a student. You are concerned about the potential consequences of this exposure to the fetus should you choose to complete the pregnancy.

Male student: After learning that your fiancée is pregnant, you must consider your options. You had a religious upbringing that valued highly the life of the unborn child, inculcating a rigorous negative judgment of those who choose abortion. But you are also concerned with the financial and emotional burden that the birth of a child would impose at precisely the time when you most need to be able to concentrate on your medical studies.

Discussion Questions: There are many viewpoints and factors affecting the consideration of this case. Who will bear the primary responsibility for the completion or termination of the pregnancy? What are the implications of the potential mother's exposure to deleterious influences on fetal development? What authority or role does the potential father have in this decision-making process? Does society have an investment in the outcome of this situation? Where do the final consequences for the decision fall?

Suggestions for Further Reading

Allen, Gina. "The ERA Won't Go Away—Nor Will Women." *The Humanist*, Vol. 38, No. 4 (July/August 1978), pp. 26–29.
> An ERA supporter, the author suggests that when ERA is passed, right of support for the homemaking spouse will be based not on sex, but on legal fact.

Ashley, Joann. *Hospitals, Paternalism, and the Role of the Nurse.* New York: Teachers College Press, 1976.
> Promotes the concept that feminist education must become an integral part of nursing education if sexism—which is dangerous to your health—is to be corrected.

Atkinson, Gary M. "Medical-Moral Dilemma: Crisis Care Vs. Health Maintenance." *Ethics and Medics,* Vol. 4, No. 2, (February 1979), p. 1.
> Explores societal policy of allocation of funds for public health through criteria of utilitarianism, distributive justice, and symbolic justice. Ethical and legal implications are discussed.

Atkinson, Gary M. "Medical-Moral Dilemma: Involuntary Hospitalization." *Ethics and Medics.* Vol. 3, No. 3, (May/June 1978), pp. 1–4.
> Provides care study analysis of involuntary hospitalization of a 30-year old housewife and mother by her husband, based on purported "mental illness." Discusses judicial and ethical implications.

Bandman, Elsie L. and Bertram Bandman. *Bioethics and Human Rights.* Boston: Little, Brown and Company, 1978.
> Fundamental theme is that the right to the enjoyment of good health is a necessity of life as vital as food, shelter, and safety. Health care is viewed as a consumer product. Functions of health providers and rights of consumers are discussed.

Bedau, Hugo Adam and Michael Zeik. "Case Studies in Bioethics—A Condemned Man's Last Wish: Organ Donation and a 'Meaningful' Death." *The Hastings Center Report,* Vol. 9, No. 1, (February 1979), pp. 16–17.
Examines issue of choosing one's own method of dying and new legal implications if "meaningful" death prospects are executed.

Black, Peter McL. "The Rationale for Psychosurgery." *The Humanist,* Vol. 38, No. 4 (July/August 1977) pp. 6, 8–9.
Discusses *pro* and *con* views on performing psychosurgery, defines psychosurgery, conclusion stated reveals techniques will not be banned provided psychosurgery remains a potentially important fact of contemporary medical care.

Brody, Baruch, Frederick S. Jaffe, Lisa Newton, and Margaret Steinfels. "Is Abortion a religious Issue?" *The Hastings Center Report.* Vol. 8, No. 4 (August 1978), pp. 12–17.
Examines religious, moral, and sociological issues, the irrelevance of religion in the abortion debate, and political implications involving related legislation regarding abortion issue.

Brody, Howard. *Ethical Decisions In Medicine.* Boston: Little, Brown and Co., 1976.
A self-instructional text focusing on the physician's interface with medical ethics. Contains a comprehensive review of medical-ethical dilemmas.

Bullough, Bonnie and Vern Bullough, eds. *Expanding Horizons for Nurses.* New York: Springer Publishing Company, 1977.
Examines recent legislative enactments and ethical problems involved in controversial clinical issues—abortion, homosexuality, and euthanasia—and the nursing profession's inherent need to stay abreast of change.

Carey, Lawrence, Steven E. Saltman, and Michael F. Epstein. *Medicine in a Changing Society.* St. Louis: The C. V. Mosby Company, 1972.
Reflection of medical students' and teachers' combined contribution in defining and exploring areas of change in the American health system, including the hospital and society, community health planning, and medicare/medicaid review.

Chapman, Elwood N. *Your Attitude is Showing—A Primer on Human Relations,* 3rd Ed., Chicago: Science Research Associates, Inc., 1977.
Basic developmental text incorporating understanding and sensitivity of individual human relations roles, emphasizing positive attitudes, self-motivation, and communication of "attitude" during the job-finding process.

Chenevert, Melodie. *Special Techniques in Assertiveness Training for Women in the Health Professions.* St. Louis: The C. V. Mosby Company, 1978.
Preparatory text of assertiveness training for women in health professions in order to challenge physicians, administrators, and other health care authorities to provide a responsible and responsive system.

Chesler, Phyllis. *Women and Madness.* New York: Doubleday and Company, Inc., 1972.

Examines mental health treatment of women based on biological definition rather than considerations of being human or adult. Attempts to view women and mental health through the eyes of a clinician.

Clark, Ann L. and Dyanne D. Affonso. *Childbearing: A Nursing Perspective.* Philadelphia: F. A. Davis Co., 1976.

Basic obstetrics text focusing on the concept of the maternity patient performing society's most essential task—childbearing. Explores psychosocial concepts, physiologic perspectives, and cultural impact of childbearing. Also examines neonatal physio-psychosocial concepts.

Claus, Karen E. and June T. Bailey. *Power and Influence in Health Care: A New Approach to Leadership.* St. Louis: The C. V. Mosby Company, 1977.

Discusses how nurses can utilize power for effective leadership. There are two major themes: The leader has capacity to use power for goal attainment; and the leader is one who takes actions, risks, and responsibility.

Cohn, Frederick and Charles E. Mortiz, eds. *Understanding Human Sexuality.* New Jersey: Prentice-Hall, Inc., 1974.

Introductory material for the non-medical layperson providing insight on current sexual practices; attempts to provide basic understanding of individual sexual motivations and needs.

Davis, Anne J. and Mila A. Aroskan. *Ethical Dilemmas and Nursing Practice.* New York: Appleton-Century-Crofts, 1978.

An introductory text for nursing's interface with ethics. Review of ethical systems and capsulization of common ethical dilemmas, including abortion, behavior control, and death and dying.

Deloughery, Grace L. and Kristine M. Gebbie. *Political Dynamics: Impact on Nurses and Nursing.* St. Louis: The C. V. Mosby Company, 1975.

Depicts the need for nurses to become committed to political action. Nurses, collectively and individually, need to participate in decision-making for social structure. Explores the political system, the nature of power, nurses' dilemmas, and preparation for action.

di la Cruz, Felix and Gerald D. La Veck, eds. *Human Sexuality and the Mentally Retarded.* New York: Brunner/Magel, Publishers, 1973.

Proceedings of "A Conference on Human Sexuality and the Mentally Retarded." Introduces concepts related to the sexual rights of the retarded, sex education for retarded, evolving social attitudes, and institutional trends.

Dolan, Edwin G. *TANSTAAFL—The Economic Strategy for Environmental Crisis.* New York: Holt, Rinehart and Winston, 1971.

Concise text for laymen, students, and professionals, encouraging ecological economics. Examines pollution, political economy of ecological action, the population explosion, and wilderness preservation.

Etzioni, Amitai. *Genetic Fix.* New York: Harper Colophon Books, 1973.
    Promotes citizen awareness of genetic research, genetic manipulation, and ethical decision-making regarding vital organ receiving. Examines eugenics, social change, and citizens' involvement.

Fulton, Robert, ed. *Death and Identity.* Bowie: The Charles Press Publishers, Inc., 1976.
    Examines meaning of death related to social structure, sociology of death, and psychosocial aspects of reactions to death by children, adults, the aged, and the terminally ill.

Gaylin, Willard, Travis Thompson, Robert Neville, and Michael Bayles. "Sterilization of the Retarded: In Whose Interest?" *The Hastings Center Report,* Vol. 8, No. 3. (June 1978), pp. 28–41.
    Thorough examination of sterilization of the mentally retarded with behavioral perspectives, philosophical arguments, and legal precedents.

Gornick, Vivian and Barbara K. Moran. *Woman in Sexist Society.* New York: Basic Books, Inc., 1971.
    Examines traditional view of woman as the subordinate member of the species. Analyzes woman in a host of contexts, including marriage, prostitution, society, and the work force. Discusses consumerism and feminism.

Gorovetz, Samuel, et al., eds. *Moral Problems In Medicine.* Englewood Cliffs: Prentice-Hall, 1976.
    Medical reference reviewing moral philosophy, physician-encountered dilemmas, legal concepts, and contemporary social problems. Collection of articles by leading scholars in each discipline. Advanced comprehension required.

Griffin, John Howard. *Black Like Me.* New York: Signet, 1964.
    Personal account of a white man living as a black in the South during the early 1960s. Startlingly sensitive revelation of the impact of racism, demonstrating pervasive effect of skin color on behavior.

Halleck, Seymour L. *The Politics of Therapy.* New York: Harper and Row, 1971.
    Suggests that psychiatry and community mental health influence the social fabric, thus giving psychiatry political meaning.

Heaton, Herbert. *Productivity in Service Organizations: Organizing For People.* New York: McGraw-Hill, 1977.
    An analysis of productivity in non-profit service institutions such as colleges or hospitals. Strongly suggests that evaluation for productivity measurement focus on service quality as opposed to quantifiable units if social goals are to be met.

Heide, Wilma Scott. "Nursing and Women's Liberation: A Parallel." *American Journal of Nursing,* Vol. 73, No. 5 (May 1973), pp. 824–27.
    A registered nurse proposes the idea that problems in nursing are symptoms of the oppression of women. She urges heightened consciousness of feminist and humanist issues.

Hepner, James O. and Donna M. Hepner. *The Health Strategy Game.* St. Louis: The C. V. Mosby Company, 1973.

Examines strategies and forces utilized by health care occupations to resist change in the health care delivery system professionally deterrent to efficient organization and management of consumer health care delivery.

Herman, Sonya J. *Becoming Assertive: A Guide for Nurses.* New York: D. Van Nostrand Company, 1978.

Comprehensive text depicting application of assertive behavior by nurses to their profession. Written especially for the nursing student. Encourages nurses to speak in a self-affirming manner and express thoughts, feelings, opinions, and beliefs honestly.

Holden, Constance. "Pain, Dying, and the Health Care System." *Science,* Vol. 203, No. 4384, (9 March 1979), pp. 984–5.

Explores management of pain and humane care of the dying as prominent concerns of the government, suggesting hospice availability and psychosocial, emotional, and spiritual aspects of patient care.

Jonas, Hans. "The Right to Die: In Twilight Zones with Anxious Choices." *The Hastings Center Report,* Vol. 8, No. 4 (August 1978), pp. 31–36.

Defines moral problems of life prolongation with aid of medical technology. Reviews the right to refuse treatment, and analyzes situations involving the terminally ill patient and the patient in irreversible coma.

Kinlein, M. Lucille. *Independent Nursing Practice with Clients.* Philadelphia: J. B. Lippincott Co., 1977.

Discusses professional nursing, need for changes in the field, conditions and steps necessary to changes which would allow for autonomy in the nursing profession. Utilizes "client-nurse" relationship. Written by a registered nurse.

Kübler-Ross, Elisabeth. *On Death and Dying.* New York: Macmillan Publishing Co., Inc., 1974.

Concise analytical interpretation of the stages of dying, an examination of attitudes on death and dying, familial response and adaptation, and several interviews with terminally ill patients.

Leininger, Madeleine. *Transcultural Nursing: Concepts, Theories, and Practices.* New York: John Wiley and Sons, 1978.

Introductory text on new subfield, transcultural nursing, incorporating cultural concepts, theories, and research findings into nursing care practices and nursing education. Elaborates on ethnoscience in the United States and in other countries.

Levine, Carol. "Ethics and Health Cost Containment." *The Hastings Center Report,* Vol. 9, No. 1 (February, 1979), pp. 10–13.

Examines service and resource allocation, ethical issues, models for health care proposed by Charles Fried and H. Jack Geiger, review of the need for psychotherapy, and the role of the expert.

Martin, Leonide L. *Health Care of Women*. Philadelphia: J. B. Lippincott Company, 1978.
    The common needs and problems of women seen in primary ambulatory care, from the viewpoint of a practitioner. Topics such as contraception, pregnancy, menstruation, and venereal disease are discussed.

McCary, James Leslie. *Human Sexuality*, Second Brief Edition, New York: D. Van Nostrand Company, 1979.
    Introductory book on human sexuality. Briefly integrates physiology, psychology, and sociology of sex, as well as the myths and fallacies surrounding human sexuality.

McCary, James Leslie. *McCary's Human Sexuality*, Third Edition, New York: D. Van Nostrand Company, 1978.
    Basic text designed to promote understanding of individual sexual needs and behavior; highlights acceptance of others whose sexual attitudes and behavior may be different from one's own. Explores sexual complications and sex and society.

"Medical-Moral Dilemma: Experimentation on Prisoners." *Ethics and Medics*, Vol. 3, No. 6 (November/December 1978) pp. 1–4.
    Reviews documented cases of research experimentation on prisoners to determine the effects of accidental radiation on the human reproductive system. Examines ethical and moral dilemmas involved in experimentation.

Miller, Michael H. and Beverly C. Flynn. *Current Perspectives in Nursing: Social Issues and Trends*. St. Louis: The C. V. Mosby Company, 1977.
    The philosophy of the text is based on the fact that health care is a social system and can be studied on various levels. Examines roles of health care providers and receivers in relation to various topical areas.

Money, John and Patricia Tucker. *Sexual Signatures On Being a Man or a Woman*. Boston: Little, Brown and Co., 1975.
    Analyzes the core of individual identity, namely gender. Examines gender identity in today's society, the impact of transvestites in society, sexual reassignment, and the sexual revolution.

Morgan, Robin, ed. *Sisterhood is Powerful—An Anthology of Writings from the Women's Liberation Movement*. New York: Random House, Inc., 1970.
    Detailed examination of the women's revolution written, edited, designed, and illustrated by women. Reviews women in a variety of situations, including medicine, religion, politics, and sexual roles.

Nelson, James B. *Human Medicine: Ethical Perspectives on New Medical Issues*. Minneapolis: Augsburg Publishing House, 1973.
    Explores a variety of ethical issues in medicine. Issues discussed are flavored by religious-humanistic overtones and the intertwining of ethical decisions is stressed.

Orem, Dorothea E. *Nursing: Concepts of Practice.* New York: McGraw-Hill Book Company, 1971.
Provides a basis for organized nursing knowledge. Proposes structural frameworks of nursing relevant to concepts and principles involving ethics, values, legalities, and nursing as a human service.

Pellegrino, Edmund D. "Medical Morality and Medical Economics." *The Hastings Center Report,* Vol. 8, No. 4 (August 1978), pp. 8–11.
Concludes that "cost containment" flavors the work of health planners, economists, legislators, and physicians. Explores traditional canons of medical morality, and cost consciousness and public policy.

Prescott, James W. "Abortion and the 'Right-to-Life': Facts, Fallacies, and Fraud." *The Humanist.* Vol. 38, No. 4, (July/August 1978), pp. 18–24.
Discusses the ethical implications of abortion, citing cross-cultural studies that indicate significant statistical support of anti-abortion views.

"Responsibility for Health." *Science,* Vol. 198, No. 4322 (December 1977), p. 1.
Suggests that responsibility for health lies with the individual. Discusses current systems of health care, and governmental involvement, in order to urge greater individual involvement of health care.

Roblin, Richard. "The Boston XYY Case." *Hastings Center Report,* Vol. 5, No. 4 (August 1975), pp. 5–8.
Documented follow-up study—psychological and behavioral—of affected children with the XYY chromosome pattern. Analyzes objections to the study and modifications to meet criticism.

Rosenhan, D. L. "On Being Sane in Insane Places." *Science,* Vol. 179, No. 4070. (January 19, 1973), pp. 250–8.
Exploration of data accumulated to attempt to define a variety of terms such as "mental illness" and "schizophrenia" through admission of pseudo-patients to psychiatric wards. Examines consequences of labeling and depersonalization.

Rowan, Carl T. "Health-Care Inhumanity." *Chicago Sun-Times,* 22 March 1979, p. 64.
Examines health care given to those patients without medical insurance and promotes the idea of a health-care system revision in order to accommodate all patients.

Royster, Vermont. "Whose Rights Shall Prevail: the Individual's or Society's?" *Chicago Sun-Times,* 19 March 1978, p. 2.
Examines how, in a free society, we can resolve the problem of the right of individuals to refuse to work, and the right of society to protect itself against striking individuals. Reviews the Taft-Hartley Law and the role of unions in collective bargaining.

Sagan, Carl. *The Dragons of Eden.* New York: Ballantine Books, 1977.
Focuses on the development of the neocortex, and our indebtedness to millions of years of evolutionary changes, resulting in an increase in the amount of genetic information as organisms increase in complexity.

Samovar, Larry A. and Richard E. Porter. *Intercultural Communication: A Reader.* Belmont: Wadsworth Publishing Co., 1972.
Core text for courses providing theoretical and practical knowledge about intercultural communication processes, as in speech-communication and political science. Supplementary text in existing basic communication skills and useful reference material for advanced communication courses.

Szasz, Thomas S. "Aborting Unwanted Behavior: The Controversy on Psychosurgery." *The Humanist*, Vol. 38, No. 4 (July/August 1977), pp. 7, 10–11.
Szasz tastefully and candidly critiques psychosurgery by endorsing the policy that physicians who advocate such a procedure constitute a threat to our personal freedom and dignity. Compares issue to abortion.

Szasz, Thomas. *The Second Sin.* New York: Anchor Press/Doubleday, 1974.
Brief collection of fresh and often humorous thoughts focusing on matters such as sex and the family, drugs, schizophrenia, and psychiatry. Szasz cites the Old Testament on the knowledge of good and evil, and calls the knowledge of clear speech the "second sin."

Toffler, Alvin. *Future Shock.* New York: Random House, 1970.
A view of society and its inability to cope with the increasingly rapid rate of change, particularly technological change. Introduces the concept of cultural lag-gap between mores, attitudes, and technologic capacity. Dated, yet excellent reading.

Visscher, Maurice B., ed. *Humanistic Perspectives in Medical Ethics.* Buffalo: Prometheus Books, 1973.
Suggests a new ethical framework resulting from advanced medical technology; reviews common ethical issues such as the right to die, human experimentation, use of psychotropic drugs, the sanctity-of-life principle, and others.

Wade, Nicholas. *The Ultimate Experiment.* New York: Walker & Co., 1977.
Defines gene splicing, the controversy surrounding genetic engineering, and the prospect of man-made evolution. Optimistic view of molecular biology's future, after reviewing both the safety and ideological considerations of gene splicing.

Warwick, Donald. "Contraceptives in the Third World." *Hastings Center Report*, Vol. 5, No. 4 (August 1975), pp. 9–13.
Examines the need for better standards governing testing and use of contraceptives, especially in less developed countries. Implicates governmental and organizational influence, such as WHO.

Wechsler, Henry, Joel Gurin, and George F. Cahill, Jr., eds. *The Horizons of Health.* Cambridge: Harvard University Press, 1977.

Attempts to define those research areas which are most important to public health. Epidemiological data and research into processes such as infection and genetic disorders are discussed. Suggests biomedical approaches to behavioral disorders, describes new techniques of diagnosis and intervention, and examines the economics of research implementation.

Wertz, Richard W., ed. *Readings on Ethical and Social Issues in Biomedicine.* New Jersey: Prentice-Hall, Inc., 1973.

Concise anthology exploring a wide variety of ethical issues, giving the arguments of both sides in most cases. Critically examines justification of issues for current practice.

Wildausky, Aaron. "Doing Better and Feeling Worse: The Political Pathology of Health Policy." *Daedalus,* Vol. 106, No. 1 (Winter 1977), pp. 105–23.

Discusses the concept of a public medical system. Examines two alternative proposals for a government health plan: the Comprehensive Health Insurance Plan and the Kennedy-Mills proposal. The quality of each program is discussed in relation to its social and individual costs.

Woods, Nancy Fugate. *Human Sexuality in Health and Illness.* St. Louis: The C. V. Mosby Company, 1975.

Examination of the biological, psychological, and social nature of human sexuality, life events that threaten sexual integrity; adaptation to interferences with sexuality and sexual function; and the role of the health professional in sexual counseling and sex education.

EPILOGUE:

ULTIMATE QUESTIONS, ULTIMATE ANSWERS

After winding your way through the morass of social problems confronting nursing and health care, digesting a few significant legal themes that impinge on health care, and reviewing ethical concepts of relevance to nursing, you may feel more confused and frustrated than when you opened this book. If this is so, then you're a good student and have experienced the usual results. There are no simple answers or final solutions to the problems that confront nursing, health care, and society in general. The very nature of the problems we seek to analyze, control, and predict does not facilitate solution. So your confusion is a healthy sign of recognition of the magnitude of the problems that confront us. Your discomfort at the inability to resolve these conundrums is a sign of your well-founded desire to do so. The discomfort and confusion are normal indices of sensitivity development.

Where do we go from here? Okay, it's great to know we have complex dilemmas requiring resolution. It's better that we recognize the requisite contribution of all groups to solution, if solution is to succeed. We would probably all acknowledge that the bottom line in choosing and designing courses of action should be an ethical base; that without development of and adherence to an ethical system for determination of right and wrong, we won't need to worry about burning in hell in a mystical afterlife. We will create a hell right here on earth.

But there is one more point worth expressing if this package is to be neatly tied: Be willing to accept new data for designing new strategies in coping with new problems. As people of good will and humane concerns focus their energies on the dilemmas that confront us, viable strategies will appear and be implemented. New problems will result. As with walking a treadmill, taking one step forward ensures the necessity of the next step. But if we aren't willing to take the first step and face the consequences of forward movement, we will still be swept along in the flow of change. The only difference will be that someone else will be directing the goals.

Get involved in decision-making. Recognize that your efforts won't always meet success, your judgments won't always be accurate, and your cause won't always win. But if you don't take the time and expend the energy, it's certain you won't contribute to guiding the outcomes. The saying, "Behold the turtle—he only makes progress by sticking his neck out," is applicable here.

Somehow I'd rather confront catastrophes of my own making than those inherited from someone else. It's easier to face the consequences of one's own actions. When we have resolved our contemporary social, legal, and ethical dilemmas, we will have to live with the results. Therefore, shouldn't we all participate in the choices that are to be made?

If people of the pro-life faction ultimately succeed in abolishing abortion rights, we will all have to cope with the result: unwanted, unloved babies; better contraceptive development; or improved social services for acquiring and caring for the resultant children. Should "pro-choice" advocates succeed, we will also cope with the impact and its mandates: competent, available, affordable abortion and contraceptive services to ensure that all segments of society are accorded access to the same safe standards of care. As you're going to have to live within whatever system evolves, it behooves you to contemplate your position and actively seek to promote it.

Similarly, we all have a stake in the changing concepts of age, dying, and death. All of us, if we are fortunate, will confront old age. All of us, though it is hard to acknowledge, will die. Should we not participate in designing the systems that will comfort us in senescence and support us as we die?

It is imperative to recognize that contemporary problems are everyone's problems, because all of us will live with the outcomes. We must all attempt to choose courses befitting our ethical standards, and we must attempt to guide our progress along the most humanly attractive paths. To paraphrase Jerry Rubin: "We may not be much, but we're all we've got."

Index